Contents

Spanish Grammar in Context
Analysis and Practice

JUAN KATTÁN-IBARRA

and

ANGELA HOWKINS

Hodder Arnold

A MEMBER OF THE HODDER HEAD

First published in Great Britain in 2003 by Hodder Education,
a member of the Hachette Livre UK Group,
338 Euston Road, London NW1 3BH

www.hoddereducation.com

British Library Cataloguing in Publication Data
A catalogue record for this book is available from the British Library

Library of Congress Cataloging-in-Publication Data
A catalog record for this book is available from the Library of Congress

ISBN 978 0 340 80790 3

6 7 8 9 10

Typeset in 10/14 pt Minion by Charon Tec Pvt. Ltd, Chennai, India
Printed and bound in Malta by Gutenberg Press

What do you think about this book? Or any other Hodder Education title?
Please send your comments to education@hodder.com

Preface

There comes a point in language study where an understanding of how a language functions is vital for progress to be made. *Spanish Grammar in Context* is designed to give students who are in the final years of school or the early stages of university study, and adult learners who are at an equivalent stage, an understanding of how Spanish functions in a practical and relevant way. More advanced students may also find the book both interesting and useful for review and revision purposes.

The starting point of each chapter, or unit, is an authentic text in which a particular grammatical point is highlighted. This focuses the student's attention on this part of speech and how it functions in context. There then follows a clear and concise explanation of both form and usage, with examples from the text or from everyday language. Differences in usage between Peninsular and Latin-American Spanish are noted. The subsequent exercises give practice of the grammar points highlighted and explained in the text. Exercises vary from the practice of form and use within the context of a single sentence through gap-fill to more open-ended communicative types of exercises. Translation exercises are included, especially where usage differs considerably from English and so can cause problems for English speakers. Except for those exercises which are of a communicative nature, a key is provided for the exercises of each unit, thus making the book ideal for self-study. In the classroom context, it can be used for the study of grammar and/or of a topic area, as the texts chosen lend themselves to exploitation beyond the study of the grammar point in question.

The texts are taken from authentic sources from all over the Spanish-speaking world. They include excerpts from contemporary literature, and from newspaper and magazine articles, including 'agony aunt' letters, and have a richness and variety which make them intrinsically interesting to read. Some exercises relate to the topic of the text, others simply practise the particular grammatical point, the aim of all types being to help students to a greater understanding of function and to a greater confidence when using the language for their own communicative purposes.

The book is divided into two main parts, one which deals with aspects of the verb, and the other which deals with nouns, adjectives, pronouns, prepositions and all other parts of speech which go to make up a sentence. Units can be studied sequentially, or in random order, according to whichever grammar point the student wishes to study, thus making it a useful and handy reference/revision tool. However, units which deal with related grammar points are grouped together (for example, the present and imperfect subjunctive), and each unit has suggested "Further Reading" for those who wish to take their study beyond the scope of the book. As each text is taken from an authentic source, it naturally produces examples of grammar not explicitly studied in that particular unit. These are indicated in the unit under the heading "Other points to note in the text" so that students may study the text beyond the confines of the grammatical point for which it has been chosen, or teachers may exploit it further in the classroom. A glossary of grammatical terms and a table of irregular verbs are also included to make the book as user friendly as possible. At the end of the book four texts with questions give students the opportunity to test their knowledge of grammar.

The book does not pretend to be exhaustive in its coverage but focuses on those areas of grammar which are important for effective communication. At all times grammar is presented not as an end in itself but as the necessary tool for effective communication. The approach encourages students not only to read for comprehension and pleasure, but also to have an awareness of how the language is used. By developing skills of observation and analysis in their studies, students will be able to enhance their productive skills and so reap the rewards that language study brings.

Acknowledgements

Thanks are due to the authors and publishers/media agents who kindly allowed to make use of their texts. Every effort has been made to trace all copyright holders of material. Any rights not acknowledged here will be acknowledged in subsequent printings if sufficient notice is given to the publisher.

Spain: *Quo*, 'Trucos para hacer turismo sin arruinarte', July 1996, 'Cómo ponerse en forma en 30 días', July 1997; *El País*, '364 días en automóvil', 23 September 2001; *El País Semanal*, 'Lo que aprendí en la escuela', 12 September 1999; *Expansión*, 'Un libro es más importante que un pan bien hecho: entrevista con Isabel Allende', 15 November 1997; *DT*, 'Esclavos de la tecnología', September 2001; *El Mundo de Catalunya*, 'Consulte a su ordenador'; *Blanco y Negro*, *ABC*, 'Entrevista: Montserrat Caballé', 29 May 1988, 'Veintiocho años, y en paro', 26 November 1995; *16*, 'A la caza del meteorito', 15 October 2000, 'Retrato', 8 September 1991; *CNR*, 'Nos estamos fumando el planeta', 20 October 1998; *Cambio 16*, 'Entrevista con Mario Molina', 15 July 1996, 'El sol, ¿amigo o enemigo?', 19 July 1998, 'La dieta mediterránea', 21 November 1988, 'La España beoda', 21 December 1987; *Tribuna*, 'Consejos para evitar incendios', 'Protagonistas: Antonio Banderas', 11–17 December 1995; *Prima*, 'Estrategias para encontrar empleo: la entrevista', October 1996; *Tiempo*, 'Retrato del nuevo español', 11 May 1987, 'Si usted quiere un hijo perfecto', 17 November 1997, 'El homo erectus, el primer balsero del estrecho de Gibraltar', 17 November 1997, 'El efecto invernadero', 14 July 1997; *Carta de España*, 'Imanol Arias: "no soy un galán" ', 1–30 August 1989; Editorial Anagrama, excerpts from *Porque éramos jóvenes* by Josefina Aldea, and 'Días felices', from *Todos mienten* by Soledad Puértolas; excerpt from the novel *Arráncame la vida* by Ángeles Mastretta, © Ángeles Mastretta, with kind permission of Mercedes Casanovas, Agencia Literaria, Barcelona; Chile: *El Mercurio*, Valparaíso, 'Latinoamericanos, los más apasionados y belicosos del mundo', 26 November 2000; *El Metropolitano*, 'Al rescate de la Amazonia', 13 October 1999; *La Tercera*, 'Dos tercios de la población mundial vivirá en ciudades en el año 2025', 6 July 2000, 'Alerta sobre alteración de costas del mundo', 24 April 2001; *El Mercurio*, Santiago, '¿Qué habría sucedido si . . . ?', 24 February 2001, 'Plácido Domingo: el artista total', 25 March 1990, 'La hora cero para los inmigrantes', 5 April 1997, '¿Para esto estudié tanto?', 26 June 1999, 'Parece que maduré, aunque no quería', 15 October 1999; 'El barco donde estaba el paraíso', 17 April 1994; *La Nación*, 'El amor es mi único discurso', 16 March 1995; Venezuela: *El Universal*, 'Automóviles y caminos inteligentes, la meta para dentro de 30 años', 9 May 1991; Bolivia: *Presencia*, 'Bosque más antiguo del planeta se encuentra en Chile', 12 March 1991; Mexico: *Este país*, Greenpeace, 'Ingeniería genética: Frankenstein o el moderno Prometeo', October 1995; *El Universal*, 'Las quejas de las esposas modernas', 23 April 2000, 'Los incas realizaban sacrificios humanos', 26 October 2000; Argentina: *Buena Salud*, 'El desmayo por estrés' and 'Las conflictivas camas solares', Nº 26; Compañía Editora Espasa Calpe Argentina S.A., Buenos Aires, excerpt from the novel *Boquitas pintadas* by Manuel Puig, © Herederos de Manuel Puig, with kind permission from Guillermo Schavelzon & Asociados, Agencia Literaria, Buenos Aires, Argentina.

Glossary of grammatical terms

Adjective   A word which provides more information about a noun: *His/her house is very **big*** Su casa es muy **grande**. *It's a **real** pity* Es una **verdadera** lástima.

Adverb   A word used to provide more information about a verb, an adjective or another adverb: *He/she treated me **badly*** Me trató **duramente**. *It was **extremely** difficult* Fue **extremadamente** difícil. *They behaved **incredibly** well* Se comportaron **increíblemente** bien.

Article   There are two types of articles, ***definite*** and ***indefinite***. Definite articles in Spanish are **el, la, los, las** *the* in English. Indefinite articles are **un, una** *a, an* in English: ***the** boy* **el** chico; *a magazine* **una** revista.

Clause   A group of words within a sentence which has its own verb. A ***main clause*** functions on its own; a ***subordinate clause*** is dependent on another clause. In *I'll tell her when she arrives* Se lo diré cuando llegue, "*I'll tell her*", the main clause, can function on its own; "*when she arrives*", the subordinate clause, is dependent on the main clause.

Conjunction   A word like *and* **y**, *or* **o**, *pero* **but**, which joins words or groups of words.

Definite article   See *Article*.

Demonstrative   Words like **este, esta** *this*, **esos, esas** *those*, are called demonstratives: ***this** book* **este** libro; ***those** ideas* **esas** ideas.

Direct object   See *Object*.

Finite verb   A verb form such as the one in *They work hard* is said to be ***finite*** because it indicates ***tense***, ***person*** and ***number***. Gerunds, infinitives and past participles are non-finite verb forms.

Gender   In Spanish, all nouns are either masculine or feminine. For example, **el** colegio *the school*, is masculine, while **la** universidad *the university*, is feminine. Nouns referring to male people are masculine and those referring to female persons are feminine.

Gerund   Refers to the forms of the verb ending in -**ando** and -**iendo**, e.g., habl**ando**, com**iendo**, viv**iendo**. Some of its uses correspond to those of the verb form ending in -*ing* in English, e.g. *She is **eating***. Está **comiendo**.

Imperative   See *Mood*.

Indefinite article   See *Article*.

Indicative   See *Mood*.

Indirect object   See *Object*.

Infinitive   The basic form of the verb, as found in the dictionary. In Spanish, infinitives end in -**ar**, -**er**, and -**ir**, e.g. habl**ar** *to speak*, com**er** *to eat*, viv**ir** *to live*.

Irregular verb   A verb which does not behave according to a set pattern.

Modal verb   An auxiliary verb which is used with another verb to convey a certain mood or intention, e.g. *We **must** do it* **Debemos** hacerlo (obligation); *We **can't** help you* No **podemos** ayudarte (possibility). Among modal verbs in Spanish we find **poder** *to be able to*, *can*, **deber** *must*, **tener que** *to have to*.

Mood   Refers to the forms verbs can take depending on how these are used. There are three moods of the verb: ***indicative***, normally associated with statements of fact, e.g. ***They are coming** tomorrow* **Vienen** mañana; ***imperative***, used for commands, directions and instructions, e.g. *Come here!* ¡**Ven** aquí!; and ***subjunctive***, normally associated with doubt, possibility, wishes, etc., e.g. *I don't think they'll **come*** No creo que **vengan**. See ***Subjunctive mood***.

Noun   A word like *table* **mesa**, *cat* **gato**, *kindness* **bondad**.

Number   Used to indicate whether something is ***singular*** or ***plural***, e.g. *the hotel* **el hotel** is singular, *the hotels* **los hoteles** is plural.

Object   In the sentence *I gave **him the keys*** **Le** di **las llaves**, the phrase *the keys*, which undergoes the action of the verb in a direct way, is said to be the direct object, while *him*, the recipient of the giving, is the indirect object. An object can be a noun or noun phrase, e.g. *the keys*, or a pronoun, e.g. *him*.

Passive and active   A sentence such as *The police caught the thief* **La policía atrapó al ladrón**, containing a subject (*the police*) carrying out the action expressed by the verb, is said to be an ***active*** sentence. In *The thief was caught by the police* **El ladrón fue atrapado por la policía**, the object of the active sentence (*the thief*), undergoing the action expressed by the verb, becomes the subject, and the agent carrying out the action (*the police*) is introduced by the preposition *by*, **por** in Spanish. This type of sentence is called ***passive***.

Personal pronoun   As the name suggests, personal pronouns refer to persons, e.g. *I* **yo**, *he* **él**, *she* **ella**, *we* **nosotros**, *him* **lo**, **le**, *us* **nos**. See ***Pronoun***.

Possessive   A word like *my* **my**, *mine* **mío**, *her* **su**, *hers* **suyo**.

Preposition   A word such as *to* **a**, *in* **en**, *between* **entre**, which provides information such as direction, location, time.

Pronoun   A word that stands in place of a noun or noun phrase which has already been mentioned, e.g., *My brother is a teacher. **He** is a teacher.* Mi hermano es profesor. **Él** es profesor. *This hotel is much better. **This one** is much better.* Este hotel es mucho mejor. **Éste** es mucho mejor. *My bedroom is small. **Hers** is big.* Mi habitación es pequeña. **La suya** es grande.

Reflexive pronoun   A word such as *myself* **me**; *yourself* **te**, **se**; *ourselves* **nos**.

Reflexive verb   When the subject and the object of a verb are one and the same, the verb is said to be reflexive, for example, *I hurt **myself*** **Me herí**. *We hid **ourselves*** **Nos ocultamos**.

Relative clause   A group of words which refers back to something previously mentioned in the sentence, a noun or a pronoun, known as the ***antecedent***. See also ***Relative pronoun***.

Relative pronoun   A word like **que** *who, whom, that, which*, **el/la cual** *that, whom, which*, **cuyo** *whose*, which introduces a relative clause. See ***Relative clause***.

Subject   In a sentence such as ***My wife** prepared a delicious meal* **Mi mujer** preparó una comida deliciosa, *my wife*, the person performing the action denoted by the verb, is the subject of the sentence. A subject can be a single word or a group of words.

Subjunctive mood   The subjunctive mood is used very rarely in modern English, but there are remnants of it in sentences such as the following: *I insist that he **come*** Insisto que **venga**.

*I wish he **were** here* Ojalá **estuviera** aquí. Spanish uses the subjunctive much more frequently than English.

Subordinate clause   See *Clause*.

Tense   Changes in the verb which indicate aspects of time are referred to as tenses, for example, present tense, future tense, preterite tense. In *He **works** in a bank* **Trabaja** en un banco, the verb is in the present tense. In *He **worked** there for a long time* **Trabajó** allí durante mucho tiempo, the verb is in the preterite tense.

Verb   A verb is a word such as *to speak* **hablar**, *to exist* **existir**, *to feel* **sentir**, which can denote actions, states, sensations, etc.

Part One:
The verb

1 | The present tense

Text

In an interview, the Spanish tenor Plácido Domingo talked about what he does before a performance, and about his spare time. The language is colloquial, and in it you will find a number of verb forms which correspond to the present tense. Read the interview for understanding first, then read it again and see how the present tense has been used.

Plácido Domingo: el artista total

– ¿Cómo **es** un día de Plácido Domingo antes de una función?

– **Intento** que sea completamente tranquilo, **procuro** no aceptar ningún compromiso, no tener que hacer absolutamente nada. Me **quedo** en casa, repasando, estudiando, leyendo algo, y **trato** de estar en silencio.

5 – ¿Qué cuidados físicos **toma** el mismo día de una presentación? ¿**Sigue** algún régimen especial?

– **Como** una comida muy ligera, **puede** ser un poquito de pollo a la parrilla, o un poco de ternera. Muy poquito, porque con el estómago lleno no se **puede** cantar.

10 – Entre sus formas de descanso, como buen español, ¿se **cuenta** la siesta?

– Me encantaría dormirla todos los días y no **puedo**, sobre todo en este país. En Estados Unidos se **arregla** uno la vida de tal forma, que no se **puede** y ¡es tan saludable!

– ¿Cuántas horas **duerme** en la noche?

15 – En días normales **duermo** como ocho horas, el día de la función **trato** de dormir hasta once, pero después de una presentación, me **es** muy difícil. Hoy eran las cinco y todavía no podía conciliar el sueño. Porque te **quedas** excitado, no sólo en el papel, sino que por la función misma.

– ¿Dónde **veranea** Plácido Domingo?

20 – **Depende**, **vamos** a la playa la mayoría de las veces, y hemos tratado de que las últimas vacaciones sean siempre en México, ya que mi madre **vive** allí. **Vamos** a Acapulco, que me **gusta** mucho.

Diario El Mercurio, Chile

♀ The present tense

1 USAGE

The present tense is used:

a To refer to an action or a state of affairs which is valid in the present.

Mi madre **vive** allí. (línea 21)   *My mother lives there.*

b To refer to something which is generally true or universal.

No **se puede** cantar. (l. 8–9)   *You can't sing.*

Other examples are **se arregla**, **puede**, **es**. (l. 12).

c To refer to habitual actions.

Duermo como ocho horas. (l. 15)   *I sleep about eight hours.*

There are a number of other examples of this use in the text. Consider for instance **intento**, **procuro** (l. 2), **me quedo** (l. 3), **toma** (l. 5).

d To refer to a timeless fact or situation.

Me gusta mucho. (l. 22)   *I like it very much.*

Also, **puedo** (l. 11), **es** (l. 12), **depende** (l. 20).

e To refer to actions taking place at the moment of speaking.

El niño **duerme**. (for 'Está durmiendo')   *The child is sleeping.*

f To express ability.

Toca el piano.   *He/she plays the piano.*

g To refer to the future, especially to pre-arranged events and, generally, with verbs of movement.

En mayo **se elige** un nuevo presidente.   *A new president will be elected in May.*
Mañana **llega** Antonio.   *Antonio is arriving tomorrow.*

h To refer to the past (historic present).

La guerra **termina** en 1939.   *The war ended in 1939.*

i To refer to an action which began in the past and is still in progress.

Hace cinco años que **viven** allí.   *They've been living there for five years.*

j As an imperative, especially in directions and instructions.

En la esquina **doblas** a la derecha.   *You turn right at the corner.*

k In requests.

¿Me **pasas** el pan?   *Will you pass the bread?*

2 FORMATION

Regular verbs

Spanish verbs fall into three categories according to the ending of the infinitive (the base or dictionary form of the verb): -**ar**, -**er** and -**ir**. Most verbs are "regular", that is, they follow a fixed pattern in their conjugation. To form the present tense, remove the -**ar**, -**er** or -**ir** of the infinitive and add the endings for the present tense:

	tom**ar**	com**er**	viv**ir**
yo	tom**o**	com**o**	viv**o**
tú	tom**as**	com**es**	viv**es**
usted/él/ella	tom**a**	com**e**	viv**e**
nosotros/as	tom**amos**	com**emos**	viv**imos**
vosotros/as	tom**áis**	com**éis**	viv**ís**
ustedes/ellos/ellas	tom**an**	com**en**	viv**en**

Stem-changing verbs

A number of verbs change their stem (the infinitive, e.g. **tomar**, minus the ending: **tom-**) in the present tense, in all but the first and second person plural, but otherwise their endings are those of regular verbs. Verbs like **contar(se)** (l. 10) *to include, be included, count,* **poder** (l. 11) *to be able to, can,* **dormir** (l. 14–15) *to sleep* and **seguir** (l. 5) *to follow,* are stem-changing, as you will see from their forms below.

o into **ue**

-ar: c**ue**nto, c**ue**ntas, c**ue**nta, contamos, contáis, c**ue**ntan.

-er: p**ue**do, p**ue**des, p**ue**de, podemos, podéis, p**ue**den.

-ir: d**ue**rmo, d**ue**rmes, d**ue**rme, dormimos, dormís, d**ue**rmen.

e into **i**

-ir: s**i**go, s**i**gues, s**i**gue, seguimos, seguís, s**i**guen.

e into **ie**

There are no examples of this type of change in the text, but there are many such verbs, e.g. **empezar** *to begin,* **pensar** *to think,* **entender** *to understand,* **querer** *to want,* **preferir** *to prefer,* **venir** *to come.* Here are the present tense forms of three of these verbs:

-ar: emp**ie**zo, emp**ie**zas, emp**ie**za, empezamos, empezáis, emp**ie**zan.

-er: ent**ie**ndo, ent**ie**ndes, ent**ie**nde, entendemos, entendéis, ent**ie**nden.

-ir: pref**ie**ro, pref**ie**res, pref**ie**re, preferimos, preferís, pref**ie**ren.

Stem changes occur not only in the present tense but also in other tenses, such as the preterite (Chapter 2), the present subjunctive (Chapter 14) and imperfect subjunctive (Chapter 15) and also in the imperative (Chapter 17) and the gerund (Chapter 9).

Spelling changes

A number of verbs, not considered irregular, undergo changes in the written form of the stem. The following examples illustrate spelling changes affecting some present tense forms, but note that spelling changes also occur in other tenses:

> **seguir** (l. 5) *to follow*, (yo) sigo; **vencer** *to conquer*, (yo) venzo; **coger** *to catch*, (yo) cojo; **conocer** *to know*, (yo) conozco; **construir** *to build*, (yo) construyo, (tú) construyes, (usted, él, ella) construye, (ustedes, ellos, ellas) construyen.

Verbs derived from these, and most verbs with a similar spelling, undergo similar changes. For spelling rules affecting verbs see pages 207–8.

Irregular first person singular

Many verbs are irregular in the first person singular (**yo**) of the present tense. Amongst these we find:

caer *to fall*	**caigo**	**salir** *to go out*	**salgo**
hacer *to do, make*	**hago**	**traer** *to bring*	**traigo**
poner *to put, place*	**pongo**	**valer** *to be worth*	**valgo**

Some are also stem-changing: **decir** *to say, tell* (digo, dices, dice…), **venir** *to come* (vengo, vienes, viene…), **tener** *to have* (tengo, tienes, tiene…), etc.

Irregular verbs

A number of verbs are called "irregular" because they do not follow a fixed pattern in their conjugation. Verbs like **ser** (l. 1) *to be*, and **ir** (l. 20) *to go*, fall within this category. The following are their present tense forms:

	ser	ir
yo	**soy**	**voy**
tú	**eres**	**vas**
usted/él/ella	**es**	**va**
nosotros/as	**somos**	**vamos**
vosotros/as	**sois**	**vais**
ustedes/ellos/ellas	**son**	**van**

See also **Irregular verbs** on pages 204–7.

OMISSION OF SUBJECT PRONOUNS

Subject pronouns (**yo, tú, él**, etc.) are usually omitted in Spanish, unless there is ambiguity, as for **usted, él, ella**, which share the same verb endings, and also for emphasis or contrast.

Usted (abbreviated **Vd.** or **Ud.**) and **ustedes** (abbreviated **Vds.** or **Uds.**) are heard more often as a sign of politeness.

LATIN AMERICAN USAGE

The **vosotros/as** subject pronoun, used for familiar address in the plural, and the corresponding form of the verb, are not used in the Spanish-speaking countries of Latin America, where **ustedes** is used in both formal and familiar address.

In the Río de la Plata area (Argentina and Uruguay), **vos** is used instead of **tú**. Regular present tense forms for **vos** are different from those of **tú** above: **vos tomás, vos comés, vos vivís.** Stem changes affecting the **tú** form of the verb, e.g. **tú tienes**, do not apply to the **vos** forms, e.g. **vos tenés**. The irregular form **eres** (from **ser**) becomes **sos: vos sos** (see also Chapters 14, 17 and 25).

Other points to note in the text

- Verb (+ preposition) + infinitive: *procuro no aceptar* (l. 2), *no tener que hacer* (l. 3), *trato de estar* (l. 4), *puede ser* (l. 7), etc. (see Chapters 8 and 28)
- Gerund: *me quedo ... repasando* (l. 3–4), *estudiando, leyendo* (l. 4) (see Chapter 9)
- Negation: *procuro no aceptar ningún compromiso* (l. 2–3), *no tener que hacer ... nada* (l. 3), *no sólo ... sino* (l. 17–18) (see Chapter 27)

See for further information:	Butt, pp. 4–6
	Butt and Benjamin, pp. 200–3
	Batchelor and Pountain, pp. 234–5
	Kattán-Ibarra and Pountain, pp. 78-9, 414–21
	Muñoz and Thacker, pp. 71–5, 213–14

EXERCISES

1 Complete these sentences by putting the appropriate present tense ending to each verb.

a Mañana (yo) sac____ las entradas y luego te llam____ ¿vale?

b Si (tú) no estudi____, no aprend____ nada.

c Plácido Domingo y su mujer visit____ a su madre que viv____ en Acapulco.

d Usted escrib____ artículos para *La Vanguardia* ¿verdad?

e En la discoteca Rosario y yo bail____ y beb____ mucho.

f El Día de Reyes los niños españoles recib____ regalos.

g Ustedes habl____ muy bien inglés.

h Oye, Rafa, ¿tú y Pili sub____ en el ascensor?

i Hace diez años que (nosotros) viv____ en Santander.

j Antes de una función, los músicos intent____ no hacer nada.

2 Put the verb in brackets into the correct form of the present tense.

   a Mi padre me (decir) _____ que yo no (conducir) _____ bien.

   b ¿No _____ (conocer, tú) a la hermana de Enrique? Yo, sí que la _____.

   c ¿A qué hora (empezar) _____ el partido?

   d ¿Cuándo (pensar, vosotros) _____ volver a Guadalajara?

   e En mis ratos libres (oír) _____ música, (leer) _____ o (salir) _____ con los amigos.

   f Si (querer, tú) _____ tocar bien el piano, (tener) _____ que dedicarle muchas horas.

   g Mariana (jugar) _____ bien al ajedrez.

   h Todavía no (saber, yo) _____ a qué hora (volver, yo) _____ el jueves.

   i ¿Me (dejar, tú) _____ tu diccionario un momento? No (tener, yo) _____ el mío.

   j (Calentar, usted) _____ el aceite, (freír) _____ las patatas* y (añadir) _____ el jamón.

   k ¡Cuánto _____ (llover) en este país!

   l Y luego (venir, ellos) _____ y nos (decir) _____ que no lo (querer) _____.

   m Como (saber, tú) _____ el camino, yo te (seguir) _____.

   n No (ir, ellos) _____ a tomar la sopa, (preferir) _____ los entremeses. Y también (pedir) _____ más pan.

   * In Latin-American Spanish: **las papas**.

3 Use one of the verbs below to complete each sentence.

pintar	ir	empezar	servir	nevar
ser	perder	comer	conducir	dormir

   a Los vegetarianos no _____ carne.

   b Un artista _____ cuadros.

   c _____ mucho en la Sierra Nevada.

   d Si _____ el pasaporte, tienes que ir a la comisaría.

   e Las corridas de toros _____ a las cinco de la tarde.

   f En días normales Plácido Domingo _____ ocho horas.

   g Ustedes _____ escoceses ¿verdad?

   h La mayoría de la gente _____ de Nueva York a Miami en avión.

   i La cena se _____ a partir de las nueve.

   j Los británicos _____ por la izquierda.

4 Translate into Spanish using the present tense to refer to the future.

'On Friday, we'll be saying goodbye to María. What shall we give her as a present?'

'She likes jewellery. Shall we give her some ear-rings?'

'Yes, why not? I'll phone her tonight to tell her that there's a party in my house Thursday night.'

'And we'll buy the ear-rings when?'

'Shall we leave it until Wednesday? I have to go to Paris and I'll not be back until Tuesday.'

'O.K. Where shall we meet? Outside the jeweller's?'

'Yes. I'll see you there at ten.'

5 After re-reading the interview with Plácido Domingo, write, as in a report, or tell a partner in Spanish what he says he does before a performance.

6 A Spanish film crew have come to your town and you have the chance to interview the director. Prepare questions to find out:

   – what time s/he starts and finishes work
   – whether s/he eats with the actors
   – to relax, what books s/he reads
   – what music s/he listens to
   – what programmes s/he watches on television
   – what sport s/he does to keep fit

You may think of other questions you can formulate using the present tense to add to this list.

7 Imagining that you are the film director, make up answers to the questions in exercise **6**.

2 | The preterite

Text

The following passage comes from a novel by the late Argentinian writer Manuel Puig, better known for his work *El beso de la mujer araña* (*The Kiss of the Spider Woman*). The main grammatical point here is the preterite tense, known in English as the simple past. Read the text and study its use.

Boquitas pintadas

El ya mencionado jueves 23 de abril de 1937 Juan Carlos Jacinto Eusebio Etchepare **se despertó** a las 9:30 cuando su madre **golpeó** a la puerta y **entró** al cuarto. Juan Carlos no **contestó** a las palabras cariñosas de su madre. La taza de té **quedó** sobre la mesa de luz. Juan Carlos **se abrigó** con una bata y **fue**
5 a cepillarse los dientes. El mal gusto de la boca **desapareció**. **Volvió** a su habitación, el té estaba tibio, **llamó** a su madre y **pidió** que se lo calentara. A las 9:55 **tomó** en la cama una taza de té casi hirviente, con la convicción de que ese calor le haría bien al pecho. **Pensó** en la posibilidad de beber constantemente cosas muy calientes y envolverse en paños calientes, con los
10 pies junto a una bolsa de agua caliente, la cabeza envuelta en una bufanda de lana con únicamente la nariz y la boca descubiertas, para terminar con la debilidad de su aparato respiratorio.

From Manuel Puig, *Boquitas pintadas*, © Herederos de Manuel Puig

---

The preterite

1 USAGE

a To refer to actions which took place and were completed at some point in the past. In this context it may be accompanied by time phrases such as **ayer** *yesterday*, **el lunes pasado** *last Monday*, **hace una semana** *a week ago*, **el verano pasado** *last summer*, **el ya mencionado jueves 23 de abril de 1937** (l. 1).

b In a narrative context it is often used alongside the imperfect tense (Chapter 3), with the preterite signalling a completed action or series of actions, and the imperfect providing a descriptive framework.

Volvió a su habitación, el té **estaba** tibio, **llamó** a su madre y **pidió** que se lo calentara.
(l. 5–6). *He returned to his room, the tea was cold, he called his mother and asked her to heat it for him.*

The description in this sentence is provided by the imperfect tense form **estaba** *it was*.

c To refer to an action which was completed before another one took place or to one which was interrupted at some point in the past.

Después que **cenó, salió** a dar un paseo. *After he/she had dinner, he/she went out for a walk.*
Trabajó allí hasta que la **despidieron.** *She worked there until she was sacked.*

d To refer to actions which took place over a prolonged period of time but ended in the past.

Vivieron en la Argentina durante quince años. *They lived in Argentina for fifteen years.*

THE PRETERITE AND THE IMPERFECT

The distinction Spanish makes between the preterite and the imperfect (Chapter 3) is very important, as this affects meaning. Note the difference between the following sentences:

Trabajé en un banco. *I worked in a bank.*
Trabajaba en un banco. *I worked/was working/used to work in a bank.*

Trabajé signals a completed past event, while **trabajaba** refers to an ongoing past action.
A suitable time phrase for the first sentence might be **desde 1995 hasta 1999** *from 1995 till 1999*.
To the second example one could add **en aquel tiempo** *at that time*.

2 FORMATION

Regular verbs

entrar	volver	vivir
entr**é**	volv**í**	viv**í**
entr**aste**	volv**iste**	viv**iste**
entr**ó**	volv**ió**	viv**ió**
entr**amos**	volv**imos**	viv**imos**
entr**asteis**	volv**isteis**	viv**isteis**
entr**aron**	volv**ieron**	viv**ieron**

Su madre **golpeó** a la puerta y **entró** al cuarto. (l. 2–3) *His mother knocked on the door and entered the room.*
No **contestó** … (l. 3) *He did not reply …*
Volvió a su habitación. (l. 5–6) *He returned to his room.*
El mal gusto de la boca **desapareció.** (l. 5) *The bad taste in his mouth disappeared.*
Vivieron allí muchos años. *They lived there for many years.*

Stem-changing verbs

a Some -**ir** verbs, like **pedir** *to ask for*, in line 6, change the **e** of the stem into **i** in the third person singular (**Vd., él, ella**) and plural (**Vds., ellos, ellas**)

> **Pidió** que se lo calentara. (l. 6)   *He asked her to heat it for him.*
> ¿Qué **pidieron**?   *What did they ask for?*

Among other verbs like **pedir** we find **corregir** *to correct*, **despedir(se)** *to say goodbye*, **divertirse** *to have fun*, **elegir** *to choose*, **mentir** *to lie*, **preferir** *to prefer*, **sentir(se)** *to feel*, **reír(se)** *to laugh*, **servir** *to serve*, **vestir(se)** *to dress*, etc.

b **Dormir** *to sleep*, like **dormirse** *to fall asleep*, and **morir(se)** *to die*, change the **o** of the stem into **u** in the third person singular and plural.

> Se **durmió** inmediatamente.   *He/she fell asleep immediately.*
> **Durmieron** toda la mañana.   *They slept all morning.*

Irregular verbs

A number of very common verbs, like **ir** *to go*, in line 4, have irregular preterite forms.

> **Fue** a cepillarse los dientes. (l. 4–5)   *He went to brush his teeth.*

The following list includes only the most common irregular verbs. For their forms see the **Irregular verbs** on pages 204–7:

andar *to walk*, **caber** *to fit, to be contained*, **dar** *to give*, **decir** *to say*, **estar** *to be*, **haber** *to have* (auxiliary), **hacer** *to do, make*, **ir** *to go* (conjugated like **ser**), **poder** *to be able*, **poner** *to put*, **querer** *to want*, **saber** *to know*, **ser** *to be* (conjugated like **ir**), **tener** *to have*, **traer** *to bring*, **venir** *to come*, **ver** *to see*.

Compounds of these verbs, for example **componer** *to compose*, **contener** *to contain*, **deshacer** *to undo*, are also irregular.

Spelling changes

A few verbs undergo spelling changes in the first person singular (**yo**) only: **c** changes to **qu** before **e**, e.g. **buscar** *to look for*, **busqué**; **tocar** *to touch, play* **toqué**.

g changes to **gu** before **e**, e.g. **llegar** *to arrive*, **llegué**; **pagar** *to pay*, **pagué**.

z changes to **c** before **e**, e.g. **comenzar** *to begin, start*, **comencé**; **empezar** *to begin, start*, **empecé**.

For other spelling rules affecting verbs see pages 207–8.

Other points to note in the text

- Prepositions: *a* (l. 2), *sobre* (l. 4), *con* (l. 4), *en* (l. 7), *para* (l. 11), etc. (see Chapter 28)
- Reflexive verbs: *se despertó* (l. 2), *se abrigó* (l. 4), *cepillarse* (l. 5), *envolverse* (l. 9) (see Chapter 12)
- Definite article: *el ... jueves* (l. 1), *a las 9:30* (l. 2) *las palabras* (l. 3), *cepillarse los dientes* (l. 5), etc. (see Chapter 18)

See for further information: Batchelor and Pountain, pp. 236–8

Butt, pp. 6–7

Butt and Benjamin, pp. 203–9

Kattán-Ibarra and Pountain, pp. 81–2, 433–7

Muñoz and Thacker, pp. 84–8, 218–20

EXERCISES

1 Complete these sentences by putting the appropriate preterite tense ending to each verb.

a (yo) Pas*é*___ dos horas viendo la tele y luego sal*í*___ a dar un paseo.

b ¿(tú) Estudi*aste* castellano en la universidad y no le*íste* El Quijote?

c La madre de Juan Carlos le prepar*ó*___ una taza de té pero él no la beb*ió*___.

d ¿A qué hora (usted) entr*ó*___ y por qué no cog*ió*___* los papeles?

e (nosotros) Viaj*amos* a Córdoba en autocar y de allí sal*imos* para Resistencia.

f ¿(vosotros) Mand*asteis* los informes pero no recib*isteis* ninguna respuesta? ¡Qué raro!

g Los amigos de Juan Carlos le llam*aron* y luego sub*ieron* a visitarle.

h Ustedes encontr*asteis* el sitio sin dificultad ¿verdad? ¿Volv*isteis* en taxi o en autobús?

** In some Latin American countries, notably Argentina, **tomar** should be used rather than*

***coger,** which has sexual connotations.*

2 Put the verb in brackets into the correct form of the preterite.

a El verano pasado (ir, yo) *fui*___ por primera vez a Cuba. (Ser) *fue*___ una experiencia maravillosa.

b Carmen no (saber) *supo*___ qué hacer y por eso no (hacer) *hizo*___ nada.

c (Andar, nosotros) _____ y (andar) _____ pero estábamos completamente perdidos y no (poder) _____ encontrar la casa.

d ¿Dónde (estar, vosotros) _____ ayer? ¿Por qué no (venir) _____ a clase?

e No nos (servir, ellos) _____ la paella como era debido así que (ir, nosotros) _____ a pedir el libro de reclamaciones pero nos (decir, ellos) _____ que no existía.

f ¿Y esto lo (traducir, ustedes) _____ cuando (estar) _____ en Bolivia?

g – Me encanta tu poncho. ¿Dónde lo (comprar, tú) _____?

– No lo (comprar) _____ yo. Me lo (traer) _____ Carlos de Argentina.

h No (tocar, yo) _____ nada. (Entrar) _____, (poner) _____ los papeles en el escritorio pero no (tocar) _____ nada.

i – El jueves (empezar, yo) _____ a trabajar a las ocho.

– No. Usted (empezar) _____ más tarde.

– No, no es verdad. (Llegar, yo) _____ a las ocho menos cuarto, (tomar) _____ un café y (ponerme) _____ a trabajar. Luego (venir) _____ Carlos y entre una cosa y otra no (tener, yo) _____ tiempo para terminarlo.

3 The following text is written using the historic present. Rewrite it using the preterite tense.

Carlos Gardel, el famoso cantante de tango, nace con el nombre de Charles Gardes en Francia a finales de 1890. Sus padres deciden probar fortuna en Argentina y el 9 de marzo de 1893 llegan a Buenos Aires. Es aquí donde nace su interés por la música y donde adopta el nombre de Carlos Gardel. Recibe clases de solfeo de algunos de los cantantes más conocidos de la época y en 1917 incorpora el tango a su repertorio y se convierte en cantor de tangos. Escribe canciones, sale en películas y llega a ser uno de los intérpretes de tango más famosos del mundo. Muere el 24 de junio de 1935 en Medellín, Colombia, cuando su avión se estrella contra otro.

4 Put the verb in brackets into the correct form of the preterite, then imagine and recount in Spanish what Juan Carlos did for the rest of that day, after he finally got up.

Esa mañana Juan Carlos no se sentía bien cuando (despertarse) _____ y por eso no (querer) _____ levantarse. Su madre le (dar) _____ un té pero en vez de beberlo (ir) _____ al cuarto de baño. El té (enfriarse) _____ y su madre (tener) _____ que prepararle otro. Después de beberlo, Juan Carlos (dormirse) _____ y (dormir) _____ hasta la hora del almuerzo cuando (levantarse) _____.

5 Read these answers that Antonio gave you about his latest holidays. Then write the questions you asked him to elicit these answers.

a Bueno, fui a La Habana, Cuba.

b Estuve una semana allí.

c No, no viajé solo. Fui con unos amigos.

d Viajamos primero en autobús hasta el aeropuerto y allí tomamos un avión que nos llevó a La Habana.

e Nos alojamos en un hotel en un complejo turístico bastante alejado del centro.

f El primer día dimos un paseo por la parte vieja de la ciudad.

g Visitamos el Museo de la Revolución y también una fábrica de tabacos.

h Por la noche no salimos, no.

i Hizo un tiempo espléndido – sol y calor todos los días.

j Compré lo típico – unas maracas, unos CDs de son cubano y habanos, por supuesto.

k Me lo pasé estupendamente bien.

6 Write an account of a real or imaginary holiday, saying where you went, with whom, how you travelled, what you did there, … .

3 | The imperfect

The Spanish film director Pedro Almodóvar was asked why he left his parents' home when he was young. As you read this, and the interviews which follow, focus attention on the use of the imperfect tense.

> ### "Parece que maduré, aunque no quería"
>
> – ¿Por qué huir?
> – Porque tanto ella como mi padre habían decidido un futuro inmediato para mí que no **era** el que yo **quería**, aunque fuera un niño. Yo ya **sabía** algunas cosas de mi vida y no **coincidían** con el futuro que ellos **proyectaban**: me habían
> 5 buscado trabajo en un banco del pueblo y les dije que no **quería**. Pero no me **dejaban** partir. Amenazaron con mandarme incluso a la Guardia Civil, pero les dije que no, que me **iba**. Después vieron que **era** en serio, que no **era** un capricho, que **estaba** dispuesto a irme a Madrid a seguir estudiando, a ser dueño de mi vida y a crear mi futuro. Entonces, como muchos chicos, me fui dándole
> 10 una patada a la puerta y estuve separado de ellos.
>
> *Revista Wikén*, Diario *El Mercurio*, Chile

The Chilean writer Isabel Allende, talked about her childhood.

> ### "Un libro es más importante que un pan bien hecho"
>
> – ¿De dónde nace su rebeldía contra la autoridad masculina?
> – De muy, muy pequeña. Yo me crié en una casa de hombres, en una familia muy severa. La vida **era** austeridad, esfuerzo, disciplina, sufrimiento. No se **discutía** nunca una decisión de mi abuelo. Después **venían** mis tíos,
> 5 que **eran** unos bárbaros. Ellos **tenían** la libertad y la autoridad que mi madre nunca tuvo. Creo que de muy chica me di cuenta de eso y me rebelé contra esa autoridad. Yo **vivía** en una sociedad donde lo que **mandaba era** siempre

masculino, y para colmo, me tocó un golpe militar. Y no hay nada más autoritario, más masculino que eso.

Diario *Expansión*, España

Text 3

Gabriel García Márquez, the Colombian writer, remembers his grandparents.

El barco donde estaba el paraíso

– *¿Qué tanta influencia tuvo tu abuela en tu formación?*
– El esposo de mi abuela, mi abuelo, **era** un coronel de las guerras civiles de fines de siglo pasado, que tuvo actuaciones verdaderamente notables de valor, de arrojo, de determinación. Así lo recuerdo ahora. En aquel momento no lo **podía**
5   juzgar: él **era** el jefe, el coronel de la casa. Yo **vivía** en el mundo de las mujeres; él **era** el único hombre en una casa llena de mujeres. Cuando llegué, yo **era** el segundo hombre, pero **estaba** entre las mujeres, y lo **veía** a él desde el punto de vista de las mujeres y me **daba** cuenta de que nadie le **hacía** caso. El mundo aquél y el mundo entero **giraban** alrededor del sol por la determinación de las
10 mujeres. Y, claro, el centro de ese universo de mujeres **era** la abuela. La abuela, que se **llamaba** Tranquilina y que **era** la persona más intranquila y más móvil que yo recuerde.

Diario *El Mercurio*, Chile

⌕ The imperfect

1 USAGE

The imperfect tense is used:

a Generally, to refer to an ongoing state or action in the past, whose beginning or end are not specified. In this context, English normally uses the simple past or, depending on the meaning, a construction with *used to*. Most imperfect tense forms in the texts correspond to this usage.

> Yo ya **sabía** algunas cosas ... (T. 1, l. 3)   *I already knew a few things ...*
> Yo **vivía** en un mundo ... (T. 3, l. 5)   *I lived in a world ...*

Consider also **era**, **quería** (T. 1, l. 3), **venían**, **eran** (T. 2, l. 4–5), **podía** (T. 3, l. 4).

b In narrative contexts, in conjunction with the preterite, where the imperfect provides the background description for the actions expressed by the preterite. In English, both correspond to the simple past.

> Yo me crié en una casa de hombres ... (T. 2 , l. 2)   *I was brought up in a house full of men.*
> La vida **era** austeridad ... (T. 2, l. 3)   *Life was austerity ...*

c To refer to past habitual actions, expressed in English through the simple past or the *used to* form.

> **Giraban** alrededor del sol. (T. 3 , l. 9)   *They revolved around the sun.*

> Similarly **se discutía** (T. 2 , l. 4), **mandaba** (T. 2 , l. 7), **veía** (T. 3 , l. 7).

d In place of the imperfect progressive.

> No **coincidían** con el futuro que ellos **proyectaban.** (T. 1 , l. 4)   *They didn't agree with the future that they were planning.*

e To refer to an action which was in progress in the past when something else happened.

> **Dormíamos** cuando sucedió.   *We were sleeping when it happened.*

> Here, **dormíamos** is equivalent to the continuous form **estábamos durmiendo**.

f In place of the present tense, to request something in a polite way.

> **Quería** hablar con usted.   *I wanted to speak to you.*

g Instead of the conditional, in colloquial speech.

> Yo que tú lo **hacía** (for **haría**).   *If I were you I'd do it.*

2 FORMATION

Regular verbs
The imperfect of -**ar** verbs is formed by adding -**aba** to the stem. The endings for -**er** and -**ir** verbs have -**ía** in all their forms.

estar	saber	vivir
est**aba**	sab**ía**	viv**ía**
est**abas**	sab**ías**	viv**ías**
est**aba**	sab**ía**	viv**ía**
est**ábamos**	sab**íamos**	viv**íamos**
est**abais**	sab**íais**	viv**íais**
est**aban**	sab**ían**	viv**ían**

> **Estaba** dispuesto a irme a ... (T. 1 , l. 8)   *I was ready to leave for ...*
> Yo ya **sabía** algunas cosas ... (T. 1, l. 3)   *I already knew a few things ...*
> Yo **vivía** en una sociedad ... (T. 2 , l. 7)   *I lived in a society ...*

Irregular verbs

There are only three irregular verbs in the imperfect. They are **ir** *to go*, **ser** *to be* and **ver** *to see*:

ir:	iba, ibas, iba, íbamos, ibais, iban.
ser:	era, eras, era, éramos, erais, eran.
ver:	veía, veías, veía, veíamos, veíais, veían.

Les dije que ... me **iba**. (T. 1, l. 6–7)   *I told them ... I was leaving.*
Era un coronel ... (T. 3, l. 2)   *He was a colonel ...*
Lo **veía** a él ... (T. 3, l. 7)   *I used to see him ...*

Other points to note in the texts

- Pluperfect tense: Text 1: *habían decidido* (l. 2), *me habían buscado* (l. 4–5) (see Chapter 5)
- Preterite tense: Text 1: *dije* (l. 5), *amenazaron* (l. 6), *vieron* (l. 7), *me fui* (l. 9), etc. Text 2: *crié* (l. 2), *tuvo* (l. 6), *di* (l. 6), etc. (see Chapter 2)
- Personal pronouns: The texts contain numerous examples of different types of pronouns, among these *ella, mí, me, les* (Text 1, lines 2, 2, 4, 5); *yo, me, ellos* (Text 2, lines 2, 2, 5); *lo, me, le* (Text 3, lines 4, 8, 8) (see Chapter 25)

See for further information:	Batchelor and Pountain, pp. 236–7
	Butt, pp. 7–9
	Butt and Benjamin, pp. 209–13
	Kattán-Ibarra and Pountain, pp. 80–1, 436–9
	Muñoz and Thacker, pp. 88–92, 220–5

✎ EXERCISES

1 Put the verbs in brackets into the correct form of the imperfect tense.

Mis abuelos (ser) _____ campesinos que (vivir) _____ en una casa pequeña que no (tener) _____ ni agua ni electricidad. Mi abuelo (cultivar) _____ sus tierras mientras mi abuela (ocuparse) _____ de la casa y también (hacer) _____ encaje. Todos los martes mi abuelo (cargar) _____ el carro y con el burro que (llamarse) _____ Sancho, (ir) _____ al mercado donde (vender) _____ sus cultivos. De vez en cuando mi abuela lo (acompañar) _____ para vender sus encajes. Los dos (estar) _____ contentos a pesar de la vida tan dura que (llevar) _____.

2 Change the verbs in the following sentences from the present tense to the imperfect tense.

  a Los domingos si hace buen tiempo doy un paseo en el parque.
  b Es baja y lleva un abrigo que le toca los pies.
  c Mientras los demás trabajan, tú charlas.

   d Estudiamos una hora cada día.

   e Cada vez que vamos a la costa llueve sin cesar.

   f Por la noche ven la tele y se acuestan tarde.

   g Sabe muy bien que no podemos hacerlo.

   h Mi padre es una persona autoritaria que no me deja hacer lo que quiero.

3 Complete these sentences using the imperfect tense to describe what the person was doing or what was happening.

   a Cuando sonó el teléfono, Juan _____.

   b Cuando llegaron sus amigos, Elena _____.

   c María vio el coche atropellar al ciclista mientras _____.

   d Laura se durmió mientras _____.

   e No abrimos la ventana porque _____.

4 Form complete sentences from these phrases adding link words where necessary and putting the verbs into the appropriate past tenses, imperfect or preterite.

   a La última vez que (yo) ver a Fernando • él estar buscando trabajo.

   b (Nosotros) entrar en el museo • llover.

   c (Yo) conocer a Isabel • tener el pelo largo y rubio.

   d Pedro y yo ir por la calle • toparnos con Ana.

   e Ser las once de la mañana • (ellos) partir para Santiago.

5 Translate into Spanish using the imperfect tense where appropriate.

   a In those days girls didn't go out after ten at night.

   b While he was waiting, he chatted with me.

   c We were very tired when we arrived.

   d I didn't realise that he was ill.

   e We used to live in a small village where everyone knew one another.

   f Everything was going well until it started to rain.

6 While on holiday, you were lucky enough to meet an octogenarian who talked to you about his life. Now write an account of your conversation which uses the imperfect tense and includes details of: his physical appearance, what he was wearing and what he said about his work, his family life and his leisure activities when he was a younger man.

7 Write or discuss with a partner the arguments you would use to defend or oppose these propositions:

   • Antes la vida era más difícil.

   • Antes la mujer no tenía tanta libertad.

   • Antes la vida para los estudiantes no era tan dura.

4 | The perfect

In this passage from a novel, the main character expresses her feelings towards an old friend in a letter. There is a note of nostalgia in the text, with the perfect tense making the events being described more vivid and closer to the present.

Porque éramos jóvenes

Nueva York, abril 1973

Querido David:
Has estado una semana en Nueva York y no nos **hemos visto**. Luché tanto hace años por que vinieras, que ahora me resulta extraño saber que **has estado** aquí.
5 **He entendido** muy bien que no trataras de encontrarme. No tenemos necesidad de vernos. No lo deseamos, ni siquiera lo tememos.
   Le **he dado** muchas vueltas al hecho de que, a pesar de todo, continuemos escribiéndonos. **He tratado** de buscar las razones de este morse prolongado con que nos enviamos señales regulares, indicios de que seguimos vivos.
10   Me parece que ésa es la clave de nuestras cartas. Escribimos para comprobar no que está vivo el otro, sino que lo estamos nosotros mismos. Tus cartas me confirman que existo. Quizá la lejanía me agudice esa necesidad de testimonio. Pero no sólo en la distancia está el destierro. Tú no te **has ido** y también reclamas cartas que dan fe de tu vida.
15   Hay un momento en que creemos poseer el hilo que nos guía hacia un destino. Nuestras cartas demuestran que lo **hemos perdido**. No es el amor y tiene poco que ver con el amor. Es la continuidad como personas lo que necesitamos, la conciencia de quiénes somos, de lo que **hemos sido** . . .

From *Porque éramos jóvenes*, © Josefina R. Aldecoa

The perfect

1 USAGE

Spanish, like English, makes a distinction between the perfect tense (e.g. *He has gone out*) and the simple past (e.g. *He went out*). Use varies from region to region, especially in the Spanish-speaking countries of Latin America, where the perfect is overall much less frequent than in Peninsular Spanish. Generally, the perfect tense is used:

a To describe past events which bear some relationship with the present.
Note that most instances of the perfect tense in the text correspond to this usage.

> **Has estado** una semana en Nueva York y no nos **hemos visto**. (l. 3)   *You've been a week in New York and we haven't seen each other.*
> **He entendido** muy bien … (l. 5)   *I've understood very well …*

Latin Americans are more likely to express the same ideas through the preterite:

> **Estuviste** una semana en Nueva York y no nos **vimos**.

b To refer to past events or actions which continue into the present.

> Le **he dado** muchas vueltas … (l. 7)   *I've thought/been thinking a lot about …*
> **He tratado** de buscar … (l. 8)   *I've tried/been trying to find …*

The continuity of the action into the present can be made more specific in Spanish through the continuous form: Le **he estado dando** …, **He estado tratando** …

c To refer to the immediate or recent past, often with adverbs such as *hoy*, *esta tarde*. Here, English may use the simple past rather than the perfect tense.

There are no examples of this use in the text.

> Esta tarde **he visto** a María.   *I saw Maria this afternoon.*
> **He desayunado** muy bien.   *I had a good breakfast.*

In Spain, you may also hear the preterite in this context, especially if the event is seen as more distant. Latin Americans, on the whole, will show preference for the preterite:

> Esta mañana **vi** a María. **Desayuné** muy bien.

d The perfect tense is not normally used with reference to events which were completed in a more distant past, for which you need to use the preterite (Chapter 2). In Spain, however, you are likely to hear sentences such as:

> ¿Dónde **ha nacido**?   *Where were you born?*
> **He nacido** en Sevilla.   *I was born in Seville.*

2 FORMATION

The perfect tense, like all compound tenses, is formed from the auxiliary verb **haber** *to have*, followed by the past participle. To form the past participle remove the -**ar**, -**er** or -**ir** ending and add -**ado** to the stem of -**ar** verbs, and -**ido** to that of -**er** and -**ir** ones. Here are two examples:

	estar	entender
yo	he est**ado**	he entend**ido**
tú	has est**ado**	has entend**ido**

Vd., él, ella	ha est**ado**	ha entend**ido**
nosotros/as	hemos est**ado**	hemos entend**ido**
vosotros/as	habeis est**ado**	habeis entend**ido**
Vds./ellos/ellas	han est**ado**	han entend**ido**

The past participle of **ir** *to go* is **ido** and that of **ser** *to be* is **sido**:

Tú no te **has ido**. (l. 13)   *You haven't gone.*

... de lo que **hemos sido**. (l. 18)   ... *of what we have been.*

IRREGULAR PAST PARTICIPLES

There are a number of common verbs whose past participle is irregular. The main ones are:

abrir	**abierto**	*opened*	morir	**muerto**	*died/dead*
cubrir	**cubierto**	*covered*	poner	**puesto**	*put*
decir	**dicho**	*said*	romper	**roto**	*broken*
escribir	**escrito**	*written*	ver	**visto**	*seen*
hacer	**hecho**	*made/done*	volver	**vuelto**	*returned*

No nos hemos **visto**. (l. 3)   *We haven't seen each other.*

Compounds of the above verbs have similar forms, e.g. **componer** *to compose*, **compuesto** *composed*; **deshacer** *to undo*, **deshecho** *undone*.

Other points to note in the text

- Subjunctive: *luché tanto ... por que vinieras* (l. 3–4), *he entendido ... que no trataras ...* (l. 5), *al hecho de que ... continuemos* (l. 7), *quizá ... me agudice* (l. 12) (see Chapters 14 and 15)
- Adverbs: *tanto* (l. 3), *ahora* (l. 4), *aquí* (l. 4), *bien* (l. 5), *sólo* (l. 13), etc. (see Chapter 21)
- Negation: *no* (numerous examples), *ni siquiera* (l. 6), *no ... sino* (l. 10–11) (see Chapter 27)

See for further information: Batchelor and Pountain, pp. 238

Butt, pp. 9–10

Butt and Benjamin, pp. 221–5

Kattán-Ibarra and Pountain, pp. 80, 430–2

Muñoz and Thacker, pp. 81–3, 216–8

✎ EXERCISES

1 Change the verb in the perfect tense according to the new subject given in brackets.

a No he entendido bien su explicación. (nosotros)

b ¿Habéis visto las fotos? (ustedes)

c ¿Has visitado Escocia alguna vez? (Carmen)

d Todavía no han llegado. (el señor Botín)

e ¿Cómo sabes que María ha recibido el paquete? (Javier y María)

f No te ha podido ayudar. (yo)

2 Change the verb in these sentences from the present to the perfect tense.

a Aprendo mucho aquí.

b ¿Vas al centro?

c Ya sale el tren.

d Vendemos la casa.

e ¿Usted llama al despacho?

f Se me cae todo.

g Ustedes tienen mucha suerte.

h ¿Entendéis?

3 Translate into Spanish.

a We have always gone on holiday to Spain.

b They haven't said anything to Pili because they haven't seen her.

c Why haven't you (**tú**) done this?

d Where have you (**ustedes**) put the bags?

e Gonzalo still hasn't come back from Paris.

4 Tomorrow you are going to visit a friend but now, unable to get to sleep, you are lying in bed going through your mental check list. Choosing an appropriate verb from the list below, fill in the gaps using the **yo** form of the perfect tense.

olvidar	cambiar	hacer	poner	poder	
envolver	dar	decir	leer	escribir	comprar

A ver si _____ todos los preparativos necesarios para el viaje. _____ el billete* y _____ a Otilia para decirle la hora de mi llegada. _____ los regalos que le voy a dar y los _____ en la maleta. _____ libras a dólares. _____ todas las guías que _____ sobre los sitios que voy a visitar. Le _____ a la vecina que voy a estar fuera quince días y le _____ la llave de la casa. Seguro que _____ hacer algo.

*In Latin-American Spanish: **el boleto**.

5 Complete the questions to these answers using the verbs in brackets.

a – ¿_____ (dormir) bien?
   – No. No he pegado ojo en toda la noche.

b – ¿_____ (comer)?
   – Todavía no. Van a comer dentro de poco.

c – ¿_____ (visitar, vosotros) Benidorm alguna vez?
   – Muchas veces. Visitamos Benidorm por primera vez hace más de diez años.

d – ¿Por qué no _____ (ir) Susana de vacaciones este año?

– Porque su madre está enferma.

e – ¿Qué tal lo _____ (pasar, ustedes)?

– Mal. Todo nos ha salido muy mal hoy.

f – ¿_____ (abrir) ya el banco?

– No. No abre hasta las diez.

g – ¿Qué _____ (hacer, usted) esta mañana?

– Nada de interés.

h – ¿_____ (llover) mucho?

– No, al contrario. Ha hecho muy buen tiempo todo el día.

i – ¿Si yo _____ (perder) alguna vez mi pasaporte?

Perderlo no, pero el año pasado en Italia me lo robaron.

6 You have some Spanish-speaking visitors staying with you and want to plan their stay to be as pleasant as possible, e.g. have they slept well, have they eaten, have they bought any souvenirs, have they been to/visited the local attractions . . .

Imagine the situation, think of and write down as many questions as you can of the kind that you would ask your visitors, using the perfect tense.

7 Think of and write down in Spanish three things that you have done and three things that you have not done in your life. Then think of other deeds/feats which you can add to this list to draw up a questionnaire ¿**Quién ha** . . . . ? to find out who, if anybody, has done these things, e.g. climbed a mountain, written to someone famous.

5 | The pluperfect

This passage from a novel by the Spanish author Soledad Puértolas contains some examples of the use of the pluperfect tense, the Spanish equivalent of *had* + past participle, as in *I had seen it*.

Días felices

Federico **había pasado** el verano en Marbella, con los tíos. Y con Bárbara y Hércules, nuestros primos. Desde el primer verano, **habían pasado** las vacaciones con ellos. Nos invitaron a todos, pero él fue el único que aceptó y repitió.

5 En Marbella se **había encontrado** con Chicho Montano, que **había sido** compañero mío durante los años escolares, sin llegar nunca a la amistad. A Chicho lo conocíamos sobre todo por la tienda de su padre, frente a la casa de los abuelos.

"Esa tienda es del padre de Chicho Montano", dijo alguien una vez,
10 señalando un escaparate pequeño colmado de las cosas más variadas. Y se nos quedó la costumbre de decirlo: "la tienda del padre de Chicho Montano", en cuanto la veíamos, antes de cruzar la calle y entrar en el portal de los abuelos. El caso es que **habíamos pronunciado** mucho ese nombre: Chicho Montano, y aunque la persona que lo llevaba era bastante ajena a nosotros, el nombre
15 nos pertenecía ...

From *Todos mienten*, © Soledad Puértolas

The pluperfect

1 USAGE

Spanish uses the pluperfect tense in much the same way as English does, that is, to refer to past events or actions which occurred before another past event or situation, in this case, the situation referred to by the narrator.

Había pasado el verano en Marbella. (l. 1)   *He had spent the summer in Marbella.*
Se **había encontrado** con ... que **había sido** compañero ... (l. 5–6)   *He had met ... who had been a classmate ...*

A clear example of the use of the pluperfect to refer to a past action which took place before another past event is in sentences like the following:

Habían cenado cuando llegamos.   *They had had dinner when we arrived.*
Ya **había salido** cuando la llamé.   *She had already gone out when I called her.*

2 FORMATION

The pluperfect indicative is formed with the imperfect of the auxiliary verb **haber** *to have* followed by the past participle. The past participle of -**ar** verbs ends in -**ado**, and that of -**er** and -**ir** verbs ends in -**ido**. For irregular past participles see Chapter 4 or **Irregular verbs** on pages 204–7.

tomar	**vivir**
había tomado	había vivido
habías tomado	habías vivido
había tomado	había vivido
habíamos tomado	habíamos vivido
habíais tomado	habíais vivido
habían tomado	habían vivido

Other points to note in the text

- Possessives and possession: *nuestros* (l. 2), *mío* (l. 6), *su* (l. 7), *la tienda de su padre* (l. 7), *los abuelos* (definite article for possessive) (l. 7–8) (see Chapter 24)
- Articles and nouns: *el verano* (l. 1), *los tíos* (l. 1), *las vacaciones* (l. 2–3), *la amistad* (l. 6), *la tienda* (l. 7), *el portal* (l. 12), etc. (see Chapters 18 and 19)
- Imperfect tense: *conocíamos* (l. 7), *veíamos* (l. 12), *llevaba* (l. 14), *era* (l. 14), *pertenecía* (l. 15) (see Chapter 3)

See for further information:	Batchelor and Pountain, p. 238
	Butt, p. 11
	Butt and Benjamin, p. 226
	Kattán-Ibarra and Pountain, p. 85, p. 439
	Muñoz and Thacker, pp. 94–6

EXERCISES

1 Put the verb in brackets into the correct form of the pluperfect, then read the sentence and study the use of the verb tenses.

   a Federico fue a Marbella porque sus tíos lo (invitar).
   b Mina y yo (repetir) los versos tantas veces que los sabíamos de memoria.

c Me pidió ayuda porque tú lo (echar) de casa.

d Cuando nos avisaron del accidente, ya (salir, vosotros).

e Ya te lo (decir, yo) mil veces pero tú no querías creerme.

f (Ver, él) la película la semana anterior pero tenía ganas de verla de nuevo.

g Todavía no (terminar, él) de construir la casa cuando murió.

h Sus hijos le (prometer) su ayuda pero al final no se la dieron.

2 Rewrite the sentences using the pluperfect tense as in the example.

Example: No le escribió. Confesé que . . .

          Confesé que no le había escrito.

a Cerraron el castillo antes de la hora indicada.

  Descubrimos que . . .

b Carmen fue al centro.

  La madre de Carmen me dijo que . . .

c No visitamos El Prado y por lo tanto no vimos *Las Meninas* de Velázquez.

  Les explicamos que . . .

d No dije la verdad.

  Tuve que confesar que . . .

e Los ladrones entraron por la ventana del comedor.

  Les dijimos a los guardias que . . .

f Le robaron la cartera en la Plaza Mayor.

  Le contó al policía que . . .

g Se encontró con unos amigos allí.

  Me contó que . . .

h No me dieron ninguna explicación por sus acciones.

  Me di cuenta de que . . .

3 Translate into Spanish:

a I was happy because Roberto had given me a present.

b He had wrapped it up and left it on my seat.

c I hadn't told him that it was my birthday.

d Later he told me that he had bought the bracelet because he had liked it.

e He hadn't thought about the price.

4 Just after Christmas you went shopping in the Sales and when you got home, found that thieves had broken into your house. Recount this incident in Spanish using the pluperfect where possible, for example to explain how the thieves had gained entry, the rooms they had gone into, how you realised what they had taken.

6 | The future

The article which follows makes some interesting predictions about the world population in the year 2025. As in Text 2 below, the style is journalistic, the future tense being common in this type of context. Read the two texts to find out what predictions are being made, then go back through them and study the language, especially the use of the future tense.

Dos tercios de la población mundial vivirá en ciudades en el año 2025

En el año 2025, alrededor de 5 mil millones de personas, es decir, dos tercios de la población mundial, **vivirán** en ciudades. La mayoría de ellas **habitará** en suburbios hacinados, con lo que se prevé la formación de muchos cordones de pobreza.

5   En un plazo de 25 años **existirán** ciudades con más de 30 millones de habitantes, **habrá** 100 ciudades con más de cinco millones de personas y **serán** 300 las urbes con más de un millón de residentes.

   La mayor parte de este crecimiento **se producirá** en los países en desarrollo, especialmente en Africa, Asia y América Latina y el Caribe, que en conjunto 10 **duplicarán** su población urbana. El incremento **se registrará** especialmente en Africa, que **duplicará** su población urbana en sólo 13 años. Para Peter Marcuse, profesor de la Universidad de Columbia, el siglo XXI **traerá** una gran división en las ciudades. "De este crecimiento, los únicos beneficiados **serán** quienes pertenecen al tercio más rico de la sociedad. La diferencia entre ricos y pobres 15 **crecerá** aún más".

Diario *La Tercera*, Chile

A new relationship between doctor and patient seems to be developing through use of the Internet. Read and find out.

Consulte a su ordenador

Es bastante probable que dentro de diez años exista un servicio de urgencia virtual. Salvo los accidentes, en los que los afectados **deberán** acudir al hospital con la mayor rapidez posible, la mayoría de los enfermos **podrá** tener comunicación directa con su médico desde su domicilio. **Bastará** con tener un
5 ordenador, una pequeña cámara de televisión y un acceso a Internet. Además de hablar y oír a través del sistema que **estará** acoplado a la pantalla del PC, el paciente **podrá** ver a su médico y éste observar el rostro de su enfermo; mirarle, incluso, el fondo del ojo y hacerse una idea de su estado.

No obstante, no **hará** falta que pase una década entera para que la relación
10 entre el cliente y su compañía de seguros médicos transite en muchas ocasiones por el ciberespacio. Casi todas las compañías de seguros médicos en EEUU tienen ya su propio "web" en Internet. De la misma forma que los computadores ya son una herramienta de trabajo en casi todas las oficinas, los ordenadores **serán** imprescindibles a la hora de obtener información. Y la información médica **será**
15 una de las que tenga mayor demanda.

Diario *El Mundo de Catalunya*, España

The future

1 USAGE

The future in English can be expressed in a number of ways. Consider for instance *They will go to Spain. She's leaving tomorrow. We are going to do it.* Spanish also uses different forms to talk about future events:

Irán a España. **Sale** mañana. **Vamos a hacerlo**.

This chapter deals with the equivalent of the *will* form, known as the future tense, which is used:

a Generally, with future meaning, to refer to future events, including predictions. This use is much more common in writing, especially in formal registers, for example the press, as in the two texts above. All the examples of the future tense in the texts correspond to this one. Here are just three of them:

Vivirán en ciudades. (T. 1, l. 2)   *They will live in cities.*
Duplicarán su población ... (T. 1, l. 10)   *They will double their population.*
Deberán acudir al hospital. (T. 2, l. 2)   *They will have to go to hospital.*

In the spoken language, especially in informal registers, reference to future actions is usually expressed with forms other than the future tense, e.g. **ir a** + infinitive:

Vamos a ir a la playa.   *We're going to the beach.*

or the present tense, generally with pre-arranged actions and with verbs of movement:

Se casan el mes que viene.   *They are getting married next month.*
Vuelvo el sábado.   *I'm coming back on Saturday.*

b To express probability and supposition.

A esta hora **estarán** en casa.   *They will/must be at home at this time.*
Tendrá tu edad.   *He/she must be your age.*

c To express uncertainty in relation to a future action.

No sé si **vendrá**.   *I don't know whether he/she will come.*
Supongo que me **llamará**.   *I suppose he/she will call me.*

d In interrogative sentences, to express speculation.

¿Qué hora **será**?   *I wonder what time it is.*
¿**Volveremos** a verlos?   *I wonder whether we'll see them again.*

e To express promises.

Te prometo que lo **haré**.   *I promise you I'll do it.*
Te juro que no **volverá** a suceder.   *I swear it won't happen again.*

OTHER WAYS OF TRANSLATING 'WILL' IN SPANISH

Note that certain constructions with *will* in English, which do not refer to future time, are normally expressed through forms other than the future in Spanish.

¿Me ayudas, por favor? (present tense)   *Will you help me, please?*
¿Quieres pasar? (**querer** + infinitive)   *Will you come in?*
No quiere escucharme. (**querer** + infinitive)   *He/she won't listen to me.*

2 FORMATION

Regular verbs

The future tense is formed with the whole infinitive, to which the endings are added. Verbs in -**ar**, -**er** and -**ir** all share the same endings. Here are three examples:

estar *to be*	estar**é**, estar**ás**, estar**á**, estar**emos**, estar**éis**, estar**án**
ser *to be*	ser**é**, ser**ás**, ser**á**, ser**emos**, ser**éis**, ser**án**
vivir *to live*	vivir**é**, vivir**ás**, vivir**á**, vivir**emos**, vivir**éis**, vivir**án**

Estará acoplado a la pantalla ... (T. 2, l. 6)   *It will be connected to the screen ...*
Serán imprescindibles ... (T. 2, l. 13–14)   *They will be essential ...*
Vivirán en ciudades. (T. 1, l. 2)   *They will live in cities.*

Irregular verbs

Some verbs have an irregular stem in the future tense, but the endings are the same as those of regular verbs. Note the following examples in the texts:

… **habrá** 100 ciudades … (T. 1, l. 6)   … *there will be a hundred cities* …
El paciente **podrá** ver a su médico … (T. 2, l. 6–7)   *The patient will be able to see his doctor* …
… no **hará** falta … (T. 2, l. 9)   … *it won't be necessary* …

The following are the most common irregular future forms:

caber *to be contained* **cabré, cabrás** …	**querer** *to want* **querré, querrás** …
decir *to say, tell* **diré, dirás** …	**saber** *to know* **sabré, sabrás** …
haber *to have* (auxiliary) **habré, habrás** …	**salir** *to go out* **saldré, saldrás** …
hacer *to do, make* **haré, harás** …	**tener** *to have* **tendré, tendrás** …
poder *to be able* **podré, podrás** …	**valer** *to be worth* **valdré, valdrás** …
poner *to put* **pondré, pondrás** …	**venir** *to come* **vendré, vendrás** …

Compounds of the above verbs are conjugated in the same way, e.g. **reponer** *to replace*, **repondré, repondrás** …; **retener** *to retain*, **retendré, retendrás** …
See also **Irregular verbs** on pages 204–7.

Other points to note in the texts

- Present subjunctive: Text 2: *es probable … que exista* (l. 1), *no hará falta que pase* (l. 9), *para que … transite* (l. 9–10), *será una de las que tenga* (l. 14–15) (see Chapter 14)
- Adjective agreement and position: Text 1: *población mundial* (l. 2), *suburbios hacinados* (l. 3), *población urbana* (l. 11), etc. Text 2: *servicio … virtual* (l. 1–2), *comunicación directa* (l. 4), *pequeña cámara* (l. 5), etc. (see Chapter 20)
- Prepositions: There are numerous prepositions in both texts, among these *en, de, con, entre, desde, a, para, por* (see Chapter 28)

See for further information: Batchelor and Pountain, pp. 235
                                      Butt, pp. 11–12
                                      Butt and Benjamin, pp. 213–16
                                      Kattán-Ibarra and Pountain, pp. 83, 422–9
                                      Muñoz and Thacker, pp. 75–8, 214–15

✎ **EXERCISES**

1 The Camino de Santiago is a famous pilgrim route in the north of Spain which every year attracts thousands of pilgrims, some who use less traditional ways of reaching Santiago.

One such pilgrim was interviewed recently and below is what he said. Change the underlined verbs to appropriate forms of the future tense.

a <u>Voy a hacer</u> el Camino en globo. Para mí, <u>es</u> la primera vez.

b Me <u>va a acompañar</u> mi amigo Eduardo. Para él, <u>es</u> la tercera vez.

c En el globo <u>vamos a llevar</u> lo mínimo. Así no <u>voy a tener</u> problemas con el peso. Yo <u>voy a guiar</u> el globo y Eduardo <u>va a sacar</u> las fotos.

d Como todos los peregrinos, <u>vamos a alojarnos</u> en los albergues. Bueno, lo <u>vamos a intentar</u>. También <u>vamos a bajar</u> en otros sitios – eso, seguro.

e ¿Que qué <u>voy a hacer</u> una vez en Santiago? Hombre, <u>voy a seguir</u> las tradiciones: primero, <u>voy a ir</u> a la catedral, <u>voy a entrar</u> por la puerta del Obradoiro, <u>voy a rezar</u> un Padre Nuestro, <u>voy a subir</u> al camarín del Apóstol y lo <u>voy a abrazar</u>. Y muy importante, <u>voy a golpear</u> la cabeza tres veces contra la imagen del santo. Esto me <u>va a dar</u> sabiduría y prudencia.

f No <u>vamos a volver</u> en seguida. <u>Vamos a quedarnos</u> unos días. Pero una vez de vuelta, Eduardo <u>va a revelar</u> sus fotos, yo <u>voy a escribir</u> el texto y <u>vamos a publicar</u> un libro sobre nuestra aventura.

g El libro <u>va a salir</u> dentro de un año. <u>Vamos a ponerle</u> por título *"A Santiago en globo"*. Le <u>va a gustar</u>.

2 Complete the questions that were asked in this interview in the future tense. Use the formal form of address: *usted* or *ustedes*.

a ¿Cómo . . . .?

b ¿Quién . . . .?

c ¿Qué . . . .?

d ¿Dónde . . . .?

e ¿Qué . . . .?

f ¿Cuánto tiempo . . . .?

g ¿Cuándo . . . .?

3 Here is an outline itinerary for a group of students who are visiting an educational establishment in a Spanish-speaking country to discuss a joint project. Rewrite the itinerary as a piece of continuous prose using the future tense.

<u>Miércoles</u>

9,00h: Llegada al Instituto. Recibimiento por parte del director. Visita de las instalaciones.

11,15h: Presentación del grupo de alumnos del Instituto.

12,30h: Salida del Centro. Visita al Ayuntamiento. Comida en el Ayuntamiento.

<u>Jueves</u>

8,30h: Trabajo en el aula.

11,50h: Trabajo en el aula con el grupo de alumnos del Instituto.

14,00h: Almuerzo en la cantina del Instituto.

16,00h: Visita turístico-cultural del centro de la ciudad.

<u>Viernes</u>

10,00h: Revisión del proyecto.

11,30h: Café.

12,00h: Planes futuros: actividades a realizar durante el resto del año hasta la próxima reunión.

14,00h: Comida. Tarde libre.

<u>Sábado</u>

Día libre para visitas y compras.

<u>Domingo</u>

8,30h: Salida al aeropuerto. Vuelo de regreso.

4 What does the future hold for us?

The two texts you have read have given you some indications. Write down your thoughts on the following questions:

¿Cómo será la ciudad del futuro en cuanto a:

– la vivienda

– los medios de transporte

– el comercio / las compras

– la seguridad?

¿Qué cambios habrá en nuestras vidas en cuanto a:

– la familia

– la alimentación

– el ocio

– el trabajo?

Discuss your views with a partner. Do you agree in your visions of the future?

7 | The conditional

In an interview, the Spanish actor Antonio Banderas talked about his Hollywood career. In this and in Text 2 below, you will find a number of examples of the conditional tense, the form of the verb usually associated with *would* in English. Note how usage differs in the two texts.

Protagonistas: Antonio Banderas

– *¿Ha colmado ya sus ambiciones en el cine americano?*
– Mis ambiciones económicas están colmadas, pero profesionalmente no soy aún el actor que me **gustaría** llegar a ser. Todavía me queda mucho por aprender. Sabía que me **costaría** llegar a donde estoy ahora, pero prefería ir despacio,
5 con papeles pequeños, antes que empezar haciendo malas películas como protagonista.

– *¿Echa usted en falta algo de su vida anterior, ahora que se ha convertido en una estrella?*
– Echo de menos todo lo que tenía antes, pero no **debería** quejarme, porque hay
10 gente que trabaja muy duro durante muchos años y no consigue ni un 2 por 100 de lo que yo tengo ahora.

– *¿Qué **haría** si se pudiera inventar un hermano gemelo, como hace su personaje en la película "Two Much"?*
– Me **inventaría** un hermano gemelo y me **tomaría** dos cervecitas, unas tapas de
15 calamares y unas gambas en la plaza Mayor. Y después me **iría** a ver una de esas películas que hacen otros.

– *Se ha vuelto usted un actor demasiado caro para el cine español. ¿Seguirá trabajando fuera de nuestro país mientras siga la racha o **haría** una "rebaja" a los directores españoles?*
20 – No **podría** trabajar en España con el mismo "caché" que tengo en Estados Unidos. Si quiero hacer una película en España, la **haría** amoldándome a las condiciones del cine español.

Revista *Tribuna*, España

Text 2

On an entirely different theme, Text 2 considers the damage caused by civilisation to the Earth's forests.

Nos estamos fumando el planeta

La Tierra ha perdido casi la mitad de sus bosques en los últimos 10.000 años, el tiempo que hace que el hombre aprendió a cultivar y dejó de recolectar su alimento. Entonces nacieron la agricultura y la ganadería, consideradas por los antropólogos como las llaves que pusieron en marcha el motor de la civilización.

5   A partir de ese momento, el ser humano **comprobaría** que era capaz de transformar su entorno. Fue un primer paso que lo **diferenciaría** para siempre del resto de los animales, pero que también **iniciaría** el camino hacia la deforestación. La agricultura no sólo mejoró su dieta y su esperanza de vida. De paso, también cambió su forma de vivir proporcionándole más tiempo para actividades que

10 **incrementarían** su calidad de vida.

    Esa situación **favorecería** la aparición de la artesanía – germen de la futura industria – que, junto a la cultura, **acabaría** por poner en marcha un aumento demográfico que no iba a retroceder jamás y que **sería** imparable. De los cinco o diez millones de habitantes que los biólogos calculan que había hace 10.000 años,

15 el planeta ha pasado a acoger a toda una población de cerca de 6.000 millones de seres humanos estimados en la actualidad.

Revista *CNR*, España

The conditional

1 USAGE

a Like the English *would*, in *I would have a couple of beers*, the Spanish conditional is used for expressing conditions.

> ¿Qué **haría** si se pudiera inventar … ? (T. 1, l. 12)   *What would you do if you could invent … ?*
> Me **inventaría** un hermano gemelo. (T. 1, l. 14)   *I would invent a twin brother.*

b To express the future in the past.

This use of the conditional is common in journalistic style. Text 2 is a good example, where all the forms of the conditional correspond to this usage.

> A partir de ese momento, el ser humano **comprobaría** … (T. 2, l. 5)   *From that moment onwards human beings were to discover …*
> Esa situación **favorecería** … (T. 2, l. 11)   *That situation was to favour …*

Another context for this use of the conditional is indirect speech.

Dijeron que este verano **irían** a Los Angeles.   *They said this summer they'd go to Los Angeles.*

The original statement here was "Este verano **iremos** a Los Angeles."

c With modal verbs like **deber**, **poder**.

No **debería** quejarme. (T. 1, l. 9)   *I shouldn't complain.*
No **podría** trabajar en España. (T. 1, l. 20)   *I couldn't work in Spain.*

d For politeness, in sentences like the following:

¿Te **importaría** cerrar la ventana?   *Would you mind closing the window?*
¿Le **molestaría** que lo deje aquí?   *Would you mind if I leave it here?*

e To express supposition with regard to something in the past.

En aquel tiempo él **tendría** veinte años.   *At that time he must have been twenty.*

2 FORMATION

Regular verbs

As with the future tense, the conditional is formed with the whole infinitive, to which the endings are added. The endings, which are those of the imperfect tense of **-er** and **-ir** verbs (**-ía**), are the same for **-ar**, **-er** and **-ir** verbs. Here are three examples from verbs in the texts:

tomar to take, have	tomar**ía**, tomar**ías**, tomar**ía**, tomar**íamos**, tomar**íais**, tomar**ían**
ser to be	ser**ía**, ser**ías**, ser**ía**, ser**íamos**, ser**íais**, ser**ían**
ir to go	ir**ía**, ir**ías**, ir**ía**, ir**íamos**, ir**íais**, ir**ían**

Me **tomaría** dos cervecitas ... (T. 1, l. 14)   *I would have two beers ...*
Sería imparable. (T. 2, l. 13)   *It would be unstoppable.*
Iría a ver una de esas películas ... (T. 1, l. 15–16)   *I would go and see one of those films ...*

Irregular verbs

Some verbs, like **hacer** *to do, make*, and **poder** *to be able to, can*, have the same irregular stem in the conditional as in the future tense (Chapter 6), but the endings are the same as those of regular verbs. Note the following examples in Text 1:

¿... **haría** una rebaja ...? (l. 18)   ... *Would you give a discount ...?*
No **podría** trabajar ... (l. 20)   *I couldn't work ...*

The following are the most common irregular conditional forms:

caber to be contained **cabría, cabrías** ...	**querer** to want **querría, querrías** ...
decir to say, tell **diría, dirías** ...	**saber** to know **sabría, sabrías** ...
haber to have (auxiliary) **habría, habrías** ...	**salir** to go out **saldría, saldrías** ...
hacer to do, make **haría, harías** ...	**tener** to have **tendría, tendrías** ...
poder to be able to **podría, podrías** ...	**valer** to be worth **valdría, valdrías** ...
poner to put **pondría, pondrías** ...	**venir** to come **vendría, vendrías** ...

Compound forms of the verbs above are irregular in the same way. For example:

proponer *to propose*   **propondría, propondrías** …

detener *to detain*   **detendría, detendrías** …

See also **Irregular verbs** on pages 204–7.

Other points to note in the texts

- *Ser* and *estar*: Text 1: *están* (l. 2), *soy* (l. 2), *ser* (l. 3), *estoy* (l. 4). Text 2: *era* (l. 5), *sería* (l. 13) (see Chapter 13)
- Adverbs: Text 1: *profesionalmente* (l. 2), *aún* (l. 2), *todavía* (l. 3), *despacio* (l. 4), etc. Text 2: *casi* (l. 1), *entonces* (l. 3), *siempre* (l. 6), etc. (see Chapter 21)
- Indefinite article: Text 1: *una estrella* (l. 7–8), *un 2 por 100* (l. 10), *un hermano* (l. 12), *unas tapas* (l. 14), etc. Text 2: *un aumento* (l. 12), *una población* (l. 15) (see Chapter 18)
- Conjunctions: There are numerous conjunctions in the texts, among these *y, o, que, pero porque*, etc. (see Chapter 29)

See for further information:	Batchelor and Pountain, pp. 236
	Butt, pp. 12–13
	Butt and Benjamin, pp. 217–19
	Kattán-Ibarra and Pountain, pp. 84–5
	Muñoz and Thacker, pp. 78–81, 215–16

✎ EXERCISES

1 Make these requests sound more polite by changing the verb to the conditional form.

  a ¿Puedes pasarme el agua?

  b ¿Puedo hablar con la señorita Blanco?

  c ¿Me hace el favor de subir el equipaje?

  d ¿Le importa esperar un momento?

  e ¿Puede decirme dónde está Correos?

  f ¿Me permiten explicarles el problema?

2 Use the conditional to rewrite and express the supposition or probability in these sentences.

  a Probablemente eran las once de la noche cuando entraron.

  b Seguramente compraba la ropa en el Rastro.

  c Probablemente había como mil personas en la manifestación.

  d Seguramente eran jóvenes los que lo hacían.

  e Seguro que al anciano le dolía la pierna, por su modo de andar.

3 When the first phase of the International Space Station was launched, a spokesperson gave out the following information.

  a 16 países participarán en el proyecto que costará más de 200.000 millones de dólares.

b Un español tomará parte en la misión.

c La estación espacial medirá lo equivalente a dos campos de fútbol y será un enorme laboratorio en el que vivirán y trabajarán siete astronautas.

d Su labor pondrá al alcance del hombre la exploración de Marte y también por medio de sus investigaciones encontraremos vida más allá de nuestro planeta.

Use the conditional to turn what the spokesperson said into indirect speech, beginning each point in the following way:

a Dijo que . . .

b Aseguró que . . .

c Afirmó que . . .

d Añadió que . . .

4 This extract is taken from a longer article profiling the modern Spanish male. Put the verbs below into the third person singular of the conditional and insert them into the text in the order given.

(1) volver   **(2) comprender**   **(3) asombrarse**   **(4) sufrir**   **(5) llegar**

Si el bisabuelo de cualquier nuevo español levantara la cabeza es seguro que, a fuerza de sobresaltos, (**a**) _____ a postrarla eternamente. No (**b**) _____ el comportamiento en casa del bisnieto varón, distribuyéndose, más o menos a la par, las tareas domésticas con la mujer. (**c**) _____ ante el afán de su descendiente por trabajar, por hacer dinero y gastar, que es la religión consumista del tiempo presente.

El bisabuelo (**d**) _____ el definitivo impacto mortal al contemplar, por ejemplo, el culto al cuerpo de su bisnieto, el armario lleno de ropas con colores de dudosa hombría, las colonias para oler bien, los aceites para poner tersa la piel, las lámparas de rayos para mantener un sempiterno bronceado . . . En fin, (**e**) _____ a la conclusión de que España había degenerado y caído en un relajamiento afeminado de las buenas costumbres.

Revista *Tiempo,* España

5 How would our great-grandparents react to our lives today? What changes would they notice and make to their lives to adapt to today's world?
Discuss with a partner or write your thoughts down using the conditional tense to express what they would do.

6 Imagine that you can do the same as Antonio Banderas in Text 1 and invent a twin brother/ sister. Complete the following using the conditional tense to describe your twin's physical appearance and to say what interests you would share and what you would do together:

• Si me pudiera inventar un/a hermano/a gemelo/a . . .

For more practice using the conditional in "if" constructions, see Chapters 15 and 16.

8 | The infinitive

The article which follows gives general guidelines on how to get fit in 30 days. You may be unfamiliar with some of the words in the text, so try to get the gist of what it says in your first reading, then go back through it, looking up some of the new words. Finally, read it again paying attention to the grammar and the ways in which infinitives have been used.

Cómo ponerse en forma en 30 días

Antes de **iniciar** un plan regular de entrenamiento, hay que **tener** en cuenta la condición física de la que partimos. Obviamente no puede **hacerlo** de la misma manera una persona que nunca ha hecho ejercicio que otra habituada a **hacer** deporte. Es imposible **compensar** en 30 días lo que no se ha hecho en
5 toda la vida.

Lo esencial es **tener** un buen estado de salud, **comenzar** con sesiones de baja intensidad, **ir** aumentando progresivamente los ejercicios y, una vez finalizado el plan, **seguir** practicando ejercicio regularmente.

La regularidad es el secreto de la forma física. La duración más recomendable
10 debe **ser** de entre 20 y 30 minutos de ejercicio aeróbico, dado que las sesiones de menor duración no suponen una mejora de la forma física.

En cuanto a la intensidad, es muy importante **hacer** el ejercicio de tal manera que nos permita **completar** la sesión de entrenamiento. Si nos cansamos pronto, la solución no es otra que **hacerlo** más despacio.
15 Entre las recomendaciones que hacen los expertos está el **mantener**, al **comenzar** un programa de entrenamiento, un nivel de ejercicio aeróbico, es decir, a una intensidad en que la energía para el trabajo realizado se obtenga en mayor proporción de la respiración. Una buena manera de **controlar** que se mantiene un ritmo adecuado consiste en que el ejercicio nos haga **sudar**, pero
20 nos permita **hablar** al mismo tiempo.

Entrenar muy intensamente – sobre todo durante las primeras sesiones – tendrá más inconvenientes que ventajas, ya que existe un mayor riesgo de lesiones, cansancio crónico y disminución del rendimiento en el trabajo o en los estudios, lo que nos puede **conducir** a **abandonar** el deporte.

> 25 Antes de **comenzar** a practicar cualquier deporte es recomendable **someterse** a un reconocimiento médico para **comprobar** que estás en perfecto estado físico. La práctica deportiva, de manera especial para aquellas personas que no están excesivamente habituadas, obliga a un esfuerzo que puede **causar** serios inconvenientes en organismos con algún tipo de problema físico. Los resultados
> 30 de las pruebas médicas nos ayudarán a **determinar** la forma, la cantidad y la intensidad de la actividad deportiva que tenemos la intención de **practicar**.
>
> Revista *Quo*, España

◯ The infinitive

USAGE

The infinitive is the full form or 'dictionary' form of the verb, which in Spanish is expressed by a single word ending in **-ar**, **-er** or **-ir** (e.g. **hablar**, **comer**, **vivir**). In English, this is made up of two words *to* + verb (e.g. *to speak*). There are a number of infinitives in the text, but their usage varies, as you will see from the notes below. Extra examples have been given in order to illustrate points not found in the article.

a As a noun, sometimes preceded by **el**, the masculine singular form of the definite article. Note here the use of the *-ing* form in English for the Spanish infinitive.

Entre las recomendaciones … está **el mantener** … (l. 15)   *Amongst the recommendations … is maintaining …*
Entrenar muy intensamente (l. 21)   *Training very intensively …*

b After prepositions and prepositional phrases.

Antes de iniciar un plan … (l. 1)   *Before starting a programme …*
Para comprobar … (l. 26)   *In order to check …*

Similarly, **a hacer** (l. 3), **de controlar** (l. 18), **de practicar** (l. 31).
Note again the use of the *-ing* form in English to translate most of these examples.

c After modal verbs such as **poder** *to be able, can, may,* **deber** *must,* **tener que** *to have to,* **haber que** *to be necessary* (Chapter 10).

Hay que tener en cuenta la condición física. (l. 1–2)   *It's necessary to take into account the physical condition.*
Debe ser de entre 20 y 30 minutos. (l. 10)   *It must be between 20 and 30 minutes.*
Puede causar … (l. 28)   *It may cause …*

d After a number of verbs, many of which may require a preposition.

Consiste en que el ejercicio nos **haga sudar**, pero nos **permita hablar**. (l. 19–20)
It consists in the exercise making us sweat but allowing us to speak.
Nos **ayudarán a determinar** … (l. 30)   *They'll allow us to determine …*

Note however that, with the exception of a few verbs (e.g. **permitir** *to allow*, **prohibir** *to forbid*, **ordenar**, **mandar**, *to order*), the infinitive cannot be used when the subject of the first verb is different from that of the second verb. In this case you need the construction **que** + subjunctive. Compare: **Conseguí hacerlo** *I managed to do it*, **Conseguí que lo hiciera** *I got him/her to do it* (see Chapters 14 and 15).

e After adjectives, in phrases such as **es imposible** *it's impossible*, **es importante** *it's important*, **es difícil** *it's difficult*, **parece fácil** *it seems easy*, **resulta caro** *it's expensive*.

> **Es imposible compensar** en 30 días ... (l. 4)   *It's impossible to make up in 30 days ...*
> **Es muy importante hacer** el ejercicio. (l. 12)   *It's very important to do the exercise.*

f Preceded by **al**, usually expressed in English with *on* + *-ing*.

> **Al comenzar** un programa ... (l. 15–16)   *On starting a programme ...*

g After **ver** *to see*, and **oír** *to hear*.

> Los **vi salir** hace un rato.   *I saw them go out a while ago.*
> Jamás la **he oído cantar**.   *I've never heard her sing.*

h In place of the imperative for giving directions and instructions.

> **Seguir** hasta el próximo semáforo.   *Continue as far as the next traffic lights.*
> No **adelantar**.   *Do not overtake.*

Other points to note in the text

- Modal verbs: *hay que tener* (l. 1), *no puede hacerlo* (l. 2), *debe ser* (l. 10), *nos puede conducir* (l. 24), *puede causar* (l. 28) (see Chapter 10)
- Adjective agreement and position: *un plan regular* (l. 1), *la condición física* (l. 1–2), *la misma manera* (l. 2–3), *un buen estado* (l. 6), *baja intensidad* (l. 6–7), etc. (see Chapter 20)
- Adverbs: *obviamente* (l. 2), *nunca* (l. 3), *progresivamente* (l. 7), *regularmente* (l. 8), *pronto* (l. 13), *despacio* (l. 14), etc. (see Chapter 21)

See for further information: Batchelor and Pountain, pp. 240
Butt, pp. 42–51
Butt and Benjamin, pp. 287–98
Kattán-Ibarra and Pountain, pp. 86–7
Muñoz and Thacker, pp. 136–140, 249–52

✎ EXERCISES

1 Make a sentence from the two parts using the preposition in brackets and making any necessary changes. Then translate the sentences into English.

Example: Salió del cuarto – no hizo ruido. (sin)

Salio del cuarto sin hacer ruido. (*S/he went out of the room without making a noise.*)

a Fueron a Salamanca – aprendieron español. (para)

b Estoy aquí – no hago nada. (sin)

c Entró en el salón – encendió la luz. (al)

d Primero cenamos – luego salimos. (después de)

e Llegaron – llamaron a sus amigos. (al)

f Se fue – no dijo nada. (sin)

g Iniciaron el programa – primero acudieron al médico. (antes de)

h Marta compró media docena de huevos – hizo una tortilla. (para)

i Primero visitaron el castillo – luego compraron recuerdos. (después de)

j Habló con Juan – primero leyó la carta. (antes de)

2 Put these words into the correct order to make meaningful sentences.

a Poder • no • ayudarte • siento.

b A • espera • Madrid • ir.

c Con • Inés • seguir • no • los • quiso • ejercicios.

d Ejercicio • es • hacer • importante • muy.

e Escuchar • aprender • que • hay • para.

f Ir • porque • no • al • tengo • gimnasio • puedo • trabajar • que.

g Ponerse • imposible • sin • es • ejercicio • en forma • hacer.

h Comprar • para • coche • quieren • España • a • un • ir.

3 Translate into Spanish – take care to use the infinitive with or without a preposition where necessary.

a As they went in, they began singing.

b I heard them singing.

c The best thing about living here is being able to go to the theatre.

d Going to the gym is a good way of getting fit.

e She is incapable of giving up smoking.

f He denies having helped the thieves.

4 Put these hostel rules into Spanish using the infinitive.

a No smoking.

b Do not use.

c No showers before 7 o'clock.

d Do not leave clothes in the changing rooms.

e Put the lights out before midnight.

f Clear the table after eating.

g Wash up.

h Beds must be made on arrival.

9 | The gerund

This article considers the main reasons for the *greenhouse effect* and its consequences. The grammar focuses on the use of verb forms such as **incrementando** *increasing*, **produciendo** *producing*, which are known as gerunds. Read the text and note how these have been used.

El efecto invernadero

La principal causa del *efecto invernadero* es la acción del hombre. Desde los inicios de la Revolución Industrial, a finales del siglo XVIII, se han estado **produciendo** y **liberando** millones de toneladas de gases y partículas, parte de las cuales se han ido **acumulando** en la atmósfera que rodea el planeta,
5 **agudizando** así el llamado *efecto invernadero*.

Es la atmósfera que recubre el planeta la que permite la existencia de formas superiores de vida en la Tierra merced a una doble acción: por un lado, filtra aquella parte de los rayos solares que son dañinos para las formas vivas, **impidiendo** que lleguen hasta la superficie; por el otro, evita que los rayos
10 del sol reboten en la corteza terrestre y se pierdan en el espacio. Gracias a la atmósfera, hasta 60 por 100 de la energía solar que llega a la Tierra queda atrapada aquí, **elevando** así la temperatura media del planeta del mismo modo que lo hacen los vidrios o los plásticos transparentes dentro de un invernadero.

Si no fuera por la atmósfera, la Tierra sería un gigantesco sorbete de hielo, con
15 una temperatura media inferior en 33 grados centígrados a la temperatura media actual, donde sólo formas de vida muy simples y primitivas podrían existir.

Pero toneladas y toneladas de gases y partículas producidas por la quema de combustibles fósiles, incendios de bosques y otras fuentes de contaminación lanzadas a la atmósfera están **incrementando** notablemente el *efecto*
20 *invernadero* **ocasionando** el recalentamiento generalizado, que ya se ha producido y seguirá **produciéndose** en los años sucesivos.

Revista *Tiempo*, España

⌕ **The gerund**

1 USAGE

Verb forms such as **hablando** *speaking*, **comiendo** *eating*, **saliendo** *going out*, are known as *gerunds*. Some of the uses of the gerund correspond to that of the *-ing* verb form in English, others are different.

a The gerund may function as a kind of adverb to refer to:

i An action which is simultaneous with or complementary to the action expressed by the main verb.

Se han ido **acumulando** ... **agudizando** así ... (l. 4–5) *They have been building up ... thus worsening ...*
Filtra ... los rayos solares ... **impidiendo** que ... (l. 7–9) *It filters the sun's rays ... preventing them from ...*

ii Cause.

Viendo que era tan tarde, decidí irme. (Como era tan tarde ...) *Seeing that it was so late, I decided to leave.*

iii Manner.

Se acercó a mí **sonriendo**. (con una sonrisa) *He/she approached me smiling.*

iv A condition.

Trabajando así llegarás muy lejos. (Si trabajas así ...) *Working like that, you'll go far.*

v Concession.

Insistió en hacerlo, **sabiendo** lo difícil que era. (aunque sabía ...) *He/she insisted on doing it, knowing how difficult it was.*

b With **estar**, in the continuous tenses.

Se han **estado produciendo** y **liberando** ... (l. 2–3) *They are being produced and released ...*
Están incrementando ... (l. 19) *They are increasing ...*

c With **ir**, to indicate that the action expressed by the verb occurs gradually.

Se han **ido acumulando** ... (l. 4) *They have been accumulating ...*

d With **seguir** and **continuar** to denote continuity.

Seguirá (or **Continuará**) **produciéndose** ... (l. 21) *It will continue occurring ...*

e With **venir**, to denote duration or repetition.

Esto **viene pasando** desde hace mucho tiempo. *This has been going on for a long time.*

f With **acabar** and **terminar** to indicate a result.

Acabaron/Terminaron divorciándose. *They ended up getting divorced.*

g With **llevar** and an expression of time, to express continuity.

Llevo dos años viviendo aquí.   *I have been living here for two years.*

h With **quedarse**, to indicate duration in the action expressed by the verb.

Se quedó mirándome fijamente.   *He/she carried on staring at me.*

i With **andar**, to express the idea of going around doing something.

Anda buscando trabajo.   *He/she's (going round) looking for work.*

SPANISH GERUND AND ENGLISH -*ING*: DIFFERENCES

There are important differences in use between the Spanish gerund and the English -*ing* form:

a The Spanish equivalent of the English -*ing* form used as a noun is normally the infinitive.

Telling him will not help at all.   El **decírselo** no ayudará en nada.

b The Spanish gerund is not normally used as an adjective.

A swimming suit.   Un traje de baño.
The falling leaves.   Las hojas que caen.

c After a preposition, Spanish uses the infinitive, not the gerund.

After having lunch …   Después de **haber** almorzado …
She left without saying goodbye.   Se fue sin **despedirse**.

d Actions involving different subjects, often expressed with -*ing* in English, require different constructions in Spanish.

I love being sent flowers.   Me encanta que me manden flores.
We like her dancing.   Nos gusta su forma de bailar.

e Different actions performed by a single subject are usually expressed in Spanish with an infinitive, not with the gerund.

I hate going to bed late.   Odio **acostarme** tarde.
We enjoy taking a walk in the evening.   Nos agrada **salir** de paseo por la tarde.

2 FORMATION

To form the gerund, remove the ending of the infinitive and add **-ando** to the stem of -**ar** verbs and -**iendo** to that of -**er** and -**ir** verbs, e.g. **habl***ando*, **com***iendo*, **viv***iendo*. A few verbs form the gerund in a slightly different way:

a -**iendo** becomes -**yendo** when the stem of the verb ends in a vowel. Common examples are: **caer** – **cayendo** (*to fall – falling*), **creer** – **creyendo** (*to believe – believing*), **leer** – **leyendo** (*to read – reading*), **oír** – **oyendo** (*to hear – hearing*).
The gerund of **ir** is **yendo**.

b Most verbs in **-ir**, which change the stem in the third person of the preterite, have a similar change in the gerund. Amongst them we find the following:

Infinitive	3rd persons, preterite	gerund	
dormir	durmió, durmieron	durmiendo	*sleeping*
morir	murió, murieron	muriendo	*dying*
pedir	pidió, pidieron	pidiendo	*asking for*
sentir	sintió, sintieron	sintiendo	*feeling*
venir	vino, vinieron	viniendo	*coming*

c The gerund of **decir** is **diciendo**, *saying*, and that of **poder** is **pudiendo**, *being able to*.

d The gerund has a past form made up of the gerund of **haber** and the past participle, e.g. **habiendo terminado**, *having finished*.

POSITION OF PRONOUNS WITH THE GERUND

Pronouns are normally added to the gerund, unless this is preceded by a finite verb, in which case the pronoun can either go before the finite verb or be attached to the end of the gerund. If the pronoun is added to the gerund, you need to place a written accent on the **a** in **-ando** or the **e** in **-iendo**.

Viéndola así, preferí no hablarle.   *Seeing her like that, I preferred not to speak to her.*
Estoy **terminándolo** *or* Lo estoy **terminando**.   *I am finishing it.*

Other points to note in the text

- Relative pronouns: *las cuales* (l. 4), *que* (l. 4 and 6), *la que* (l. 6) (see Chapter 26)
- *Por* and *para*: *por un lado ... por el otro* (l. 7–9), *para las formas* (l. 8), *si no fuera por* (l. 14), *producidas por* (l. 17) (see Chapter 28)
- Subjunctive, present and imperfect: *impidiendo que lleguen* (l. 9), *evita que ... reboten ... y se pierdan* (l. 9–10), *si no fuera por* (l. 14) (see Chapters 14 and 15)

See for further information: Batchelor and Pountain, pp. 241
Butt, pp. 51–5
Butt and Benjamin, pp. 304–13
Kattán-Ibarra and Pountain, pp. 87–8
Muñoz and Thacker, pp. 142–6, 253–5

EXERCISES

1 Choose a verb from the list and put it into the gerund form to complete the sentences.

usar   dormir   sustituir   trabajar   correr

a – ¿Los niños están en el jardín?
– No, están en su cuarto, _____.

b – ¿Cómo va a pasar el verano Rosario?

– _____ en un bar.

c – ¿Qué le dijiste al policía?

– Que vi a dos jóvenes que salieron _____ de la tienda.

d – ¿Cómo puedo ahorrar energía?

– _____ estas bombillas por unas de bajo consumo.

e – Y ¿cómo puedo ahorrar agua?

– _____ la ducha en lugar de la bañera.

2 Replace the underlined words by gerunds, making other adjustments where necessary.

a El Presidente salió al balcón y saludó a las masas.

b Si me escribes a esta dirección, la carta llegará.

c Al mismo tiempo que nos ayudas, aprenderás.

d Seguimos utilizando nuestros coches, aunque sabemos del daño que esto causa al entorno.

e Pasó la noche en el tren y leyó _La muerte de Artemio Cruz_.

f Mientras descansaba en el Pirineo, se olvidó de todos sus problemas.

3 Form sentences from the constituent parts as in the example, then translate into English.

Example: Elvira • un año • reformar su casa.

Elvira lleva un año reformando su casa.

(_Elvira has been renovating her house for a year._)

a Los agricultores • dos años • plantar bosques.

b Sofía • seis meses • ir al trabajo en autobús.

c Los oficinistas • año y medio • reciclar el papel.

d Nosotros • mucho tiempo • reducir nuestro consumo de electricidad.

e Los ecologistas • más de treinta años • crear conciencia sobre los peligros que corre el planeta.

4 Rewrite these sentences using the bracketed verb to make a gerund construction.
Then study each one, thinking about the meaning.

a La suciedad se acumula en el fondo del mar. (estar)

b La situación mejora. (ir)

c Notamos un aumento del nivel del mar desde hace varios años. (venir)

d Según los ecologistas, el hombre destruirá el planeta. (acabar)

e El hombre contamina la atmósfera desde los inicios de la Revolución Industrial. (venir)

f Los municipios instalan contenedores específicos para los distintos tipos de basura. (estar)

g Los fabricantes de vidrio apoyarán el reciclado como una medida activa a favor del medio ambiente. (seguir)

h Poco a poco estamos cambiando nuestros hábitos al tirar la basura. (ir)

5 Rewrite these sentences using **andar, ir, seguir, quedarse** or **venir** + gerund according to which seems the most appropriate to the context.

a Mi hermano dice a todo el mundo que soy tonta.

b Poco a poco estamos aprendiendo.

c Todavía estás fumando a pesar de lo que te ha dicho el médico.

d Fernando y Javier buscan un apartamento.

e Estuvimos charlando hasta altas horas de la noche.

f Poco a poco estoy conociendo la ciudad.

g Todavía tiramos la basura sin separarla.

h Escribía todo lo que oía.

6 Translate the English into Spanish to complete these sentences.

a Por efecto del calentamiento global los polos *will end up melting*.

b Muchos científicos desmienten el pésimo estado de salud de la Tierra *accusing the environmentalists of sensationalism*.

c Se sabe que si la emisión de gases de efecto invernadero no se limita, las temperaturas *will carry on increasing*.

d Ahora tenemos que separar la basura, *depositing plastics and tins in one bag and throwing organic material into another bag*.

e Las lavadoras de alta tecnología detectan automáticamente la cantidad y tipo de ropa a lavar *consuming only the necessary water and electricity*.

f *By recycling glass* se ahorra la materia prima con que se fabrica el cristal.

g En las selvas tropicales la deforestación *is threatening the indigenous populations*.

h En los más de 150 años que *temperatures have been recorded* los años más calurosos corresponden a los años más recientes.

See also Chapter 8, **The Infinitive**, for ways that English -*ing* can be rendered in Spanish.

10 | Modal verbs

A reader whose husband fainted due to stress wrote to a health magazine seeking advice. This letter and Text 2 below contain several examples of modal verbs, such as **soler** *to be accustomed to*, **deber** *must*, **tener que** *to have to*, which are followed by an infinitive. Read the letters and study the way in which they have been used.

El desmayo por estrés

Desde hace un mes mi marido tiene un nuevo trabajo que le exige mucho desgaste tanto físico como psicológico. Llega todas las noches cansado, y por la mañana **suele levantarse** sin fuerzas, pero sigue adelante con todo. Hace una semana estábamos desayunando y de repente, cuando **quiso pararse*** se cayó. El

5 médico dijo que fue un simple desmayo y que **se tenía que relajar**, pero yo no quedé muy conforme con esta respuesta. ¿Me **podrían aclarar** qué fue lo que pasó y qué **debe hacer**?

Graciela Pérez, Revista *Buena Salud*, Argentina

* *Peninsular Spanish* **levantarse**.

Text 2

This text presents a letter from someone asking for advice on sunbeds.

Las conflictivas camas solares

Estoy muy asustada porque todo el invierno fui a la cama solar y hace un tiempo leí que era muy malo y que **podía provocar** algunas enfermedades en la piel. **Quisiera saber** si esta información es real y qué opinan los médicos con respecto al tema de las camas solares. Además, quisiera que me digan cuánto tiempo

5 **se puede tomar** sol así y qué cuidados **hay que tener**.

Florencia Massini, Revista *Buena Salud,* Argentina

Modal verbs

USAGE

Modal auxiliary verbs are used with the infinitive to express a certain intention or mood with regard to the accompanying infinitive. Below are the main Spanish modal verbs and their specific usage. Extra examples have been given to illustrate usage not found in the texts.

a **Soler** (**o** changes into **ue**) *to be accustomed to, usually,* is used for expressing habitual actions in relation to the present (in the present tense) or the past (in the imperfect tense), as an alternative to using the present and the imperfect. This modal verb is generally infrequent in Latin America.

> **Suele levantarse** sin fuerzas. (T. 1, l. 3) (for **Se levanta** ...)   *He usually gets up without energy.*
> **Solían visitarnos** a menudo. (for **Nos visitaban** ...)   *They used to visit us often.*

b **Querer** (**e** changes into **ie**) normally translates *to want,* but depending on the context it can have other meanings as well. The forms **quisiera** and **querría** *I'd like* are common in polite offers and requests, while the imperfect tense form **quería** *wanted to,* is also used in polite address. The preterite form **quiso** normally translates *tried to.*

> Cuando **quiso pararse** se cayó. (T. 1, l. 4)   *When he tried to get up he fell.*
> **Quisiera** (o **quería**) **saber** si ... (T. 2, l. 3)   *I'd like to know if ...*

c **Tener que** *to have to,* expresses obligation and strong need.

> **Se tenía que relajar**. (T. 1, l. 5)   *He had to relax.*

d **Poder** *to be able to, to manage, can, may,* is used to express:

> **i** Requests which, when used in the conditional, convey more formality and politeness, the equivalent of *could you ...?* or *would you ...?* in English.

> > ¿Me **podrían aclarar** ... ? (T. 1, l. 6)   *Could you explain ...?*

> **ii** Possibility.

> > **Podía provocar** ... (T. 2, l. 2)   *It could cause ...*
> > ... se **puede tomar** sol así. (T. 2, l. 4–5)   *... one can sunbathe this way.*

Note the use of the imperfect in the first example. The conditional **podría** *could,* and the present form **puede** *can,* are equally valid in this context.

> **iii** Permission, usually translating *may* or *can* in English.

> > ¿**Podemos pasar?**   *May we come in?*

> **iv** Ability.

> > No **pude entenderle**.   *I didn't manage to understand him/her.*

The use of the imperfect, No **podía entenderle**, would change the meaning of this sentence into *I couldn't understand him/her.*

e **Deber** expresses:

  i Obligation.

   ¿Qué **debe hacer**? (T. 1, l. 7)   *What must he do?*
   Deberías ir con ella.   *You ought to go with her.*

  ii Supposition.
   Strictly speaking, when expressing supposition, **deber** should be followed by the preposition **de**. Most Spanish speakers, however, will use it without **de**.

   Deben (de) ser las seis.   *It must be six o'clock.*
   Debe (de) estar en casa.   *He/she must be at home.*

f **Haber que** *to be necessary*, is an impersonal form, used in the third person singular.

   ... qué cuidados **hay que tener**. (T. 2, l. 5)   ... *what precautions it's necessary to take.*
   Habrá que venderlo.   *It'll be necessary to sell it.*

g **Haber de** *must, to have to*, indicates mild obligation, and is generally uncommon in colloquial speech in Spain. In México, it is used for expressing supposition.

   Hemos de terminarlo hoy. (Obligation)   *We have to finish it today.*
   Ha de haber salido. (Supposition)   *He/she must have gone out.*

h **Saber**, followed by the infinitive, means *to know how to.*

   No **sé conducir/manejar**. (L. Am.)   *I don't know how to drive.*

USING *QUERER* AND *PODER* WITH THE SUBJUNCTIVE

Note that **querer** and **poder** can also be followed by a subordinate clause introduced by **que**, with a verb in the subjunctive (see Chapters 14 and 15). This kind of construction occurs when the subject of the main verb is different from that of the subordinate clause.

   Quisiera que me digan. (T. 2, l. 4)   *I'd like you to tell me.*
   Puede que lleguen hoy.   *It's possible that they may arrive today.*

SABER FOLLOWED BY *QUE*

Saber is followed by **que** when meaning *to know.*

   Sé que me ayudarán.   *I know they will help me.*

Other points to note in the texts

- Present tense indicative: Text 1: *tiene* (l. 1), *exige* (l. 1), *llega* (l. 2), *suele* (l. 3), *sigue* (l. 3), etc. Text 2: *estoy* (l. 1), *es* (l. 3), *opinan* (l. 3) (see Chapter 1)

- Preterite and imperfect tenses: Text 1: *estábamos desayunando* (l. 4), *cuando quiso pararse se cayó* (l. 4), *el médico dijo que fue* ... (l. 4–5), *que se tenía que relajar* (l. 5), etc. Text 2: *fui a la cama* (l. 1), *leí que era malo* (l. 2), *que podía provocar* (l. 2) (see Chapters 2 and 3)
- *Ser* and *estar*: Text 1: *estábamos desayunando* (l. 4), *fue un simple desmayo* (l. 5), ¿ ... *qué fue lo que pasó* ... ? (l. 6–7). Text 2: *estoy muy asustada* (l. 1), *era muy malo* (l. 2), *si* ... *es real* (l. 3) (see Chapter 13)

See for further information:	Batchelor and Pountain, pp. 243–7
	Butt, pp. 60–3
	Butt and Benjamin, pp. 314–20.
	Kattán-Ibarra and Pountain, pp. 109–13
	Muñoz and Thacker, pp. 121–3, 239–40

✎ EXERCISES

1 Correct these sentences.

   a Quiero voy a México de vacaciones.

   b ¿Cuánto tiempo podemos nos quedamos aquí?

   c Debéis habláis con Juan cuanto antes.

   d ¿Quieres vienes conmigo?

   e Debemos tomamos las cosas con calma.

2 Rewrite the following sentences using the verb **soler** or **deber** according to context.

   a Normalmente juego un partido de ajedrez después de la cena.

   b De costumbre los abuelos echaban la siesta después de comer.

   c Es importante que no tomes el sol entre las dos y las seis.

   d Por lo general vamos a la piscina dos veces por semana.

   e ¿Por qué no pedís ayuda?

   f Lo mejor es tomar una aspirina si te duele la cabeza.

   g Generalmente tomábamos las vacaciones con los amigos.

   h Jorge no sale; supongo que está estudiando.

3 **Tener que/hay que/deber**. Complete the following sentences with the most appropriate verb for the context.

   a El médico le dijo al marido de Graciela que _____ relajarse.

   b _____ tener cuidado con las camas solares.

   c No se _____ tomar el sol en exceso.

   d Tengo hora con el médico dentro de diez minutos. _____ irme ahora mismo.

   e Florencia no _____ usar la cama solar con tanta frecuencia.

   f Para encontrar un buen trabajo _____ saber hablar otros idiomas.

g En este país _____ preocuparnos por aprender otros idiomas.

h María _____ estudiar mucho si quiere aprobar los exámenes; _____ estudiar al menos cinco horas diarias.

4 Translate the following sentences into Spanish.

   a Can you play the guitar?
   b We usually spent the morning on the beach.
   c Why have you got to go?
   d If you want to sunbathe, you should use a good sun cream.
   e It must not be forgotten that the sun's rays can be harmful.
   f He used to work ten hours a day until the doctor told him that he had to relax.
   g To travel on the AVE, you have to book your seats in advance.
   h Pepe, you should pay more attention.
   i Of course I know how to cook!
   j We'll have to get up early tomorrow.

5 When on holiday, think of and write down:

   a a thing that you want to do
   b a thing that you can do
   c a thing that you usually do
   d a thing that you should do
   e a thing that you have to do
   f a thing that has to be done.

Compare and comment on your list with a partner.

11 | Passive and impersonal sentences

Text 1

Text 1 warns about the threat posed to coastal areas by population increase, industrial pollution and tourism. The grammar in this text and in Text 2 below focuses on passive sentences, expressed in English through the construction *to be* + the past participle, as in *It is done, They will be built.*

Alerta sobre alteración de costas del mundo

De acuerdo con los análisis efectuados por el Instituto Mundial de Recursos, cerca del 30% del territorio adyacente a los ecosistemas costeros del mundo **ha sido alterado** o **destruido** debido principalmente a la creciente demanda por terrenos que luego **son destinados** a la construcción de casas, a la industria
5 y a la recreación. Las poblaciones costeras están aumentando y, a medida que **se incrementan**, la presión sobre los ecosistemas costeros también crece.

　　Se estima que más de 70 mil productos químicos sintéticos **han sido descargados** en los océanos del mundo. Sólo un pequeño porcentaje de ellos **ha sido controlado**, y éste corresponde a aquéllos relacionados con salud
10 humana y no con impacto ecológico.

　　El organismo señala que, de continuar la permanente modificación o destrucción de esas áreas, **se pondrá** en grave peligro la capacidad de las costas para mantener la biodiversidad, proveer pesca, hogares y negocios y reducir la polución y la erosión.

Diario *La Tercera*, Chile

Text 2

The article which follows looks at the destruction of the Amazon and outlines the plans being established by the Brazilian government to halt and revert the process of destruction.

Al rescate de la Amazonia

La Tierra pierde cada año 11,2 millones de hectáreas de bosque nativo. **Se estima** que cada dos segundos **se pierde** una superficie equivalente a una cancha de fútbol. En cuatro minutos **se habrán destruido** 90 hectáreas de árboles, lo que explica por qué sólo queda vivo el 22% de los bosques originarios del planeta.

5   La Amazonia no ha estado exenta de la destrucción en serie. El 80% de la madera que **se extrae** de esta zona **se corta** sin permiso. La contribución de los bosques amazónicos a la producción total de madera brasileña ha crecido en dos décadas del 14% al 85%.

Para rescatar esta región de características únicas, que posee el 10% de las

10 especies del mundo, el gobierno de Brasil, con el apoyo del Banco Interamericano del Desarrollo, implementará un proyecto de ecoturismo que pretende el rescate económico, medio-ambiental y social de la región. **Se prevé** la construcción de 21 grandes obras de infraestructura, **se crearán** veinte parques y áreas de protección ambiental. También **se incluye** la capacitación de unos mil residentes que se

15 encargarán de llevar adelante el plan y de recibir a los turistas internacionales. **Se construirán** puertos, ferrocarriles y aeropuertos.

Dentro del plan **se pretende** incluir a toda la comunidad para que los beneficios sean también sociales. Por ejemplo, en la ciudad Presidente Figueredo **se llevará a cabo** una remodelación de las instalaciones de agua potable y de

20 alcantarillado.

Diario *El Metropolitano*, Chile

Passive and impersonal sentences

1 ACTIVE AND PASSIVE SENTENCES

Spanish, like English, has active and passive sentences. A sentence such as **El turismo ha destruido las zonas costeras** (*Tourism has destroyed coastal areas*) is an active sentence, with an active subject, **el turismo**, carrying out the action expressed by the verb.

In **Las zonas costeras han sido destruidas por el turismo** (*Coastal areas have been destroyed by tourism*), the direct object of the active sentence, **las zonas costeras**, has become the subject of what is a passive sentence. The agent performing the action, **el turismo**, occupies a secondary place in a phrase introduced by **por** *by*. The construction with **ser** *to be* + past participle here is similar to the one used in English.

Alternatively, you may use a sentence like **Se han destruido las zonas costeras** (*Coastal areas have been destroyed*), another type of passive sentence, much more common than the one above, introduced by **se**, in which the agent performing the action is not mentioned.

2 PASSIVE SENTENCES WITH *SER* + PAST PARTICIPLE

a The past participle must agree in gender (masculine and feminine) and number (singular or plural) with the noun it refers to.

Cerca del 30% del territorio **ha sido alterado** o **destruido**. (T. 1, l. 1–3)   *Nearly 30% of the territory has been altered or destroyed.*

... terrenos que **son destinados** ... (T. 1, l. 4) ... *land which is used* ...

See also **han sido descargados** (T. 1, l. 7–8) *they have been dumped*, **ha sido controlado** (T. 1, l. 9) *it has been monitored.*

b The passive with **ser** is found more frequently in written language. It is uncommon in the spoken language, except in a very formal style, for example a formal speech.

c If the agent performing the action of the verb is important, and you wish to name it, then use the passive with **ser**, e.g. **Ha sido destruido por el hombre** *It has been destroyed by man.*

d English passive sentences such as *I was told he was here*, *She was asked why she'd done it*, cannot be expressed in Spanish with the construction **ser** + past participle. To convey these ideas use the impersonal third person plural **Me dijeron que** ... , **Le preguntaron por qué** ...

3 PASSIVE SENTENCES WITH *SE*

a The verb agrees in number (singular and plural) with the subject.

> **Se corta** sin permiso. (T. 2, l. 6)   *It is cut without permission.*
> **Se construirán** puertos. (T. 2, l. 16)   *Ports will be built.*

See also **se habrán destruido** (T. 2, l. 3) *they will have been destroyed*, **se extrae** (T. 2, l. 6) *it is extracted*, **se crearán** (T. 2, l. 13) *they will be built*, **se incluye** (T. 2, l. 14) *it is included.*

b Passive sentences with **se** are common in all forms of language.

c Do not use this construction when the agent of the action expressed by the verb needs to be specified. Use the passive with **ser** instead, as in (**c**) above.

4 IMPERSONAL USE OF *SE*

Not all sentences with **se** are passive. **Se** is also used in impersonal sentences, the Spanish equivalent of *one/we/they/people*, **on** in French and **man** in German. In the text we find

> **Se pretende** incluir ... (T. 2., l. 17)   *They hope to include* ...
> **Se estima** ... (T. 1, l. 7; T. 2, l. 1)   *It is estimated* ...
> **Se prevé** ... (T. 2, l. 12)   *They are planning* ...

For the use of **se** as an object pronoun in place of **le, les**, see **Personal pronouns**, Chapter 25. For the use of **se** with reflexive verbs see **The reflexive**, Chapter 12.

5 OTHER IMPERSONAL SENTENCES

Impersonal sentences can also be formed by using one of the following devices:

a **Tú** form of the verb:

> **Tienes** que estar muy alerta.   *You have to/one has to be very alert.*

b Third person plural of the verb:

Dicen que el conflicto empeorará.   *They say the conflict will get worse.*

c **Uno**

Uno tiene que estar muy seguro.   *One has to be very sure.*

d **La gente**

La gente no sabe lo que dice.   *People don't know what they say.*

Other points to note in the texts

- Future tense: Text 1: *pondrá* (l. 12). Text 2: *habrán* (l. 3), *implementará* (l. 11), *se crearán* (l. 13), *se encargarán* (l. 14–15), *se construirán* (l. 16), *se llevará a cabo* (l. 19) (see Chapter 6)
- Perfect tense: Text 1: *ha sido alterado* (l. 2–3), *han sido descargados* (l. 7–8), *ha sido controlado* (l. 9). Text 2: *no ha estado exenta* (l. 5), *ha crecido* (l. 7) (see Chapter 4)
- Prepositions: There are numerous prepositions in both texts, among these *de, con, por, a,* etc. (see Chapter 28)

See for further information: Butt, pp. 64–6

Butt and Benjamin, pp. 380–97

Kattán-Ibarra and Pountain, pp. 123–6

Muñoz and Thacker, pp. 131–4, 244–7

EXERCISES

1 Change these sentences from passive to active constructions.

a *La Regenta* fue escrito por Leopoldo Alas.

b El camionero fue interrogado por el policía.

c Los cristales fueron rotos por los chicos.

d El motor ha sido desmontado por Agustín.

e El campeonato no será emitido por Tele-Mundo.

f Estas casas fueron construidas por mi padre.

g La casa de mis sueños será diseñada por mi hermano.

h Los árboles han sido cortados por los agricultores.

2 Change the verb in brackets into the passive form, **ser** with the past participle, to complete these sentences.

a Estos restos incaicos (excavar) _____ el año pasado por un equipo internacional de arqueólogos.

b Los pueblos (repoblar) _____ por familias jóvenes.

c Todos los datos (analizar) _____ antes de publicarlos.

d Mucha gente (invitar) _____ a la inauguración del nuevo teatro.

   e Los robots (programar) _____ para tomar fotografías de la superficie de Marte.

   f La manifestación del martes pasado (organizar) _____ por los estudiantes.

3 Rewrite these sentences replacing the passive construction, **ser** with the past participle, with **se**.

   a La catedral fue construida en el siglo XV.

   b Este libro no ha sido traducido al inglés.

   c Las películas serán conservadas en cajas metálicas.

   d Las estatuas fueron destruidas en el bombardeo.

   e La noticia del accidente fue difundida por televisión.

4 Translate the following sentences into Spanish using the passive construction with **se**.

   a Twenty parks and conservation areas will be created.

   b Ports, railways and airports will be built.

   c 80% of the wood which is extracted from this area is cut down without permission.

   d Every two seconds, a surface area equivalent to a football pitch is lost.

   e In four minutes, 90 hectares of trees will have been destroyed.

   f Redevelopment of the drinking water and sewerage systems will be carried out.

5 Translate into Spanish using the third person plural to render the English passive.

   a We have not been paid this month.

   b I have been given a lot of support.

   c They weren't helped very much.

   d The cause of the accident was investigated.

   e A new cinema is going to open here.

   f The lift has been mended.

6 Rewrite these sentences replacing the passive construction, **ser** with the past participle, with **se** or with the third person plural. Make any other necessary changes.

   a El turrón es elaborado en Jijona.

   b Una nueva vida extraterrestre será descubierta en un futuro próximo.

   c Hoy día muchos libros son fotocopiados y pirateados.

   d Una nueva autopista será construida pronto.

   e Tras el accidente el conductor fue hospitalizado.

   f Las ciudades fueron bombardeadas.

   g El alpinista fue rescatado a última hora.

7 Below is an outline of a robbery. Add detail to the elements and use **ser** with the past participle, **se** or the third person plural where possible and appropriate to give an account of the incident.

una joyería asaltada • la alarma dada • dos jóvenes corriendo por la calle • dos jóvenes atropellados • alhajas por la calle • llegada de la policía • los jóvenes detenidos y llevados a la comisaría • motivo del asalto desconocido.

12 | The reflexive

This passage from a Spanish magazine describes the daily routine of Martín López Zubero, a swimmer. As you read the text, focus attention on the verb forms in bold, which are known as reflexive.

Retrato

Martín López Zubero **se levanta** todos los días a las seis a.m. y **se ducha**. Media hora después **se zambulle** en la piscina, donde entrena hasta las 8,30. A esa hora vuelve a casa y, antes de desayunar un yogur con frutas, **se remoja** de nuevo en agua caliente y jabón. **Se va** a clase a la universidad y hacia las 15,00 regresa a
5   consumir un almuerzo frugal. A lo mejor **se da** otra ducha antes de **ponerse** de nuevo el traje de baño y nadar durante las tres horas siguientes. A las 18,00 deja la piscina, **se aplica** una ducha más y **se dedica** a estudiar. Cena algo ligero, ve televisión y al llegar las 23,00 ya **se va** a dormir.

No será un modo de vida muy impresionante, pero a Martín le ha producido
10 los resultados más emocionantes de su vida: medallas de todos los metales en diversos campeonatos de natación. De hecho, Martín es el único español que ha batido récords mundiales en el agua.

Problema: Martín López nació en Jacksonville (Estados Unidos) el 23 de abril de 1969; ha vivido siempre en Estados Unidos; estudia y entrena en Estados Unidos;
15 su director es norteamericano; mide 1,90 de estatura; habla perfecto inglés y no **se expresa** bien en castellano. ¿Puede **considerarse** español? ¿Podemos pensar que sus triunfos en las piscinas son triunfos españoles?

Respuesta: Sí. Martín López Zubero no sólo lleva nombre y apellidos sino también sangre española. El país de su cariño es el de sus mayores, y por eso
20 agrega siempre a su firma la palabra *España*. Martín tiene, pues, títulos suficientes para llevar, como ha llevado, la representación deportiva española en certámenes internacionales.

Revista semanal, *Diario 16*, España

Text 2 is part of an interview with the Spanish actor Imanol Arias. Note the use of reflexive verbs in this text.

Imanol Arias: "no soy un galán"

*¿Cuáles fueron las razones que le impulsaron a **convertirse** en actor?*
Primero, la posibilidad de **dedicarme** a algo artístico y poco rutinario y perder de vista la profesión a la que estaba abocado, que era la industria. En el País Vasco existía una gran tradición de músicos, escultores y artistas y yo ni dibujaba bien,
5 ni sabía cantar, ni tenía ninguna habilidad manual. Sólo **me veía** capacitado para ser actor. Por eso **me vine** a Madrid.

¿Cómo fueron sus primeros años de trabajo?
Espantosos. Al principio **me** lo **pasé** muy mal, apenas podía **mantenerme** económicamente y, además, estaba lleno de dudas. Llegué a temer seriamente
10 no estar a la altura de las circunstancias, no estar capacitado para mi trabajo. De hecho, hay muchos que trabajan o que **se quedan** a medio camino. **Convertirse** en un buen actor exige un esfuerzo enorme, una dedicación profunda. Si no tienes cualidades y no las desarrollas, es absolutamente imposible llegar a ser algo en esta profesión.

Revista *Carta de España*

The reflexive

1 USAGE

Verbs such as **expresarse** *to express oneself*, **considerarse** *to consider oneself*, **mantenerse** *to support oneself*, are known as ***reflexive*** or ***pronominal*** verbs because they are accompanied by an object pronoun (see **Forms** below) which refers back to the subject of the verb. The term ***reflexive***, however, is not strictly correct, as this has other uses as well. But you may already be familiar with this label, so it is this one rather than the term ***pronominal***, used in some grammar books, which has been adopted here. The notes below describe the various uses of the reflexive:

a In sentences such as

No **se expresa** bien en castellano. (T. 1, l. 15–16)   *He doesn't express himself well in Spanish.*
¿Puede **considerarse** español? (T. 1, l. 16)   *Can he consider himself Spanish?*
Apenas podía **mantenerme** ... (T. 2, l. 8)   *I could hardly support myself ...*

usage corresponds to that of English, with the object pronouns *se himself* and **me** *myself*, in these examples, referring back to the ***subject*** of the verb. All three verbs above can be used without the reflexive pronoun, but then the action would refer not to the subject but to something or someone outside:

Lo **expresa** muy bien.   *He/she expresses it very well.*
Apenas podía **mantener** a sus hijos.   *He/she could hardly support his/her children.*

b   The use of the reflexive may change the meaning of certain verbs. Compare for example the meaning of the following verbs from Text 1 with that of the non-reflexive forms. As is the case with other uses of the reflexive below, the reflexive pronoun is not here translated in English.

levantarse (T. 1, l. 1) *to get up*	**levantar** *to lift*
irse (T. 1, l. 4) *to leave*	**ir** *to go*
ponerse (T. 1, l. 5) *to put on*	**poner** *to put*
convertirse (T. 2, l. 1, 11) *to become*	**convertir** *to convert*

c   Some verbs are used only in their reflexive form, without actually having a reflexive meaning. In Text 1, line 2 we find **zambullirse** *to dive*, **se zambulle en la piscina** *he dives in the swimming pool*. Other verbs of this kind are **arrepentirse** *to repent*, **atreverse** *to dare*, **ausentarse** *to stay away, to be absent*, **jactarse** *to boast*, **quejarse** *to complain*, **suicidarse** *to commit suicide*.

d   The reflexive form of certain verbs translates *to get* or *to become* in English. Compare the following pairs of verbs: **aburrirse** *to get bored*, **aburrir** *to bore*, **arreglarse** *to get ready*, **arreglar** *to tidy (up), to fix*, **asustarse** *to become frightened*, **asustar** *to frighten*, **emborracharse** *to become drunk*, **emborrachar** *to get someone drunk*, **ensuciarse** *to get dirty*, **ensuciar** *to soil*, **enfadarse** *to get angry*, **enfadar** *to annoy*.

e   The reflexive, used with a verb in the plural, can denote a ***reciprocal*** action. In English, this meaning is usually expressed with phrases such as *one another, each other*. Compare the following sentences, in which the second example of each pair corresponds to the reciprocal use.

Se da otra ducha. (T. 1, l. 5)   *He takes another shower.*
Se dieron de patadas.   *They kicked each other.* (reciprocal)
Sólo **me veía** capacitado … (T. 2, l. 5)   *I only saw myself as capable …*
Nos veíamos a diario.   *We saw each other daily.* (reciprocal)

Reciprocal meaning can be made clear in Spanish with phrases such as **el uno al otro** or **los unos a los otros** *one another*, or with a word such as **mutuamente**.

Se insultaron el uno al otro/mutuamente.   *They insulted each other.*

f   The reflexive **se** can be used with a passive meaning, with a verb in the third person singular or plural (see Chapter 11).

Se construyeron en 1998.   *They were built in 1998.*
La carta **se envió** por correo electrónico.   *The letter was sent by electronic mail.*

g In impersonal sentences, with an indefinite subject, the reflexive **se** is used with a verb in the third person singular (see Chapter 11).

> Aquí no **se trabaja** mucho.   *People don't work much here.*
> ¿Por dónde **se va** al aeropuerto?   *How does one get to the airport?*

The impersonal **se** is not used where the verb is already accompanied by **se**. The alternative here is to use words such as **la gente** *people,* **uno** *one* or **tú** *you.*

> La gente/uno **se divierte** mucho allí.   *People have/One has a lot of fun there.*

Se, here, is part of the verb **divertirse** *to enjoy oneself, to have fun.*

h The reflexive is used with certain verbs as an intensifier.

> **Se leyó** todo el libro.   *He/She read the whole book.*
> **Me comí** todo lo que había.   *I ate up everything there was.*
> ¡**Bébete** la leche!   *Drink up your milk!*

2 FORMS

The infinitive of a reflexive verb has the pronoun **se** added to it, e.g. **ponerse** (T. 1, l. 5) *to put on,* **considerarse** (T. 1, l. 16) *to consider oneself.* The reflexive pronouns show agreement with the subject of the verb. Here is an example:

(yo)	**me** levanto	*I get up*
(tú)	**te** levantas	*you get up*
(usted/él/ella)	**se** levanta	*you get up, he/she gets up*
(nosotros/as)	**nos** levantamos	*we get up*
(vosotros/as)	**os** levantáis	*you get up*
(ustedes/ellos/ellas)	**se** levantan	*you/they get up*

Note that Latin Americans do not use the **vosotros/as** form, as **ustedes** *you* (plural) is used in familiar and polite address. The reflexive pronoun for this will be **se** instead of **os**.

POSITION OF REFLEXIVE PRONOUNS

The pronoun comes before the verb, except with the infinitive, the gerund and positive imperative forms. Note the following examples with **irse, considerarse, ducharse** and **levantarse**.

> **Se va** a clase. (T. 1, l. 4)   *He goes to class.*
> ¿Puede **considerarse** español? (T. 1, l. 16)   *Can he consider himself Spanish?*
> (or ¿**Se** puede **considerar** ... ?)
> Está **duchándose**.   *He/she is taking a shower.*
> (or **Se** está **duchando**.)
> ¡**Levántate**!   *Get up!*
> (but No **te levantes**.)

Other points to note in the texts

- Present indicative: Text 1: *se levanta* (l. 1), *se ducha* (l. 1), *se zambulle* (l. 2), *se remoja* (l. 3), etc. (see Chapter 1)
- Preterite and imperfect tenses: Text 2: *fueron* (l. 1), *existía* (l. 4), *dibujaba* (l. 4), *sabía* (l. 5), *tenía* (l. 5), *veía* (l. 5), *me vine* (l. 6) *me lo pasé* (l. 8) (see Chapters 2 and 3)
- Negation: Text 1: *no será* (l. 9). Text 2: *ni dibujaba bien, ni sabía cantar, ni tenía ninguna habilidad* (l. 4–5), *apenas podía* (l. 8), *imposible* (l. 13), etc. (see Chapter 27)
- Infinitives: Text 1: *antes de desayunar* (l. 3), *a consumir* (l. 4–5), *antes de ponerse . . . y nadar* (l. 5–6), *se dedica a estudiar* (l. 7), *al llegar* (l. 8), etc. Text 2: *a convertirse* (l. 1), *de dedicarme . . . y perder* (l. 2), *ni sabía cantar* (l. 5), *para ser* (l. 5–6), etc. (see Chapter 8)

See for further information:	Batchelor and Pountain, pp. 286–93
	Butt, pp. 66–76
	Butt and Benjamin, pp. 352–74
	Kattán-Ibarra and Pountain, pp. 119–22
	Muñoz and Thacker, pp. 134–6, 247–9

✎ EXERCISES

1 Complete the following sentences with an appropriate reflexive pronoun.

a Manolo, ¿por qué no ____ has afeitado esta mañana?

b ¡Cómo ____ ensucian los niños cuando juegan!

c Cuando hace calor, no ____ baño; prefiero duchar____.

d Siento mucho que usted no ____ considere experto en la materia.

e ____ divertíamos tanto que no ____ acordamos de la hora y Raquel ____ enfadó con nosotros.

f No ____ vayan ustedes. Quéden____, por favor.

g Niños, si no ____ dormís en seguida, mañana no podréis levantar____.

h – ¿Dónde está Rosario?

– En el cuarto de baño, maquillándo____.

2 Complete these sentences by choosing a verb from the list and putting it into the correct form.

preocuparse	**quejarse**	**sentarse**	**levantarse**
parecerse	**aburrirse**	**ponerse**	**acostarse**

a Pablo y Pedro son hermanos pero no _____ en nada.

b Cuando suena el despertador lo apago porque no quiero _____.

c Esa gente nunca está contenta; siempre está _____ de algo.

d ¡Cuánto _____ (nosotros) en la clase de religión! El profesor es tan pesado.

e ¿Tienes mucho sueño? ¿A qué hora _____ anoche?

f Si ustedes _____ en ese sofá, estarán más cómodos.

g ¿Por qué _____ usted tanto de su hijo? No le pasará nada.

h ¡Sois tontos! Debéis _____ las botas.

3 Translate these sentences into Spanish.

a I had an awful time at Carlitos's party.

b First I had an aperitif with Juanjo in the Bar Florida.

c Then, arriving at Carlitos's house, I slipped and fell.

d Carlitos's mother gave me a brandy, and although I don't like it, I drank it.

e I danced for a while and then I fell asleep.

f When I woke up, Juanjo had gone.

4 Study these sentences and say whether the function of **se** in each one is *reflexive* or *reciprocal*.

a Aunque eran hermanos, se peleaban mucho.

b Roberto y Ana se escribieron durante dos años.

c Muchos de los presos se suicidaron.

d Se cayeron al agua.

e Los amigos se visitaban todos los veranos.

f Se cansaron mucho.

g Se mataron.

h No se querían y por eso se divorciaron.

5 Rewrite these sentences using impersonal **se**.

a Aquí respiramos aire puro.

b Mandas la factura a esta dirección.

c Según lo que dicen, en Escocia beben mucho.

d En España cenan tarde.

e Han destruido el centro de la ciudad.

f ¿Dónde hay que bajar para la Plaza Mayor?

6 Write an account of what Alberto did yesterday, incorporating these verbs, and as many more reflexive verbs as your account will take.

levantarse • vestirse • prepararse • reunirse • reírse • enfadarse • irse • sentarse • ducharse • acostarse.

For exercises which practise the use of **se** with <u>passive</u> meaning, see Chapter 11. For exercises which practise the use of **se** functioning as an <u>indirect object pronoun</u>, see Chapter 25.

13 | *Ser* and *estar*

Text

This article looks at the effects of a new immigration law on the Hispanic community in the United States. As you read the text, focus attention on the uses of **ser** and **estar**, the main grammatical point in this unit.

La hora cero para los inmigrantes

Juan Ceballos tiene sus papeles en orden. Hace más de quince años que **está** en los Estados Unidos y desde hace cinco **es** ciudadano norteamericano.
Sin embargo, él **es** una de las personas que más trabajo ha tenido durante las últimas tres semanas. Él **es** funcionario de un registro civil en Los Angeles
5 y sostiene que "nunca había visto tantos matrimonios como en los últimos días."

Lo que pasa **es** que la entrada en vigencia de la nueva ley de inmigración ha desatado una masiva ola de matrimonios entre ciudadanos y personas indocumentadas temerosas de **ser** deportadas.

Las calles donde la mayoría de los ilegales acuden diariamente a conseguir
10 trabajo **están** desiertas. El mismo vacío **están** experimentando muchos colegios y hospitales públicos, donde los inmigrantes, por temor a **ser** deportados, han preferido no aparecer.

La nueva regulación establece que la gente que **esté** ilegalmente en EE.UU. deberá obtener un permiso de trabajo, visa o haber solicitado la residencia
15 permanente o el asilo político.

Washington, por su parte, **está** mirando de cerca cómo funciona la nueva ley de inmigración. Los principales cambios **serán** vistos en los aeropuertos y en las fronteras, donde la gente que llegue sin los papeles adecuados **será** expulsada del país.

20 Lo cierto **es** que la mayoría de los consulados, y en especial el mexicano, **están** estudiando la ley con mucha detención para saber cómo se va a aplicar y cómo va a afectar a su comunidad.

A pesar de que los mexicanos **son** los más afectados con esta nueva legislación, la comunidad hispana ha concentrado todos sus esfuerzos en informar
25 y ayudar a la población. Tanto los medios de comunicación como los organismos

diplomáticos y servicios de asistencia judicial **están** abiertos para responder las dudas.

Diario *El Mercurio*, Chile

Ser and estar to be

1 GENERAL

Spanish has two words meaning *to be*, **ser** and **estar**, which are clearly differentiated by native speakers. The generalisation sometimes found in textbooks that **ser** is used to refer to permanent characteristics and **estar** to temporary states is true only to some extent, and it can in fact be misleading. It seems more appropriate to look at each use separately. The article above contains several examples of the use of these two verbs. The notes below cover these and other uses not found in the text.

2 USING SER

a With a noun, a pronoun or an infinitive.

Es ciudadano norteamericano. (l. 2)   *He's an American citizen.*
Él **es** funcionario de un registro civil. (l. 4)   *He's an employee in a registry office.*
Es ella.   *It's her.*
Lo difícil **es** entender.   *The difficult thing is to understand.*

b With a clause.

Lo que pasa **es** que ... (l. 6)   *What happens is that ...*
Lo cierto **es** que ... (l. 20)   *The truth is that ...*

c To identify someone or something.

Es una de las personas ... (l. 3)   *He's one of the people ...*
¿Dónde dijiste que **era**?   *Where did you say it was?*

See also: **son** los más afectados (l. 23).

d With a past participle, to form passive sentences (see Chapter 11).

... temerosas de **ser** deportadas (l. 8)   *... fearful of being deported*
... **serán** vistos (l. 17)   *... they will be seen*

See also: **ser** deportados (l. 11), **será** expulsada (l. 18).

e With adjectives, to refer to a characteristic which is considered as permanent or intrinsic.

Es guapa.   *She's pretty.*

f To indicate price, time, material and origin.

Son diez euros/pesos.   *It's ten euros/pesos.*
Es la una/tarde.   *It's one o'clock/late.*

Es de plata.   *It's made of silver.*
Son de Madrid.   *They are from Madrid.*

g To indicate possession.

> **Es** tuyo.   *It's yours.*

h To say where and when an event is taking place.

> La fiesta **es** aquí/mañana.   *The party is here/tomorrow.*

Asking and giving personal information

Note that much personal information such as who you are, your nationality, origin, occupation and even religion and political affiliation, as well as questions related to this, can be given with **ser**. Marital status accepts **ser** or **estar**. Latin Americans tend to use **ser**, while Spaniards show preference for **estar**, unless a definition rather than a state is implied:

> **Es** un hombre casado.   *He's a married man.*

2 USING *ESTAR*

a To indicate position or location.

> **Está** en los Estados Unidos. (l. 1–2)   *He's in the United States.*

b To indicate marital status.

> **Está** soltera/casada/divorciada.   *She's single/married/divorced.*

c To indicate existence.

> Y también **está** el problema del desempleo.   *And there's also the unemployment problem.*

d With gerunds, to form progressive tenses.

> **Están** experimentando ... (l. 10)   *They are experiencing ...*
> **Está** mirando ... (l. 16)   *It is looking ...*

See also: **están** estudiando (l. 21).

e With adjectives and past participles to indicate a state or condition which is the result of a process or action.

> Las calles ... **están** desiertas. (l. 9–10)   *The streets are deserted.*
> **Están** abiertos. (l. 26)   *They are open.*
> ¡Qué grande **está** tu hijo!   *Your child looks very big!*

f With adjectives, showing that a state or condition is regarded as temporary, or implying a change from usual circumstances.

> El día **está** muy frío.   *The day is very cold.*
> **Estás** muy elegante.   *You're looking very elegant.*

g To indicate cost, when prices fluctuate.

¿A cuánto/cómo **están** las peras?   *How much are the pears?*

h With prepositional phrases.

Están de vacaciones.   *They are on holiday.*
Estoy a régimen.   *I'm on a diet.*

i To denote a physical or mental state or condition.

Están muy bien/contentos.   *They are very well/happy.*

j With expressions of time.

Estamos a 5 de abril/en primavera.   *It's the 5th of April/spring.*

Other points to note in the text

- Adjective agreement and position: *ciudadano norteamericano* (l. 2), *últimas tres semanas* (l. 4), *una masiva ola* (l. 7), *ciudadanos y personas indocumentadas* (l. 7–8), *el mismo vacío* (l. 10), *colegios y hospitales públicos* (l. 10–11), etc. (see Chapter 20)
- Present subjunctive: *la gente que esté ilegalmente* (l. 13), *la gente que llegue* (l. 18) (see Chapter 14)
- Passive: *ser deportadas* (l. 8), *ser deportados* (l. 11), *serán vistos* (l. 17), *será expulsada* (l. 18) (see Chapter 11)
- Indefinite article omission: *es ciudadano norteamericano* (l. 2), *es funcionario* (l. 4) (see Chapter 18)

See for further information:	Batchelor and Pountain, pp. 271–9
	Butt, pp. 77–80
	Butt and Benjamin, pp. 398–406
	Kattán-Ibarra and Pountain, pp. 114–18
	Muñoz and Thacker, pp. 127–31, 242–4

✎ EXERCISES

1 Use **ser** or **estar** to complete the following sentences.

a – ¿_____ interesante ese libro?
– No. _____ aburridísimo.

b – ¿Sabes dónde _____ Miguel?
– _____ en el jardín, leyendo.

c – ¿Quién _____ ese chico tan guapo?
– _____ mi amigo Carlos. _____ argentino. Todos los argentinos _____ guapos.

d Las calles de los pueblos blancos _____ estrechas y en verano los balcones _____ repletos de flores.

e Nada _____ fácil en esta vida.

f María y yo _____ contentos de verlos.

g ¿De quién _____ ese bolso? ¿_____ tuyo?

h – ¿Quién _____ ?

 – _____ yo.

i Diego _____ de Teruel pero ahora _____ en Valladolid. _____ estudiando filosofía.

j – ¿A cuánto _____ las sardinas?

 – Hoy _____ a 3 euros el kilo. _____ muy frescas.

k – ¿De cuándo _____ ese diario?

 – _____ de ayer.

 – ¿Dónde _____ el de hoy?

l Los obreros _____ en huelga pero _____ una huelga que no les sirve para nada.

m La última vez que Ignacio _____ en La Habana, el Museo de Bellas Artes _____ cerrado por obras.

n Este vestido _____ de seda y _____ carísimo pero el color _____ muy de moda. Voy a comprármelo.

o Cállate, _____ mejor que no hables. ¿No ves que Juan _____ furioso?

2 Fill in the gaps with **ser** or **estar**.

a Paco _____ aburrido; el trabajo que hace _____ aburrido.

b Gloria _____ una chica muy guapa pero esta noche _____ más guapa que nunca.

c En este restaurante la comida suele _____ buena; hoy _____ riquísima.

d Mi abuelo no _____ muy mayor pero por lo que le ha pasado _____ bastante viejo.

e Mi tío _____ una persona alegre; ahora _____ muy alegre porque le ha tocado la lotería.

f A Silvia le gusta _____ a la moda aun cuando _____ una moda que no le va.

g Ya sé que Felipe _____ enfermo pero os digo que ahora _____ enfermo de peligro.

h Mira, ya _____ borracho Antonio. _____ que _____ un borracho perdido.

3 Write the result of these actions.

a El banco ha abierto.

b Mi gato se ha muerto.

c Se ha enfriado la sopa.

d Los niños han perdido la llave.

e Voy a servir la cena.

4 Cross out the incorrect verb.

Era/estaba fotógrafo pero como su hija era/estaba recién nacida y no quería ser/estar fuera tanto tiempo, era/estaba de técnico en electrodomésticos. Sus suegros no eran/estaban nada contentos. Era/estaba lógico entonces, que al poco tiempo fuera/estuviera divorciado.

5 Of the following sentences, four are incorrect. Identify them and correct them.

   a ¿Usted cree que este sistema es el más seguro?

   b Allí es donde vivíamos cuando era niño.

   c Nuestro aniversario está en junio.

   d El dinero siempre es más seguro en el banco.

   e El incendio fue provocado.

   f La sopa era muy sosa.

   g La fábrica era un edificio imponente que fue demolido el año pasado por estar en malas
   condiciones.

   h Soy sin dinero porque gasté todo lo que tenía en el billete.

6 Translate into Spanish.

   a The house was quite far from the station.

   b It was late and we were tired when we arrived.

   c We are not going to go out because it is raining.

   d The streets are very busy today.

   e The mirror is broken.

   f Do you like this picture? It's not bad, is it?

   g It's not good to be so discontented.

   h At what time is the concert? It's in the Town Hall, isn't it?

   i The coffee will be cold and Marga will be in a bad mood if you don't come right now.

   j The hotel was full, which was a pity.

7 You have been asked to contribute to a Spanish magazine by writing an article about your
favourite town/city in which you describe its location, its character, the places of interest:
where they are in the town and what they are like, and the reasons why you like it.

14 | The present subjunctive

This text considers the frustrations often felt by young university graduates on taking up their first job. The main grammatical point here is the present subjunctive. Read the article and then, with the help of the notes which follow the text, study the way in which the verbs in bold have been used.

¿Para esto estudié tanto?

Con su mejor traje y el estómago apretado, el novato se presenta a tomar posesión de su nuevo puesto de trabajo. Si tiene suerte, puede que alguien lo **salude** y le **indique** donde sentarse. Pero también es posible que nadie **esté** enterado de su llegada, que la recepcionista lo **mire** con extrañeza

5   y le **pregunte** a quien espera. Es posible que **termine** ocupando algún rincón improvisado, leyendo aburridos documentos para interiorizarse "mientras tanto". Pueden pasar días antes de que alguien lo **introduzca** a su nuevo cargo. Y aunque no **sea** así, sus ilusiones y expectativas tal vez **disminuyan** considerablemente.

10   En las semanas que siguen podrá comprobar la diferencia entre la teoría y la realidad, entre lo que le enseñaron en la universidad y las tareas que tendrá que cumplir. Es común que para comenzar se le **ocupe** en tareas rutinarias, aquéllas que los que llevan más tiempo en la institución ya no están dispuestos a realizar.

Es frecuente que su jefe **sea** una persona con mucha experiencia, pero quizás

15   **tenga** una preparación académica inferior a la suya, y le **sea** difícil entender sus proposiciones. "¿Para esto estudié tanto?" se pregunta el novato y comienza a sentir una leve depresión.

Por otra parte, el joven deberá hacer importantes ajustes en su vida personal. Para muchos no es fácil adquirir esa disciplina. Además, es común que

20   los jóvenes **se casen** cuando ingresan a su primer trabajo o que **se independicen** económicamente de sus padres y **se instalen** por su cuenta o con amigos. De la actitud del joven en este trance dependerá en parte su carrera laboral futura. Si es capaz de sobreponerse a la frustración y enfrentar con entusiasmo esta etapa, es probable que **comience** a recibir poco a poco

25 responsabilidades más interesantes que le **permitan** demostrar sus verdaderas capacidades.

Revista *El Sábado*, Diario *El Mercurio*, Chile

The present subjunctive

1 USAGE

Verbs can take different forms depending on how they are used. There are three basic forms of the verb, traditionally referred to as ***moods***: the ***indicative*** mood (all the tenses you have learnt so far), used in statements, the ***imperative*** mood, for expressing orders and instructions (Chapter 17), and the ***subjunctive*** mood, generally used to refer to things which are uncertain or unreal. In English, the subjunctive is very little used, e.g. *I wish she were here*, but in Spanish it is common.

The four main tenses of the subjunctive – ***present***, ***imperfect***, ***perfect*** and ***pluperfect*** – are found in all forms of language, formal and informal, spoken and written. General usage is much the same for all, so most of the notes below, illustrated here with the present subjunctive, will be valid for the rest of the tenses. The future subjunctive is a special case, as this is very little used nowadays, except in very formal written language and in legal documents.

a The subjunctive in subordinate clauses

i By far the most frequent general use of the subjunctive is within subordinate clauses introduced by **que** (most examples in the text), e.g. **Puede que alguien lo salude** (l. 2–3) *It's possible that someone may greet him.* More specifically, the presence of the subjunctive in the subordinate clause is determined by two main factors: one is the nature of the main verb, and the other is the fact that the subject of the main verb and that of the verb in the subordinate clause are different (as in the example above).

ii Amongst the verbs calling for the use of the subjunctive in the subordinate clause there are those expressing possibility/impossibility, uncertainty, permission and prohibition, hope, wishes, requests, necessity, thinking (in negative sentences), and those indicating some kind of emotion, for example **alegrarse** *to be glad*, **molestar**, *to bother*, **detestar** *to detest*, **gustar** *to like*, **temer** *to fear*.

Es posible que nadie **esté** enterado ... (possibility, l. 3–4) *It's possible that no-one may be aware ...*

See also **indique** (l. 3), **mire** (l. 4), **pregunte**, **termine** (l. 5).

Esperan que **vengas**. (hope) *They hope you come.*
Quiere que **esté** aquí. (wish) *He/she wants me to be here.*
No creo que **vuelvan**. (thinking) *I don't think they'll come back.*
Me alegro de que **llames**. (emotion) *I'm glad you're calling.*

iii Ser + adjective/noun + **que** + subjunctive

The construction **ser** + adjective/noun + **que**, as in **Es natural/normal/mejor/injusto** ... , **Es una pena/lástima** ... , often used to express some kind of value judgement, usually calls for the use of the subjunctive in the subordinate clause.

Es frecuente que su jefe **sea** ... (l. 14)   *It's common for his boss to be* ...

See also **es posible** ... (l. 3), **es común** ... (l. 19), **es probable** ... (l. 24).

b The subjunctive after conjunctions

i The subjunctive is used after conjunctions indicating time, such as **antes (de) que** *before*, **después (de) que** *after*, **cuando** *when*, **hasta que** *until*, but only when these refer to the future. Note the following example from the text:

Antes de que alguien lo **introduzca** ... (l. 7)   *Before someone introduces him* ...

Note that if the action referred to is a fact, the indicative and not the subjunctive must be used. Compare these two sentences:

Cuando tenga tiempo la visitaré.   *When I have time I'll visit her.*
Cuando tengo tiempo la visito.   *When I have time I visit her.*

ii Conjunctions expressing concession, among these **aunque**, *although, even if*, **aun cuando**, *even if*, take the subjunctive when denoting uncertainty. When reference is to a fact, you need an indicative verb.

Y **aunque** no **sea** así ... (l. 7–8)   *And even if it isn't like that* ...
Y **aunque** no **es** así ... (a fact)   *And although it isn't like that* ...

For other conjunctions used with the subjunctive see Chapter 15.

c The subjunctive in relative clauses

The subjunctive is used in relative clauses when the relative pronoun, e.g. **que**, refers back to something which is non-existent, indefinite or unknown. Otherwise, you must use an indicative verb.

... responsabilidades ... **que** le **permitan** ... (l. 25)   *... responsibilities which may allow him* ...
Buscan a alguien **que hable** ruso.   *They're looking for someone who can speak Russian.*

Compare the examples above with the following ones:

... responsabilidades **que** le **permiten** ...   *... responsibilities which (actually) allow him* ...
Buscan a alguien **que habla** ruso.   *They're looking for someone who speaks Russian.*

d The subjunctive in main clauses

i The subjunctive is used in independent clauses introduced by words such as **quizá(s)**, **tal vez** *perhaps*. With these two words its use is optional, the indicative being used when there is a greater degree of certainty.

A lo mejor, also meaning *perhaps,* always takes an indicative verb.

Quizás tenga ... (l. 14–15) *He may perhaps have ...*
Tal vez disminuyan ... (l. 8) *They may perhaps diminish ...*

But **A lo mejor tiene/disminuyen** ...

ii Expressions of wish introduced by **que** or **ojalá (que)** are followed by a verb in the subjunctive.

Que tengas suerte. *I hope you are lucky.*
Ojalá (que) consigas entradas. *I hope you get tickets.*

iii The subjunctive is used as the imperative form for **usted** and **ustedes** and for negative familiar commands (see **Imperative**, Chapter 17).

Llámeme mañana. *Call me tomorrow.*
No se lo **digan** a nadie. *Don't tell anyone.*
No se lo **cuentes**. *Don't tell him/her.*
(but **Cuéntaselo**. *Tell him.*)

SEQUENCE OF TENSES WITH THE PRESENT SUBJUNCTIVE

The present subjunctive in the subordinate clause is normally dependent on a main clause verb in the present indicative, future, perfect, for example:

¿Quieres que te **acompañe?** *Do you want me to accompany you?* (present)
Les **diré** que **se vayan**. *I'll tell them to go.* (future)
Ana me **ha pedido** que le **escriba**. *Ana has asked me to write to her.* (perfect)

For more information on the use of the subjunctive see Chapters 15 and 16.

2 FORMATION

Regular verbs

llamar	comer	vivir
llam**e**	com**a**	viv**a**
llam**es**	com**as**	viv**as**
llam**e**	com**a**	viv**a**
llam**emos**	com**amos**	viv**amos**
llam**éis**	com**áis**	viv**áis**
llam**en**	com**an**	viv**an**

Note that -**er** and -**ir** verbs have the same endings. Note too that, except for the first person (**yo**), the endings of -**ar** verbs are like those of the present indicative of -**er** verbs, while those in -**er** and -**ir** have endings which are similar to those of the present indicative of -**ar** verbs.

Stem-changing and irregular verbs

To form the present subjunctive of stem-changing and irregular verbs, drop the -**o** from the stem of the first person singular of the present indicative and add the endings of regular verbs. Stem-changing verbs keep the stem of the infinitive in the first and second person plural, as in the present tense. Here are some examples:

infinitive	1st person pres. indicative	present subjunctive
decir	digo	diga, digas, diga, digamos digáis, digan
querer	quiero	quiera, quieras, quiera, queramos, queráis, quieran
venir	vengo	venga, vengas, venga, vengamos, vengáis, vengan

A few verbs form the present subjunctive in a different way.

infinitive	present subjunctive
dar *to give*	dé, des, dé, demos, deis, den
estar *to be*	esté, estés, esté, estemos, estéis, estén
haber *to have*	haya, hayas, haya, hayamos, hayáis, hayan
ir *to go*	vaya, vayas, vaya, vayamos, vayáis, vayan
saber *to know*	sepa, sepas, sepa, sepamos, sepáis, sepan
ser *to be*	sea, seas, sea, seamos, seáis, sean

See also **Irregular verbs** on pages 204–7.

Spelling-changing verbs

Verbs ending in -**car**, -**gar**, -**ger**, -**zar**, change their spelling in all persons of the present subjunctive. Among these we find **buscar** *to look for* (**busque, busques** …), **llegar** *to arrive* (**llegue, llegues** …), **recoger** *to pick up* (**recoja, recojas** …), **empezar** *to begin, start* (**empiece, empieces** …).

For other spelling rules affecting verbs see pages 207–8.

LATIN AMERICAN USAGE

The present subjunctive forms for **vos**, used in the Río de la Plata area in place of **tú** (see Chapters 1, 17 and 25), are slightly different, with the stress falling on the last syllable: **vos llamés, vos comás, vos vivás**. Stem changes do not apply in this case, e.g. **vos empecés, vos volvás** for **tú empieces, tú vuelvas**, while irregular verbs of more than one syllable simply undergo a shift in stress, e.g. **vos vengás, vos vayás**.

Other points to note in the text

- Direct and indirect object pronouns (3rd person singular, masculine form): *lo salude* (l. 3), *le indique* (l. 3), *lo mire* (l. 4), *le pregunte* (l. 5), *lo introduzca* (l. 7), *le enseñaron* (l. 11), *se le ocupe* (l. 12), *le sea difícil* (l. 15), *le permitan* (l. 25) (see Chapter 25)
- *Por* and *para*: *para* (l. 6, 12, 16, 19), *por* (l. 18, 21) (see Chapter 28)

- Possessives: There are numerous examples in the text, among these *su mejor traje* (l. 1), *inferior a la suya* (l. 15), *sus proposiciones* (l. 15–16), *sus . . . capacidades* (l. 25–6), etc. (see Chapter 24)
- Adjective agreement and position: There are a number of examples in the text. Note in particular *su mejor traje* (l. 1), *el estómago apretado* (l. 1), *su nuevo puesto* (l. 2), *algún rincón improvisado* (l. 5–6), *aburridos documentos* (l. 6), *tareas rutinarias* (l. 12), *su carrera laboral futura* (l. 22–3), etc. (see Chapter 20)

See for further information:	Batchelor and Pountain, pp. 248–70
	Butt, pp. 20–35
	Butt and Benjamin, pp. 238–77
	Kattán-Ibarra and Pountain, pp. 90–101
	Muñoz and Thacker, pp. 96–103, 226–34

EXERCISES

As you do these exercises, study the sentences carefully and think about their equivalent meanings in English.

1 Put the verb in brackets into the correct form of the present subjunctive.

a No quiero llamar a Juan. Prefiero que tú lo (llamar) _____.

b La madre les prohibe a sus hijos que (jugar) _____ en la calle.

c Le recomendamos que (abrir) _____ una cuenta corriente en el Banco Exterior.

d Me ha pedido que (escribir) _____ una carta a su padre.

e Queremos que usted nos (preparar) _____ los informes cuanto antes.

f Nos sugiere que (hablar) _____ con el gerente.

g Mi padre quiere que (estudiar, yo) _____ Derecho pero mi madre prefiere que (ver) _____ mundo.

h Os digo que (dejar) _____ los zapatos allí.

i ¿Quieres que (mirar, nosotros) _____ esto juntos o no?

j El profesor exige a todos sus estudiantes que (hablar) _____ en castellano.

k Les aconsejo a ustedes que no (llegar) _____ tarde.

l Por el momento no quiero que (cerrar, tú) _____ el libro.

2 Link the two phrases to form a complete sentence, making whatever adjustments are necessary.

a	Siento mucho	•	Gloria no se encuentra bien.
b	Nos extraña	•	mienten.
c	¿Os molesta	•	decimos la verdad?
d	Temen	•	hay un accidente.
e	Está muy contento	•	nos conocemos.
f	No me sorprende	•	lo han pasado bien en México.
g	Me alegro	•	te dan un aumento de sueldo.

h No creo	• viene Pedro a la hora indicada.
i No le gusta	• su hijo sale con Marta.
j No creo	• este trabajo es muy duro.
k Dudamos	• saben mucho sobre el incidente.
l Odio	• la gente no dice la verdad.

3 In Column B below is a list of recommendations to a new employee. You can link an element from Column A with one from Column B without changing the verb from the infinitive in Column B but by so doing you are making a general statement. To personalise the advice (It is important that <u>you</u> …), you need to use the subjunctive. Personalise the advice given by choosing a phrase from Column A to go with one from Column B and write a complete sentence, making the necessary changes and additions. Use the formal form of address: **usted**.

A	B
es importante	proponer nuevas ideas en el trabajo
es aconsejable	aprender o perfeccionar un idioma
es bueno	reconocer tanto sus puntos fuertes como sus puntos débiles
es mejor	esforzarse por hacer siempre bien el trabajo
es necesario	aceptar las críticas sin enfadarse
hace falta	desconectarse del trabajo una vez en casa
es imprescindible	no almorzar en el área de trabajo
es recomendable	acudir a cursillos de especialización
es fundamental	cuidar su aspecto personal
conviene	decir "no" a un exceso de trabajo

4 Make meaningful sentences by combining a phrase from Column A with one from Column B.

A	B
a Cuando encuentre trabajo	**1** no salen
b Tenemos que terminar esto	**2** después de que esté allí un par de meses
c Habla con Pepe	**3** hasta hartarte
d Cuando llueve	**4** después de casarse
e Nos quedaremos aquí	**5** daré una fiesta
f Cuando lleguemos	**6** mientras espero
g Van a comprarse una casa	**7** podremos descansar
h Todo el mundo lo conocerá	**8** mientras haya dinero
i Hago esto	**9** antes de irte
j En esa casa comes	**10** antes de que venga Pepe

5 Change these sentences so that they express a greater degree of uncertainty.

a No lo entiendo. Tal vez no tengo todos los datos.

b No ha llegado Roberto. Quizás viene mañana.

c Tal vez nos invitan a cenar.

d No nos contesta. Quizás no está en casa.

e Todavía no me ha llamado Alfonso. Quizás me llama esta tarde.

6 Write the correct form of the verb in brackets.

   a Gabriel García Márquez escribió una novela que tituló "El Coronel no tiene quien le (escribir) _____ ".

   b No tengo nada que (poder) _____ serviros.

   c ¿Conoces a alguien que (dar) _____ clases de violín?

   d Necesitamos un piso que (ser) _____ bueno pero barato.

   e Cómprate algo que te (gustar) _____ .

   f Mariana está dispuesta a casarse con cualquiera que se lo (pedir) _____ .

7 Fill in the blanks using one of the verbs from the list.

pasar	**aprobar**	**tocar**	**tener**	**ir**
llegar	**haber**	**ser**	**dormir**	**mejorar**

   a Necesito la ayuda de Alberto. ¡Ojalá _____ pronto!

   b Queremos dejar de trabajar. ¡Ojalá nos _____ la lotería!

   c Susana tiene un exámen mañana. ¡Ojalá _____ ¡

   d La niña lleva mucho tiempo llorando. ¡Ojalá se _____ pronto!

   e Hace calor y la mochila pesa. ¡Ojalá _____ camas libres en el albergue!

   f – El lunes Félix empieza su nuevo trabajo.

      – ¡Que _____ suerte!

   g – Mañana nos vamos de vacaciones.

      – ¡Que lo _____ bien!

   h – Tengo una entrevista muy importante.

      – ¡Que te _____ bien!

   i – Me caso la semana que viene.

      – ¡Que _____ muy feliz!

   j – Julio no se encuentra bien.

      – ¡Que se _____ pronto!

8 Correct these sentences and say in each case why the subjunctive is needed.

   a Queremos que Eduardo va a Roma el jueves.

   b Espero que están ustedes bien.

   c Les rogamos a los señores pasajeros que se abrochan los cinturones de seguridad.

   d No conozco a nadie que toca el piano como tú.

   e Me pide que le doy mis apuntes.

   f No le gusta a la gente que uno tiene éxito.

   g Es muy buena idea que visitan la destilería antes de marcharse.

   h No vamos a empezar hasta que viene Rodrigo.

   i No me extraña que a Paloma no le gusta su trabajo.

   j Cuando voy a Madrid ¿quieres que te traigo algo?

   k Es imposible que van ustedes antes de que vuelve mi jefe.

9 Translate the following sentences into Spanish.

    a I'm sorry you are not well; I hope to see you when you are better.

    b I don't think there is anyone here who will help us.

    c It's not necessary to see it but it's important for us to know how it works.

    d Perhaps he can tell us what's happening before Juan gets back.

    e Even if he gets a job, Julio will have to carry on studying.

    f Samuel may have more experience but it's not very likely that he has studied as much as you.

10 Imagine and write down the advice you would give to Michael who wants to learn a foreign language. Use as much as possible expressions which require the use of the subjunctive, e.g. **te aconsejo que**, **te recomiendo que**, **te sugiero que**, **no creo que**, **es importante que**, etc.

15 | The imperfect subjunctive

Las quejas de las esposas modernas

Long-established male attitudes in marriage are the subject of the passages which follow. The problem is presented here through the voice of two women from Mexico, who discuss their relationships. Read and find out what their complaints are, then go back through the texts again and focus attention on the use of the imperfect and the present subjunctive.

1 "Mi marido no tolera mis éxitos profesionales"

Ana Luisa, licenciada en comunicación, 34 años

"Tengo cinco años de casada. Luis, mi esposo, es un hombre educado a la antigua y, aunque me duele reconocerlo, macho.

Nos conocimos en la universidad, donde los dos cursábamos la carrera de comunicación. Solíamos estudiar juntos y le daba mucho gusto que yo **sacara**
5 buenas notas . . . claro, siempre y cuando no **fueran** superiores a las de él. No obstante, lo quería tanto que hasta llegué a cometer errores intencionales para que él no se **sintiera** tan mal.

Luis no tolera que yo **sea** más que él. No soporta que yo **gane** más y **tenga** más éxitos. Nuestros pleitos son constantes y mi suegra opina que yo debo dejar el
10 empleo, pues lo único que consigo es que mi marido **se sienta** inferior. En un principio pensé hacerlo, pero amo demasiado mi trabajo. Si lo **hiciera** me arrepentiría.

Me gustaría que mi marido **fuera** más participativo, que **se sintiera** más orgulloso de mí y **considerara** mis logros como suyos. Sin embargo, por su
15 manera de ser nos alejamos cada vez más y temo que un día no muy lejano **nos separemos**."

2 "Mi esposo no colabora conmigo en los quehaceres hogareños"

Lucía, secretaria, 35 años

"Luego de mi matrimonio dejé mi empleo de secretaria porque Alberto, mi marido, me pidió que lo **hiciera**. Pero cuando vino el primer hijo, a veces no teníamos dinero ni para la leche. Alberto aseguraba que todo se

arreglaría y quería que yo **siguiera** en la casa. Al llegar el segundo hijo
5 nuestra situación económica se agravó y a regañadientes mi marido aceptó que
regresara al trabajo.

Los primeros meses fueron terribles. Entraba a las 8 de la mañana y muchas
veces me daban las 10 de la noche en la oficina. A Alberto le molestaba que yo
volviera tarde. Yo me indignaba más porque, pese a la hora y a mi cansancio,
10 aún debía limpiar la casa, cocinar, lavar ropa y plancharla. Nuestra situación
económica mejoró, pero yo me sentía agobiada por las presiones laborales, las
tareas domésticas, el descuido de mis hijos y los celos de mi marido.

Quiero mucho a Alberto y no deseo perderlo. Si me **dejara** no sé qué haría.
Hablé con él y aceptó que **contratáramos** una persona para que me **ayudara** en
15 casa (él jamás lo hará). Además, mi jefe accedió a que yo **saliera** más temprano.
Alberto está mucho más complacido."

Diario *El Universal*, México

The imperfect subjunctive

1 USAGE

General usage of the imperfect subjunctive corresponds with that of the subjunctive as a whole,
so the uses of the subjunctive outlined in Chapter 14 are also valid here. One important
exception is the use of the imperfect subjunctive (and the pluperfect subjunctive) in **si** (*if*)
clauses (see below).

There are a number of subjunctive forms in the texts, the majority of them in the imperfect,
but a few also in the present. In Text 1, note the use of **sea**, **gane** and **tenga** (l. 8), **se sienta**
(l. 10) and **nos separemos**, (l. 15–16), which are forms of the present subjunctive used in
subordinate clauses.

Use of the subjunctive in subordinate clauses has already been covered in Chapter 14, except
that tense sequence with the imperfect subjunctive is different, as you will see from the examples
which follow (see also 'Sequence of tenses with the imperfect subjunctive').

a Subjunctive in subordinate clauses, with the verb in the main clause expressing:

i Some kind of emotion.

Le daba mucho gusto **que** yo **sacara** buenas notas. (T. 1, l. 4–5)   *He was very pleased that
I got good marks.*
Le molestaba **que** yo **volviera** tarde. (T. 2, l. 8–9)   *He was annoyed that I should be late home.*

ii Wishes, requests.

Me gustaría **que** mi marido **fuera** más participativo … (T. 1, l. 13)   *I wish my husband
were more co-operative …*

See also ... **que se sintiera ... y considerara** (T. 1, l. 13–14), **que lo hiciera** (T. 2, l. 2), **que siguiera** (T. 2, l. 4).

iii Permission.

Aceptó **que regresara**. (T. 2, l. 5–6)   *He agreed that I should go back.*

See also **que yo saliera** (T. 2, l. 15).
For further information on the use of the subjunctive in subordinate clauses see Chapters 14 and 16.

b Subjunctive after conjunctions.

i Conjunctions expressing conditions: **siempre y cuando, siempre que** *as long as,* **en caso de que** *if, in case,* **a menos que,** *unless,* etc.

Siempre y cuando (*or* **siempre que**) no fueran ... (T. 1, l. 5)   *As long as they weren't ...*

ii Conjunctions indicating purpose: **para que, de modo/manera/forma que,** etc.

... **para que** él no **se sintiera** tan mal. (T. 1, l. 6–7)   *... so that he wouldn't feel so bad.*

See also **para que** me **ayudara** (T. 2, l. 14).
For other conjunctions used with the subjunctive see Chapter 14.

iii Imperfect subjunctive in **si** *if* clauses.
The imperfect subjunctive occurs in **si** *if* clauses, with the verb in the main clause in the conditional. Note that English uses the simple past in the *if* clause.

Si lo **hiciera** me arrepentiría. (T. 1, l. 11–12)   *If I did it I'd regret it.*
Si me **dejara** no sé que haría. (T. 2, l. 13)   *If he left me I don't know what I would do.*

In the examples above, the conditions are seen as remote or unlikely to be fulfilled. But the same construction can be used to express conditions which cannot be met:

Si fuera más joven conseguiría trabajo.   *If he/she were younger he/she would get work.*

See also **si** + pluperfect subjunctive, in Chapter 16.

SEQUENCE OF TENSES WITH THE IMPERFECT SUBJUNCTIVE

The imperfect subjunctive in the subordinate clause is normally dependent on a main clause verb in the imperfect indicative, preterite, pluperfect indicative, conditional, for example:

Me alegré de que **vinieran**. (preterite)   *I was glad they came.*
Yo te **había dicho** que lo **terminaras**. (pluperfect indicative)   *I had told you to finish it.*
Nos **gustaría** que nos **ayudaras**. (conditional)   *We would like you to help us.*

2 FORMATION

Regular verbs

The imperfect subjunctive is formed from the stem of the third person plural of the preterite tense, to which the endings are added. There are two sets of endings for the imperfect subjunctive, which are interchangeable. Note that -**er** and -**ir** verbs share the same endings.

tomar	comer	vivir
tom**ara/ase**	com**iera/iese**	viv**iera/iese**
tom**aras/ases**	com**ieras/ieses**	viv**ieras/ieses**
tom**ara/ase**	com**iera/iese**	viv**iera/iese**
tom**áramos/ásemos**	com**iéramos/iésemos**	viv**iéramos/iésemos**
tom**arais/aseis**	com**ierais/ieseis**	viv**ierais/ieseis**
tom**aran/asen**	com**ieran/iesen**	viv**ieran/iesen**

Irregular verbs

Irregular verbs form the imperfect subjunctive in the same way as regular ones, as you will see from these examples:

Infinitive	*Preterite* (3rd pers. pl.)	*Imperfect subjunctive*
decir *to say*	dijeron	dijera/dijese, dijeras/dijeses ...
poner *to put*	pusieron	pusiera/pusiese, pusieras/pusieses ...
tener *to have*	tuvieron	tuviera/tuviese, tuvieras/tuvieses ...

Other points to note in the texts

- Present subjunctive: Text 1: *no tolera que yo sea* (l. 8), *no soporta que yo gane ... y tenga* (l. 8), *lo único que consigo es que ... se sienta ...* (l. 10), *temo que ... nos separemos* (l. 15–16) (see Chapter 14)
- Preterite and imperfect tenses: Text 1: *nos conocimos* (l. 3), *cursábamos* (l. 3), *solíamos* (l. 4), *llegué* (l. 6), etc. Text 2: *dejé* (l. 1), *pidió* (l. 2), *vino* (l. 2), *teníamos* (l. 3), etc. (see Chapters 2 and 3)
- Adverbs and adverbial phrases: Text 1: *a la antigua* (l. 1), *juntos* (l. 4), *claro* (l. 5), *tanto* (l. 6), *hasta* (l. 6), *tan* (l. 7), *demasiado* (l. 11), etc. (see Chapter 21)
- Conditional: Text 1: *me arrepentiría* (l. 11–12), *me gustaría* (l. 13). Text 2: *se arreglaría* (l. 3–4), *no sé qué haría* (l. 13) (see Chapter 7)
- Possessives: There are numerous possessives in both texts.

See for further information:	Batchelor and Pountain, pp. 248–70
	Butt, pp. 20–35, 42
	Butt and Benjamin, pp. 238–77, 345–51
	Kattán-Ibarra and Pountain, 90–101, 320–1
	Muñoz and Thacker, pp. 96–103, 105–8, 226–37

✎ **EXERCISES**

As you do these exercises, study the sentences carefully and think about their equivalent meanings in English.

1 Put the verb in brackets into the imperfect subjunctive.

  a Yo no esperaba que Laura me (escribir) _____.

  b Les mostramos las fotos porque queríamos que (ver, ellos) _____ la casa.

  c No era posible que lo (hacer, nosotros) _____ en el tiempo previsto.

  d Nos sorprendió mucho que Paco os (hablar) _____ de tal manera.

  e Tuvo que ocultarlo como si (ser) _____ una cosa inadmisible.

  f Tenía que darle cuanta información (pedir, él) _____.

  g Mandó a su hijo al pueblo para que (ayudar, él) _____ a los abuelos.

  h Se marchó sin que nadie (despedirse) _____ de él.

  i ¡Ojalá (saber, nosotros) _____ su paradero!

  j Puede que (salir, ellos) _____ antes de que (llover) _____.

2 Rewrite these sentences in the past.

  a A Luis no le gusta que Ana Luisa saque mejores notas que él.

  b Ana Luisa no quiere que su marido se sienta inferior a ella.

  c Es importante que Luis reconozca los éxitos de su esposa.

  d Siendo macho, es lógico que Luis tenga celos.

  e Alberto le prohibe a Lucía que trabaje fuera de casa.

  f Es una pena que los ingresos de Alberto no sean suficientes para mantener a la familia.

  g A Luisa le duele que su marido no le dé apoyo.

  h No está bien que Alberto no ayude en casa.

  i Lucía le exige a Alberto que contraten una persona que haga las tareas domésticas.

3 Complete these sentences using the imperfect subjunctive.

  a La suegra de Ana Luisa no quería que . . .

  b Lucía le pidió a su marido que . . .

  c No les gustó a los niños que . . .

  d Era importante que . . .

  e Era extraño que . . .

  f A Lucía no le gustaba que . . .

4 Translate these sentences into Spanish.

  a What did she expect her husband to do?

  b She asked him to look after the children.

  c In those days it was not normal for women to work.

  d Many women did not eat so that their children would not go hungry.

e They lived in that house without anyone knowing that they existed.

f Everyone left before Juan arrived.

g We were very sorry that you (familiar, plural) could not come to the party.

5 Complete the sentences by putting the verb in brackets into the correct form.

a Preferíamos que (acabar, tú) _____ lo más pronto posible.

b Nos gustaría que (quedarse, vosotras) _____ más tiempo.

c Quisiera que no (ser) _____ así.

d Me gustaría que me (acompañar, tú) _____ cuando vaya a Santiago.

e Claro que les gustaría que (ganar) _____ su equipo pero no lo ven muy probable.

f Aunque me (ofrecer, ellos) _____ un sueldo magnífico, no trabajaría allí.

6 Cross out the inappropriate verb in each sentence.

a Si tuve/tuviera tiempo, iría.

b Si fumaras/fumas menos, te sentirías mejor.

c Si podemos/pudiéramos, os ayudaríamos.

d Si dijera/dijo la verdad, estaríamos dispuestos a creerlo.

e Si vinieron/vinieran, les gustaría.

f Si te pide/pidiera dinero, se lo darías.

7 Complete these sentences as remote conditions.

Example: Compraría una casa . . .

　　　　　Compraría una casa si me tocara la lotería.

a Estaríamos más contentos si . . .

b Habría menos contaminación si . . .

c Me enfadaría si . . .

d Haría un recorrido por Sudamérica si . . .

e Sería fantástico si . . .

See also Chapter 7, **Conditional tense**. See Chapter 16, **Pluperfect Subjunctive and Conditional Perfect**, for practice of unfulfilled conditions.

16 | The pluperfect subjunctive and conditional perfect

Text

February 23rd 1981 marked a turning point in Spanish political history. Lieutenant-Colonel Antonio Tejero occupied the Congress building with the intention of overthrowing the government. What would have happened if the *Tejerazo* or *23-F*, as it came to be known, had succeeded? This is the subject of this article. As you read the text, note the way in which Spanish expresses ideas such as *What would have happened if it had . . . ?*, *If it had . . . it would have . . .*

¿Qué habría sucedido si . . . ?

El 23 de febrero de 1981 pasó a la historia de España porque un grupo de militares al mando del teniente coronel Antonio Tejero decidió irrumpir en el Congreso e intentar, pistola en mano, tomarse el poder.

Más de veinte años después, los españoles intentan imaginar qué **habría**
5 **pasado** si la intentona **hubiese triunfado**. ¿Cómo sería España ahora? ¿**Habría entrado** en la Unión Europea? ¿Quién sería el presidente? Probablemente, las cosas serían muy diferentes si Tejero **se hubiera salido** con la suya.

Aunque resulta difícil determinar el curso que **habrían tomado** los acontecimientos, los analistas políticos coinciden en que escasamente España
10 **habría conseguido** el grado de desarrollo económico que ha alcanzado en los últimos 20 años y menos aún **habría formado** parte de la Unión Europea. Porque si el golpe **se hubiera consolidado** España **habría vuelto** a estar bajo una dictadura militar al menos unos años y eso **habría impedido** su integración en la Europa democrática. El país no **se habría beneficiado** de los fondos para
15 el desarrollo que ha recibido desde mediados de los '80 de sus socios comunitarios y su economía se parecería mucho más a la de países como Argentina.

Las noticias serían también muy diferentes si el golpe **hubiese triunfado**. La mayoría de los españoles cree que si el golpe del 23-F **se hubiera consumado**, muchos de los periódicos que hoy existen no **hubieran visto** la luz, ni tampoco las
20 cadenas de TV privadas, mucho más difíciles de controlar por una dictadura.

De haberse concretado el golpe, **habría cambiado** la historia de España. Gracias al fracaso del 23-F, la democracia se encuentra consolidada y sólo un 20% de los españoles cree que existe algún riesgo de que los militares vuelvan al poder.

Diario *El Mercurio*, Chile

○ **The pluperfect subjunctive**

1 USAGE

a *Si* **+ pluperfect subjunctive**
The pluperfect subjunctive is used in a construction with **si** *if* and the conditional perfect in the main clause, to express unfulfilled conditions in relation to the past. The text as a whole focuses on the idea that had the coup succeeded, things would have been different. Note the following example:

> ¿Qué **habría pasado si** la intentona (de golpe de Estado) **hubiese triunfado?** (l. 4–5)   *What would have happened if the attempted coup had succeeded?*

The coup did not succeed, therefore the condition here is an unfulfilled one.
Other sentences in the text express a similar idea. Note the following example in which **haber** takes the **-ra** ending instead of **-se**. In the **si** clause the two forms are interchangeable.

> … las cosas serían muy diferentes **si** Tejero **se hubiera salido** con la suya. (l. 7)   *… things would be very different if Tejero had had his way.*

The same usage of the pluperfect subjunctive is found in lines 12, 17–18.

b **Pluperfect subjunctive for conditional perfect**
In conditional sentences such as those above, the **-ra** form of the pluperfect subjunctive can replace the conditional perfect in the main clause, with exactly the same meaning. Note the following example from the text:

> **Si** el golpe **se hubiera consumado**, muchos de los periódicos … no **hubieran visto** la luz. (l. 18–19).   *If the coup had succeeded many of the newspapers … would not have been published.*

In this sentence, **hubieran visto** and **habrían visto** mean the same. Although the pluperfect subjunctive and the conditional perfect are interchangeable in the main clause, this is not the case in the **si** clause, where only the pluperfect subjunctive can be used.

c *De* **+ perfect infinitive for** *si* **+ pluperfect subjunctive**
An alternative to the construction **si** + pluperfect subjunctive is the construction with **de** followed by the perfect infinitive. This can be used when the subject of the **si** clause and that of the main clause are in the same person of the verb.

> **De haberse concretado** el golpe, habría cambiado la historia de España. (l. 21)   *Had the coup succeeded, the history of Spain would have changed.*

d **Other uses of the pluperfect subjunctive**
Usage of the pluperfect subjunctive outside conditional sentences corresponds to that of the subjunctive as a whole, for example in subordinate clauses, independent clauses, after certain conjunctions, etc. (see Chapters 14 and 15). Generally, though, it is less frequent than the present or the imperfect subjunctive.

2 FORMATION

The pluperfect subjunctive is formed from the imperfect subjunctive of **haber** followed by the past participle.

	cambiar	comer	salir
hubiera/iese			
hubieras/ieses			
hubiera/iese	cambiado	comido	salido
hubiéramos/iésemos			
hubierais/ieseis			
hubieran/iesen			

SEQUENCE OF TENSES WITH THE PLUPERFECT SUBJUNCTIVE

The pluperfect subjunctive in the subordinate clause is normally dependent on a main clause verb in the preterite, imperfect, conditional, conditional perfect and pluperfect, for example:

No **pensé** que me **hubieran visto**. *I didn't think they would have seen me.*
Sentía mucho que te **hubieses ido**. *He/she was very sorry you had gone.*
No **creyó/creía** que yo lo **hubiera hecho** solo. *He/she didn't believe I had done it on my own.*
Me **habría gustado** que la **hubieras visto**. *I would have liked you to have seen her.*
No me **extrañaría** que ya **se hubiese enterado**. *I wouldn't be surprised if he/she had already found out.*
Me **habría encantado** que **hubiesen venido**. *I would have loved it if they had come.*

♀ The conditional perfect

1 USAGE

The conditional perfect is used in the main clause in unfulfilled conditions (see **a** above), to refer to a hypothetical situation, to what *would have happened* given certain circumstances. There are a number of examples in the text, not all used alongside the **si** clause, which is understood.

... qué **habría pasado** si ... (l. 4–5) ... *what would have happened if* ...
¿**Habría entrado** en la Unión Europea? (l. 5–6) *Would it have joined the European Union?*

In conditional sentences such as the above, the conditional perfect has the same meaning as the -ra form of the pluperfect subjunctive in the main clause (see **b** above).
Note also the use of the conditional perfect in **habrían tomado** (l. 8), **habría conseguido** (l. 10), **habría formado** (l. 11), **habría vuelto** (l. 12), **se habría beneficiado** (l. 14), **habría cambiado** (l. 21).

2 FORMATION

The conditional perfect is formed from the conditional of **haber** followed by the past participle.

	cambiar	comer	salir
habría			
habrías			
habría	**cambiado**	**comido**	**salido**
habríamos			
habríais			
habrían			

Other points to note in the text

- Definite article: There are a number of examples in the text, but note particularly *el 23 de febrero* (l. 1), *los españoles intentan* (l. 4), *las cosas serían* (l. 7), *si . . . se hubiera salido con la suya* (l. 7) (see Chapter 18)
- Finite verb + infinitive: *decidió irrumpir . . . e intentar* (l. 2–3), *intentan imaginar* (l. 4), *habría vuelto a estar* (l. 12) (see Chapter 8)
- Verb + preposition: *irrumpir en* (l. 2), *entrado en* (l. 6), *coinciden en* (l. 9), *habría vuelto a* (l. 12), *no se habría beneficiado de* (l. 14), *se parecería . . . a* (l. 16) (see Chapter 28)

See for further information:	Batchelor and Pountain, pp. 248–70
	Butt, pp. 21
	Butt and Benjamin, pp. 238–77
	Kattán and Pountain, pp. 90–101, 321
	Muñoz and Thacker, pp. 96–103, 226–34

EXERCISES

As you do these exercises, study the sentences carefully and think about their equivalent meanings in English.

1 Put the verb in brackets into the correct form of the pluperfect subjunctive.

a Jacobo no estaba convencido de que le (dar, ellos) _____ las mismas oportunidades que a Fidel.

b Consuelo había deseado que (venir, ellos) _____.

c ¡Ojalá (comprar, él) _____ una casa en el campo! Allí (vivir, nosotros) _____ felices.

d Gastó dinero como si (heredar) _____ una fortuna.

e Aunque (traer, tú) _____ el televisor, no podríamos haber visto el partido.

f Lamentaba que no (ver, nosotros) _____ su nueva película.

2 Rewrite the following sentences as in the example.

Example: Todo esto ha pasado porque no me hicisteis caso.

Nada de esto hubiera pasado si me hubierais hecho caso.

a No sabía que llovía tanto y no he traído un impermeable.

b No me quedé y por eso no me encontré con el cineasta.

c No hizo buen tiempo y por eso no salimos de excursión.

d No se lo dije porque no vinieron.

e No acudieron a la cita porque nadie les avisó.

f No te ha salido bien porque no me has hecho caso.

3 Change the phrases underlined to a construction using **de** + perfect infinitive.

a ¡Qué pena que el museo esté cerrado! Si lo hubiéramos sabido, no hubiéramos venido.

b Pepe tardó mucho en hacer el trabajo. Si lo hubiera hecho de otra forma, no hubiera tardado tanto.

c No sabía que estuviste solo en casa ayer. Si me lo hubieras dicho, te hubiera llamado.

d El cónsul no sabía que nuestros visados habían llegado. Si se hubiera dado cuenta, nos hubiera avisado.

e No sabemos lo que hubiera hecho el rey si el golpe de estado se hubiera consolidado.

f Si hubieras seguido mis instrucciones, no te encontrarías ahora en este apuro.

4 Complete the sentences using a pluperfect subjunctive or conditional perfect.

a Si el golpe de estado no hubiera fracasado, ...

b Si España no hubiera entrado en la Unión Europea, ...

c Si Cristobal Colón no hubiera navegado hacia el oeste, ...

d Si Napoleón hubiera ganado la batalla de Waterloo, ...

e Si no me hubiera puesto a estudiar español, ...

f Si hubiera ido al cine anoche en vez de quedarme en casa, ...

5 Translate the following sentences into Spanish.

a If he had time, he would go to the cinema.

b If he had had time, he would have gone to the cinema.

c If I did it, I would regret it.

d If I had done it, I would have regretted it.

e If we were rich, we would take you on a journey.

f If we had been rich, we would have taken you on a journey.

g If they read more books, they would understand much more.

h If they had read more books, they would have understood much more.

i When I saw him, I wouldn't have believed that he was ill.

17 | The imperative

The following article warns about the dangers of excessive exposure to the sun and gives recommendations on how to avoid them. As you read the text, note the way in which formal imperative forms have been used.

El sol, ¿amigo o enemigo?

Que el sol se convierta en un enemigo en la época de las vacaciones sólo depende de usted. Para no iniciar relaciones turbias, no **abuse** de él. El cáncer y el envejecimiento prematuro de la piel son dos consecuencias más que suficientes para intentar evitar esos problemas.

5   Si desea broncearse y no tener que acudir a un médico **procure** tomar el sol comedidamente, aunque sea en la terraza, antes de salir de vacaciones.

Es fundamental que lo haga progresivamente y muy prudente, al principio. Si no quiere deshidratarse **beba** agua, **muévase** y **báñese** y, aunque ya esté bronceado, **extienda** siempre sobre la piel una capa de crema

10 protectora eficaz.

Si sufre una quemadura solar, **refúgiese** en la sombra y no **vuelva** a echarse aceite o crema solar. Mejor **aplique** un poco de hielo en la zona lesionada y **compre** en la farmacia una crema apropiada. Los médicos aconsejan desconfiar del sol. Por eso, **utilice** un protector con un índice de protección en función de

15 la sensibilidad de su piel. **Aplíquelo** antes de la exposición y **repita** la operación con frecuencia. **Cuídese** de los productos de bronceado solar. Si le provocan picores, no los **utilice** y **vigile** su piel.

Revista *Cambio 16*, España

This text looks at job interviews and gives advice on how to confront them. As you read it, note the use of the familiar form of the imperative.

Estrategias para encontrar empleo: la entrevista

- **Prepárala** a fondo. **Consigue** todos los datos que puedas sobre la empresa en cuestión.
- **Acude** a la entrevista relajado/a y sereno/a. **Evita** tomar café.
  La presencia, impecable, pero no te **arregles** en exceso.
5 - No importa si tu interlocutor es más joven o de tu misma edad, **háblale** de usted.
- **Responde** a sus preguntas sin rodeos y **sé** sincero/a. **No te justifiques** nunca.
- **Habla** tranquilo/a, vocalizando, no hay prisa. **Piensa** antes de hablar y **deja** largos intervalos antes de contestar.
- Tu actitud hacia la empresa debe ser positiva. **Deja** claro que tienes ganas de
10 trabajar y muchas ideas que aportar.
- **Argumenta** un cambio de aires antes que hacer el papel de víctima parado/a a quien nadie quiere contratar.
- **No te contradigas** en nada **ni des** explicaciones sobre tu salud, familia, novio/a . . .
15 - **Habla** de tus aficiones siempre que éstas tengan algo que ver con la actividad de la empresa. **Di** sólo lo necesario.
- **No acabes** tú la entrevista. Cuando concluya, **agradéceles** que te hayan recibido y **muéstrate** encantado de haberles conocido.

Revista *Prima*, España

The imperative

1 USAGE

Verb forms such as **habla** *speak*, **beba** *drink*, **repita** *repeat*, are known as imperative or command forms. The imperative, which is more widely used in Spanish than in English, is found in contexts like the following ones:

a Recommendations and advice. All the examples in Texts 1 and 2 fall into this category.

b Directions and instructions.

> **Siga** todo recto.   *Go straight on.*
> **Tome** una cucharada antes de cada comida.   *Take one spoonful before each meal.*

c Commands and prohibition.

> **Haga** lo que digo.   *Do as I say.*
> No lo **deje** aquí.   *Don't leave it here.*

d Requests.

> **Pásame** la sal, por favor.   *Pass the salt, please.*

2 FORMATION

Unlike English, Spanish uses different imperative forms depending on who you are talking to (formal or familiar form) and whether you are speaking to one or more than one person (singular or plural form).

a Formal imperative

Positive and negative commands for **usted** and **ustedes** are taken from the third person of the present subjunctive (Chapter 14). This is itself formed by removing the -**o** of the first person singular of the present tense indicative, to which the endings are added. This rule applies to all regular verbs and, with a few exceptions, to irregular and stem-changing verbs.

Present indicative (1st person)	*Formal imperative* (Vd./Vds.)
habl**o** *I speak*	habl**e/n** *speak*
beb**o** *I drink*	beb**a/n** *drink*
repit**o** *I repeat*	repit**a/n** *repeat*
teng**o** *I have*	teng**a/n** *have*
dig**o** *I say*	dig**a/n** *say*

Irregular forms and spelling changes

Amongst irregular forms we find **dé/n** *give* (from **dar**), **esté/n** *be* (from **estar**), **vaya/n** *go* (from **ir**), **sepa/n** *know* (from **saber**), **sea/n** *be* (from **ser**).

Note also spelling changes in verbs ending in -**car**, -**gar**, -**ger**, -**zar**, for example **aplicar** *to apply*, **aplique/n**; **pagar** *to pay*, **pague/n**; **coger** *to take, catch*, **coja/n**; **empezar** *to begin, start*, **empiece/n**.

All the examples in Text 1 correspond to the formal imperative.
Note that the negative command is formed by placing **no** before the verb.

> ... no **abuse** ... (T. 1, l. 2)   ... *do not abuse* ...
> ... **procure** tomar el sol ... (T. 1, l. 5)   ... *try to sunbathe* ...
> ... **beba** agua ... (T. 1, l. 8)   ... *drink water* ...
> ... **repita** la operación ... (T. 1, l. 15)   ... *repeat the operation* ...
> ... **aplique** un poco de hielo ... (T. 1, l. 12)   ... *apply some ice* ...

The use of the formal imperative may sound abrupt in some contexts so, to avoid this, use courtesy forms such as **por favor** *please*, **si es Vd. tan amable** *if you would be so kind*.

> Por favor **tenga** cuidado.   *Please be careful.*
> **Venga** aquí un momento, si es Vd. tan amable.   *Come here a moment, if you would be so kind.*

b Familiar imperative

Negative familiar commands are taken from the present subjunctive, just as formal commands above, but positive familiar ones have special forms.

Infinitive	Positive	Negative	
hablar	habla	no hables	(tú)
	hablad	no habléis	(vosotros/as)
responder	responde	no respondas	(tú)
	responded	no respondáis	(vosotros/as)
acudir	acude	no acudas	(tú)
	acudid	no acudáis	(vosotros/as)

Note that the **tú** positive imperative derives from the second person singular of the present indicative, without its final -s, e.g. **tú hablas** *you speak*, **habla** *speak*. The **vosotros/as** positive command is like the infinitive, but with a final -**d** instead of an -**r**, e.g. **hablar** *to speak*, **hablad** *speak*.

> **Acude** a la entrevista ... (T. 2, l. 3) *Go to the interview ...*
> **Responde** a sus preguntas ... (T. 2, l. 6) *Answer his questions ...*
> **Habla** tranquilo/a ... (T. 2, l. 7) *Speak in relaxed way ...*

Irregular forms

Some verbs form the ***singular positive*** familiar imperative in an irregular way: **di** *say* (from **decir**), **haz** *do, make* (from **hacer**), **ve** *go* (from **ir**), **pon** *put* (from **poner**), **sal** *go out* (from **salir**), **sé** *be* (from **ser**), **ten** *have* (from **tener**), **ven** *come* (from **venir**).

> **Sé** sincero/a. (T. 2, l. 6) *Be sincere.*
> **Di** sólo lo necesario. (T. 2, l. 16) *Say only what's necessary.*

See also **Irregular verbs** on pages 204–7.

The ***plural positive*** imperative and negative commands follow the ***regular*** pattern for familiar forms, for example **decid** (for **vosotros/as**), **no digas** (for **tú**), **no digáis** (for **vosotros/as**), from **decir** *to say*.

> No te **contradigas** ... (T. 2, l. 13) *Don't contradict yourself ...*

LATIN AMERICAN USAGE

Latin Americans do not use the **vosotros/as** form, which is replaced by the **ustedes** form in both formal and familiar address.

Regular familiar imperative forms for **vos**, used in the Río de la Plata area in place of **tú** (see Chapters 1, 14 and 25), are mostly similar, except that the stress falls on the last syllable. Below are the positive and negative forms for **hablar**, **comer** and **partir**:

hablá	**comé**	**partí** (for **parte**)
no hablés	**no comás**	**no partás**

c Command forms including the speaker

Command forms including the speaker, as in *Let's work*, correspond to the first person plural of the present subjunctive (Chapter 14), e.g. **trabajemos** (from **trabajar**) *let's work*, **comamos** (from **comer**) *let's eat*, **no subamos** (from **subir**) *let's not go up*. When **nos** is added, the final -**s** of the verb is removed, e.g. **bañémonos** *let's bathe*, **vámonos** *let's go*.

PRONOUNS WITH IMPERATIVES

Object and reflexive pronouns precede negative imperatives but are attached to positive ones. In the case of object pronouns, the indirect one must come first. There are a number of examples of this in the texts. Note that an accent may need to be added to the positive form to indicate that the stress remains in the same place.

... **muévase** y **báñese** ... (T. 1, l. 8)   ... *move and bathe* ...
Apliquelo antes ... (T. 1, l. 15)   *Apply it before* ...
Prepárala a fondo. (T. 2, l. 1)   *Prepare it thoroughly.*
No **te arregles** en exceso. (T. 2, l. 4)   *Don't over-dress.*
No **te justifiques** ... (T. 2, l. 6)   *Don't justify yourself* ...
Hagámoslo.   *Let's do it.*
No lo hagamos.   *Let's not do it.*

Other points to note in the text

- Prepositions: There are numerous prepositions in both texts, including among others *en*, *de*, *para*, *sobre*, *con*, *sin*. (see Chapter 28)
- Verb + preposition: Text 1: *se convierta en* (l. 1), *depende de* (l. 1–2), *no abuse de* (l. 2), *acudir a* (l. 5), *cuídese de* (l. 16) (see Chapter 28)
- Adverbs: There are numerous adverbs in the texts. In Text 1, note *sólo* (l. 1), *más* (l. 3), *comedidamente* (l. 6), *progresivamente* (l. 7), etc. (see Chapter 21)
- Present subjunctive: Text 1: *que el sol se convierta* (l. 1), *aunque sea* (l. 6), *es fundamental que lo haga* (l. 7), *aunque ya esté* (l. 9). Text 2: *los datos que puedas* (l. 1), *siempre que éstas tengan* (l. 15) (see Chapter 14)

See for further information:	Batchelor and Pountain, pp. 249–50
	Butt, pp. 36–40
	Butt and Benjamin, pp. 278–86
	Kattán-Ibarra and Pountain, pp. 88–9, 395, 399, 403, 405
	Muñoz and Thacker, pp. 108–13, 237–9

✎ **EXERCISES**

1 Put the following infinitives into the formal imperative forms (**usted** and **ustedes**), positive and negative.

a pasar   _____ _____

b leerlo   _____ _____

c oír   _____ _____

d sentarse   _____ _____

e tener   _____ _____

f venir   _____ _____

g probarlo   _____ _____

h ser   _____ _____

2 Put the following infinitives into the singular familiar imperative form (**tú**), positive and negative.

a mirar   _____ _____

b acostarse   _____ _____

c aprenderlo   _____ _____

d dármela   _____ _____

e hacerlo   _____ _____

f decirnos   _____ _____

g ponérselos   _____ _____

h irse   _____ _____

3 Put the same verbs into the plural familiar imperative form (**vosotros/as**), positive and negative.

4 Change these questions into inclusive command forms, *let's* . . .

a ¿Empezamos? Sí, _____

b ¿Por qué enfadarnos? No _____

c ¿Leemos? Sí, _____

d ¿Nos sentamos? Sí, _____

e ¿Nos acostamos? No, no _____

f ¿Seguimos? Sí, _____

5 Here is some advice on what to do and not do when writing a curriculum vitae. Rewrite the advice using the **tú** form of the imperative.

a Procurar no escribir más de 1 o 2 folios.

b Utilizar frases cortas.

c No usar siglas ni abreviaturas.

d Cuidar la ortografía, sintaxis y signos de puntuación.

e Destacar los aspectos que puedan despertar interés.

f No mentir.

g No escribirlo a mano.

h No mandar una fotocopia del original.

i No incluir una fotografía a no ser que se la haya pedido.

j Recordar firmarlo.

6 Rewrite the following text addressing the reader in the formal singular form (**usted**).

Trucos para hacer turismo sin arruinarte

- Viaja fuera de las fechas que se consideran temporada alta. Un par de días de diferencia pueden significar precios más baratos.
- Elige agencias especializadas en el destino escogido. Además de conocer todas las tarifas, y acceder a precios más baratos que los mayoristas, te ayudarán a planear mejor el viaje. Las oficinas de turismo de cada país tienen listados de estas agencias.
- Pide los precios por separado si prefieres contratar un paquete turístico (viaje, traslados con guía y alojamiento): a veces la tarifa global oculta que te cobran a precio de oro los transportes del aeropuerto al hotel, y viceversa. En estos casos, ir en taxi te puede salir mucho más económico.
- La fórmula más barata suele ser "avión + alojamiento". Si eres un viajero experimentado y sabes moverte con soltura en otros países, no dudes en contratarla.
- Haz tu reserva con antelación y, para mayor tranquilidad, contrata en la propia agencia un seguro de cancelación del viaje.
- Aprovecha las ofertas de última hora si tienes la suerte de no tener que ajustar tus vacaciones a unas fechas determinadas. Pero ten en cuenta que, contratando una semana antes de salir, difícilmente podrás elegir el destino que más te guste.
- Si quieres hacer un "tour" por varios países, siempre te saldrá más económico contratar un viaje organizado que ir por libre.

Revista *Quo*, España

7 Recipes can be written in a variety of ways. Rewrite this one, which gives instructions on how to make a potato omelette, using the **vosotros/as** form of the imperative.

   a Córtense las patatas en láminas finas y fríanselas en aceite.
   b Bátanse unos huevos y una vez cocidas las patatas, mézclese todo.
   c Póngasele la sal necesaria.
   d Caliéntese un poco de aceite en una sartén y cuando esté caliente, échese la mezcla.
   e Cuando la tortilla esté dorada por un lado, désele la vuelta.

8 Your friend is going for an interview. While Text 2 gives advice on how to behave at an interview, there are also things you should do before you get there, like preparing questions to ask, rehearsing answers to the kind of questions you may be asked, to more practical points like polishing your shoes, cleaning your nails, going to the hairdresser's, not using too much perfume/aftershave. Prepare a list of points for your friend, using the familiar form of the imperative.

Part Two:
Grammar essentials

Text

This extract from an article in a Spanish magazine expresses concern over drinking habits among young people in Spain. As you read the text, look at the way in which articles, the Spanish equivalent of *the* and *a/an*, have been used.

La España beoda

Por lo menos veintiséis millones de ciudadanos consumen cotidianamente alcohol en este país. España es **una** sociedad alcohólica, y **los** españoles beben, según **los** parámetros europeos, de manera desmedida y creciente. La imagen que muchos visitantes extranjeros se llevan de los españoles es **la** de individuos reunidos
5 multitudinariamente en bares, que sostienen copas en **la** mano. Hay más bares en España que en **el** resto de toda Europa y éstos no están poblados, precisamente, por bebedores de leche.

La tendencia a beber es claramente ascendente. En España **el** consumo de alcohol se ha disparado entre **los** adolescentes, **los** jóvenes y **las** mujeres. [. . .]
10 Existe **un** verdadero proceso de alcoholización en **la** juventud.

El consumo de alcohol es más frecuente entre personas con mayor nivel de estudios e ingresos. Entre **los** que tienen estudios medio-superiores se da **una** mayor proporción de bebedores frecuentes, **el** 59 por ciento, y menos de abstemios, **el** 21 por ciento.

15 Entre **el** 30 y **el** 39 por ciento de **los** jóvenes españoles bebe a diario, y **el** 45 por ciento lo hace **los** fines de semana. En **los** hogares **los** chicos toman cerveza como otra costumbre más y se sigue despachando alcohol a **los** menores con toda impunidad.

José P.L. tiene veintidós años, es técnico en electrónica e intenta acudir a
20 diario a Alcohólicos Anónimos. Su caso ilustra el drama d**el** alcoholismo en **la** juventud española, porque son muchos **los** casos como **el** suyo. José, que sigue sin abandonar **la** bebida, es alcohólico de fin de semana. Comenzó a beber a **los** diecisiete años para superar cierto problema psíquico. Actualmente, al llegar **el** sábado bebe hasta caer al suelo . . .

Revista *Cambio 16*, España

♀ The definite article

1 FORMS

There are two types of articles, *definite* and *indefinite*. In English, the definite article is *the*. Spanish uses four different forms:

	singular	*plural*
masculine	**el**	**los**
feminine	**la**	**las**

Note that **a** + **el** become **al**, and **de** + **el** become **del**.

Note also that Spanish has a neuter form of the definite article, **lo**, but this is not used with nouns. (See "The neuter form *lo*" below.)

2 USAGE

The Spanish definite article agrees in gender (masculine/feminine) and number (singular/plural) with the noun. **El** and not **la** is used before singular feminine nouns beginning with stressed **a-** or **ha-**: **el arte** *art* (but **las artes**), **el habla** *language, speech*. Spanish and English differ substantially in the way in which they use the definite article, as you will see from the notes and examples below:

a With plural nouns used in a general sense.

> **los españoles** (l. 2)   *Spaniards*
> **los jóvenes** (l. 9)   *young people*

b With abstract nouns.

> **la juventud** (l. 10, 20–1)   *young people*

c With words denoting subjects, sciences, sports, arts, illnesses.

> **el alcoholismo** (l. 20)   *alcoholism*

d With parts of the body, in place of a possessive.

> en **la mano** (l. 5)   *in their hand*

e With days of the week and other expressions of time.

> al llegar **el sábado** (l. 23–4)   *when Saturday comes*

f With words indicating measure, weight and percentages.

> **el 30** y **el 39 por cient**o (l. 15)   *30 and 39 per cent*

g With age, when there is a relationship between this and a certain event.

> Comenzó a beber a **los 17 años** (l. 22–3)   *He started drinking at 17*

h In place of a noun, meaning *that/those of, the one/s from/belonging to*. The article must show agreement in number and gender with the noun it refers to.

… es **la** de individuos … (l. 4)   *… it is that of people …*
Entre **los** que tienen … (l. 12)   *Amongst those who have …*

i With possessive pronouns. (See **Possessives**, Chapter 24.)

… los casos como **el** suyo … (l. 21)   *… cases like his …*

j With singular nouns denoting substances, and names of food, drinks and meals.

La cerveza mexicana es buena.   *Mexican beer is good.*
El desayuno es a las 9.00.   *Breakfast is at 9.00.*

But:

Bebe cerveza.   *He/she drinks beer.*

k With titles and words like **señor, señora, señorita**, except in direct address.

el señor y **la señora** Díaz   *Mr and Mrs Díaz*

l With names of languages, unless the name is preceded by **hablar** *to speak* or **aprender** *to learn*.

El chino es difícil.   *Chinese is difficult.*
Hablan español.   *They speak Spanish.*

m With the names of certain countries, although this use is now mostly optional.

(el) Perú, (el) Ecuador, (la) Argentina, but
la India, el Reino Unido

n With words denoting colours.

El rojo te va/queda bien.   *Red suits you.*

o With infinitives to form nouns. (See **The Infinitive**, Chapter 8.)

El beber demasiado es malo para la salud.   *Drinking too much is bad for your health.*

The neuter form *lo*

The neuter form **lo** is used:

a Before adjectives and adverbs as an intensifier

No sabes **lo** hermoso que es.   *You don't know how beautiful it is.*
No te imaginas **lo** bien que está.   *You can't imagine how well he/she is.*

b With adjectives, to form abstract nouns.

Lo extraño es que no nos dijo nada.   *The strange thing is that he/she didn't tell us anything.*

The indefinite article

1 FORMS

In English, the indefinite article is *a/an*. Spanish has four different forms, with the plural forms translating *some*.

	singular	*plural*
masculine	**un**	**unos**
feminine	**una**	**unas**

2 USAGE

The Spanish indefinite article agrees with the noun in gender (masculine/feminine) and number (singular/plural). Before a singular feminine noun beginning with a stressed **a-** or **ha-**, use **un** instead of **una**: **un arma** *weapon* (but **las armas**), **un habla** *language, speech*. Usage of the indefinite article in Spanish and English does not differ greatly, but there are a few important points to note:

a Generally, the indefinite article is not used in the construction **ser** + noun, unless the noun is qualified. This rule applies with a number of categories of nouns, such as those denoting nationality, religion, occupation.

> Es técnico en electrónica. (l. 19)   *He's an electronics technician.*
> Es **un** buen técnico en electrónica.   *He's a good electronics technician.*

b The indefinite article is not used after **tal** *such*, **qué** *what*, **medio/a** *half*, **de manera/forma/modo** *in a way*.

> ... **de manera** desmedida y creciente (l. 3)   ... *in an excessive and increasing way*
> Beben de **tal** manera.   *They drink in such a way.*
> ¡**Qué** lástima!   *What a pity!*

c The indefinite article is not used before **otro** *another* and **cierto** *certain*, **cien** *a hundred* (except with percentages) and **mil** *a thousand*.

> **otra** costumbre (l. 17)   *another custom*
> **cierto** problema psíquico (l. 23)   *a certain psychological problem*

d The indefinite article is omitted with **tener** *to have* and **llevar** *to wear*, when the accompanying noun is used in a general sense. If the noun is qualified, **un** or **una** cannot be omitted.

> No tengo coche.   *I haven't got a car.*
> Tiene **un** coche muy caro.   *He/she has a very expensive car.*
> Llevaba corbata.   *He was wearing a tie.*
> Llevaba **una** corbata roja.   *He was wearing a red tie.*

Other points to note in the text

- Comparison: *más . . . que* (l. 5–6), *más frecuente* (l. 11), *con mayor nivel* (l. 11), *una mayor proporción* (l. 12–13), *menos . . . abstemios* (l. 13–14) (see Chapter 22)
- Adjective agreement and position: *una sociedad alcohólica* (l. 2), *los parámetros europeos* (l. 2–3), *visitantes extranjeros* (l. 4), *un verdadero proceso* (l. 10) (see Chapter 20)
- Adverbs and adverbial phrases: *cotidianamente* (l. 1), *de manera desmedida y creciente* (l. 3), *multitudinariamente* (l. 5), *precisamente* (l. 7), *claramente* (l. 8), *a diario* (l. 15), etc. (see Chapter 21)

See for further information:	Butt, pp. 82–90
	Butt and Benjamin, pp. 28–50
	Kattán-Ibarra and Pountain, pp. 20–5
	Muñoz and Thacker, pp. 12–16, 183–6

✎ EXERCISES

1 Put the appropriate definite article in the blank where necessary.

a Nunca salgo ____ sábados por ____ noche; prefiero ver ____ tele en ____ casa.

b En España se sirve ____ cena más tarde que en ____ países nórdicos.

c Se ha roto ____ pierna.

d A pesar de ____ frío que hacía, no se puso ____ abrigo.

e A Luis lo metieron en ____ cárcel ____ semana pasada.

f Julio no se encuentra bien; está en ____ cama.

g ____ año que viene Gonzalo va a estudiar en ____ universidad de Hamburgo.

h ____ abuela viene ____ fin de semana en ____ tren.

i ____ señores de Cortés vivían en ____ calle Pez.

j ____ veintitantos de marzo en ____ hemisferio norte, empieza ____ primavera.

k Me gusta ____ marisco pero no me gustan ____ aceitunas.

l En Escocia se cultiva ____ cebada para hacer ____ whisky.

m ____ tomates están a 2 euros ____ kilo.

n A Pepe le gusta ____ azul pero mi color preferido es ____ rojo.

o Me gusta más la chaqueta verde que ____ marrón.

2 Translate these sentences into Spanish.

a Alcohol consumption is prevalent among today's youth.

b Women are also drinking more than before.

c Over 40% of young people drink at weekends.

d Beer is a popular drink.

e Ramón, José's best friend, began drinking at the age of twelve.

f Doctor Justino León thinks that unemployment causes many problems.

g Girls now drink as much as boys.

h Statistics show that cycling and swimming are good for your health.

3 Rewrite these sentences inserting **lo** in the correct place, then study them for meaning.

   a Importante es viajar.

   b Hay que ver bonitos que son.

   c Mío es mío y suyo es suyo.

   d Bueno era que se dio cuenta de mezquina que era Patricia.

   e Pepe prefiere picante y yo dulce.

4 Translate these sentences into Spanish.

   a You can't imagine how good-looking she is.

   b I don't want to tell you how bad the film was.

   c The best thing is to wait.

   d The interesting bit is coming.

   e The difficult bit was not so difficult.

5 Put the appropriate indefinite article in the blank where necessary.

   a Fernando era ____ diseñador; era ____ diseñador ingenioso.

   b Silvio es ____ nicaraguense; es ____ músico.

   c Queremos ____ casa con ____ jardín.

   d En el frigorífico sólo hay ____ leche.

   e En el frigorífico sólo hay ____ botella de leche.

   f Mi abuelo tiene ____ paciencia formidable.

   g Dame ____ otro pedazo de pan.

   h Hay ____ poema de Machado que es ____ recuerdo de cuando era ____ profesor.

   i Los niños cantaban ____ cien veces, ____ mil veces, ____ cien mil veces.

   j Antonio no llevaba ____ abrigo cuando salió. Luego, se compró ____ abrigo de piel.

   k No tengo ____ coche. Todo el mundo me dice que tengo que comprar ____.

   l Este año vamos a Costa Rica; ____ otro año iremos a Guatemala.

6 Translate into Spanish.

   a Paco was a really good engineer.

   b A certain young man was asking for you.

   c I don't want to repeat such an experience.

   d What a noise! We left after half an hour.

   e Jules is French, is a doctor and doesn't have a girlfriend.

   f And another thing – he always wears a ring.

7 Insert the appropriate article, definite or indefinite, in the gaps where necessary.

____ verano pasado estuvimos ____ días en Buenos Aires, ____ capital de Argentina, con ____ amiga nuestra. ____ domingo, después de tomar ____ desayuno, visitamos ____ barrio de San Telmo donde había ____ mercado con ____ puestos que vendían ____ antigüedades y ____ cosas de ____ segunda mano. También vimos a ____ pareja mayor que bailaba ____ tango y ____ otra pareja más joven que bailaba con ____ público. ____ malo de Buenos Aires era ____ tráfico y por tanto ____ ruido constante, pero es ____ ciudad que nos encantó.

8 On the basis of the following information, write a description of María, using the article as and when appropriate.

Nombe: María
Apellidos: González Posada
Fecha de nacimiento: 21.04.84
Domicilio: Santa Ana
País: El Salvador
Actividades y deportes: cine; música; lectura; voleibol; baloncesto
Bebida preferida: cerveza
Plato favorito: arroz con frijoles
Color preferido: amarillo
Mayor cualidad: generosidad
Mayor defecto: pereza
Preocupaciones: medio ambiente; protección de animales; pobreza en el mundo

19 | Nouns

This article tells about the discovery in southern Chile of the oldest forest in the world, with **alerces**, *larch trees*, more than 4000 years old. The main grammatical point in this unit is nouns. As you read the text, list them according to their gender (masculine and feminine) and look at the ways in which plurals have been formed.

El bosque más antiguo del planeta

El **bosque** más antiguo de la **Tierra**, con **alerces** que superan los 4.000 **años**, se encuentra en la **Cordillera** de Los **Andes**, a mil **kilómetros** de Santiago de Chile, según un **estudio** efectuado por **científicos** y **ecologistas**.

La **expedición** fue organizada por la **fundación** *Ancient Forest International* y
5 su **objetivo** era explorar las **áreas** naturales vírgenes del **bosque** húmedo templado más austral del **mundo**.

El **grupo**, integrado por 92 **profesionales** visitó nueve **zonas**, a fin de determinar la urgente **necesidad** de preservar **sectores** forestales poco estudiados hasta ahora y que se encuentran bajo fuerte **presión** de la
10 **industria** papelera.

En el **volcán** *Hornopirén*, a 800 **metros** sobre el **nivel** del **mar**, el **ecólogo** chileno Daniel González encontró **alerces** cuya **edad** promedio fue determinada entre 1.600 y 2.000 **años**, sin poder, por **razones** climatológicas, explorar **áreas** más altas. Las diferentes **condiciones** de la **topografía** y el **clima** existentes a
15 mayor **altitud** hacen presumir a los **expertos** que los **alerces** que ahí se encuentran superan los 4.300 **años**. Con **anterioridad** a estas **investigaciones** se consideraba que los **árboles** más antiguos del **planeta** eran los famosos *sequoias gigantes* de California.

La **representante** de *AFI* en Chile dijo que la **institución** tiene **interés** en
20 comprar 200.000 **hectáreas** del **bosque** y destinarlas a un **parque** para la **humanidad** y explicó que por ser éste un **ecosistema** único en el **mundo**, existe a **nivel** internacional mucho **interés** por preservarlo.

Diario *Presencia*, Bolivia

♀ Nouns

1 GENDER

All nouns in Spanish are either masculine or feminine. The following simple rules will help you to differentiate a masculine noun from a feminine one. Study the notes and check how the nouns in the text fit each rule. Then do the same for the section on "Number" below.

a Most nouns ending in **-o** are masculine and most nouns ending in **-a** are feminine, e.g.
el mundo (l. 6) *world*, **la zona** (l. 7) *zone*.
But, **el clima** (l. 14), **el planeta** (l. 17) *planet*, **la mano** *hand*.

b Nouns referring to males will be masculine and those referring to females will be feminine. To form the feminine of nouns which refer to people, you normally change **-o** to **-a** or add **-a** to the final consonant. e.g. **el ecólogo/la ecóloga** (l. 11), **el experto/la experta** (l. 15) *expert*, **el doctor/la doctora** *doctor* (but **el/la profesional**). Some nouns have a fixed gender and they may be used to refer to a male or to a female, e.g. **el bebé** (masc.) *baby*, **la persona** (fem.) *person*.

c Some nouns referring to people remain invariable, no matter whether they refer to a man or to a woman. Amongst these we find those ending in **-ista** and many nouns ending in **-e**, e.g. **el/la ecologista** (l. 3) *ecologist*, **el/la representante** (l. 19) *representative* (but **el jefe/la jefa** *boss*).

d Some nouns have different forms for each sex, e.g. **el yerno** *son-in-law*, **la nuera** *daughter-in-law*, **el padre** *father*, **la madre** *mother*.

e Nouns ending in **-or** and **-aje** and in a stressed vowel are usually masculine, e.g. **el sector** (l. 8) *area*, **el aterrizaje** *landing*, **el alelí** *wallflower*.

f Nouns ending in **-ción**, **-sión**, **-ie**, **-iza**, **-dad**, **-tad**, **-tud**, **-umbre** are usually feminine, e.g. **la expedición** (l. 4) *expedition*, **la pasión** *passion*, **la serie** *series*, **la hortaliza** *vegetable*, **la edad** (l. 12) *age*, **la humanidad** (l. 20–1) *humanity*, **la altitud** (l. 15) *altitude*, **la muchedumbre** *crowd*.

g A number of nouns ending in **-ma** are masculine, but some are feminine, e.g. **el clima** (l. 14) *climate*, **el ecosistema** (l. 21) *ecosystem*, **la forma** *shape*, **la yema** *yolk*.

h The following classes of noun are normally masculine: names of languages (e.g. **el español**), mountains and volcanoes (e.g. **Los Andes**, l. 2, **el volcán Hornopirén**, l. 11), rivers and seas (e.g. **el Amazonas, el Pacífico**), substances (e.g. **el oro** *gold*, but **la plata** *silver*), colours (e.g. **el rojo** *red*), days of the week (e.g. **el viernes** *Friday*), points of the compass (e.g. **el sur** *south*), fruit trees (e.g. **el manzano** *apple tree*, but **la manzana** *apple*).

i The following classes of noun are normally feminine: islands (e.g. **las islas Baleares** *the Balearic Islands*), letters of the alphabet (e.g. **la be** *b*).

j Some nouns change meaning according to gender (e.g. **el policía** *policeman*, **la policía** *the police*).

2 NUMBER

a Nouns ending in a vowel normally form the plural by adding **-s**, e.g. **el año/los años** (l. 1) *year/s*.

b Nouns ending in a consonant add -**es**, e.g. **el profesional/los profesionales** (l. 7) *professional/s*, **el sector/los sectores** (l. 8).

c Nouns ending en -**z** change -**z** to -**c** and add -**es**, e.g. **el pez/los peces** *fish*.

d Nouns ending in -**í** and -**ú** add -**es**, e.g. **marroquí/marroquíes** *Moroccan*, **hindú/hindúes** *Hindu, Indian* (but **el menú/los menús** *menu/s*).

e Nouns carrying a written accent on the last syllable, lose this in the plural, e.g. **la razón/las razones** (l. 13) *reason/s*, **el volcán** (l. 11)/**los volcanes** *volcano/es*.

f Nouns which end in -**en**, with the stress on the penultimate syllable, gain a written accent in the plural, e.g. **el joven/los jóvenes** *young man/young people*.

g The masculine plural of some nouns may be used to refer to members of both sexes, e.g. **los padres** *parents*, **los hermanos** *brothers and sisters*.

h Some nouns are used in the plural only, e.g. **los alrededores** *outskirts*, **las vacaciones** *holidays*.

i Some nouns with a plural sense function as singular nouns, e.g. **la gente es** … *people are* …

j A few nouns have the same form for singular and plural, **el análisis/los análisis** *analysis/analyses*, **el miércoles/los miércoles** *Wednesday/s*.

Other points to note in the text

- Superlative: *el bosque más antiguo de la Tierra* (l. 1), *el bosque húmedo templado más austral del mundo* (l. 5–6), *los árboles más antiguos del planeta* (l. 17) (see Chapter 22)
- *Por* and *para*: *efectuado por* … (l. 3), *organizada por* … (l. 4), *por razones* … (l. 13), *para la humanidad* (l. 20–1), *por ser* … (l. 21), *interés por preservarlo* (l. 22) (see Chapter 28)
- Relative pronouns: *alerces que superan* … (l. 1), *sectores forestales* … *que* … (l. 8–9), *alerces cuya edad* … (l. 12), etc. (see Chapter 26)

See for further information: Batchelor and Pountain, pp. 157–71

Butt, pp. 91–103

Butt and Benjamin, pp. 1–27

Kattán-Ibarra and Pountain, pp. 11–19

Muñoz and Thacker, pp. 17–21, 187–91

EXERCISES

While these are not vocabulary exercises, use your dictionary to check meanings of words you are not sure of.

1 Give the gender of the following groups of nouns.

  a región; habitación; recepción; manifestación

  b moto; foto; bici; mano

c calor; dolor; color; motor

d coraje; garaje; viaje; equipaje

e bondad; sinceridad; amistad; mitad

f jabón; jamón; balcón; pantalón

g jueves; viernes; martes; miércoles

h taxi; avión; camión; tranvía

i costumbre; certidumbre; pesadumbre; muchedumbre

j azul; verde; marrón; gris

2 Although all these nouns end in **-a**, only four are feminine. Identify them.

norma	programa	clima	sistema
tema	pijama	idioma	víctima
problema	síntoma	trama	cima

3 Identify which of the following nouns are <u>not</u> feminine.

calle	serie	bronce	hambre	peine
fraude	aire	nieve	cine	catástrofe
sangre	base	parque	tarde	este

4 Say whether the noun is masculine (m) or feminine (f).

catedral	pan	noche	nariz	planeta
luz	dólar	día	agua	estrés
garaje	ciudad	régimen	lesión	césped
deber	labor	sur	flor	porvenir
valor	énfasis	sol	mes	tarde
virtud	imagen	mapa	cárcel	sed

5 Write these nouns in the plural.

bar _____   lápiz _____

crisis _____   hotel _____

paraguas _____   deber _____

examen _____   origen _____

francés _____   nación _____

altavoz _____   orden _____

mes _____   pie _____

país _____   cuarto de baño _____

6 Write these nouns in the singular.

regiones _____   aviones _____

quehaceres _____   ingleses _____

coles _____   jóvenes _____

luces _____   sofás _____

convoyes _____   caracteres _____

records _____   rubíes _____

vírgenes _____   ilusiones _____

violines _____   imágenes _____

7 Give the feminine equivalents of these nouns.

a padre _____   **g** actor _____

b hombre _____   **h** emperador _____

c alcalde _____   **i** poeta _____

d príncipe _____   **j** rey _____

e macho _____   **k** traductor _____

f toro _____   **l** escritor _____

8 Some nouns have a masculine form and a feminine form. What difference in meaning is there between the following nouns?

a el puerto _____   la puerta _____

b el libro _____   la libra _____

c el punto _____   la punta _____

d el pato _____   la pata _____

e el pago _____   la paga _____

f el herido _____   la herida _____

9 Some nouns have the same form (homonyms) but different meaning according to gender. Say what the meanings of these nouns are.

a el capital _____   la capital _____

b el guía _____   la guía _____

c el mañana _____   la mañana _____

d el orden _____   la orden _____

e el cura _____   la cura _____

f el policía _____   la policía _____

20 | Adjectives

Text 1

This article tells about the recent discovery in the Peruvian Andes of embalmed mummies, in a site which was probably used for human sacrifice. This text serves to illustrate the use of adjectives, whose function is to identify or describe nouns.

Los incas realizaban sacrificios humanos

El **reciente** hallazgo de **tres** momias **embalsamadas** en un pico **nevado** de la cordillera **andina peruana** abre la posibilidad de una **profunda** investigación **científica** en una región en la que, al parecer, los incas celebraban sacrificios **humanos**.

5   Las víctimas de estos sacrificios habrían sido jóvenes **vírgenes**, entre los 14 y 16 años, integrantes de culturas **incas** que dominaban la zona **sur** del Perú, según las **primeras** indagaciones.

    Al parecer, las jóvenes eran sacrificadas para evitar la erupción de los volcanes y así neutralizar la "ira de la naturaleza". Sus cuerpos están **momificados**,

10 cubiertos por elementos y vestimentas **funerarios** y en **virtual** estado de congelamiento.

    Este **sorprendente** descubrimiento pone en evidencia que la cultura **inca** fue la **única** civilización en el mundo que construyó edificaciones a más de **seis mil** metros de altura para realizar rituales **mágico-religiosos**.

Diario *El Universal*, México

Text 2

Text 2 looks at the use of computers in cars and roads. Read the text and study the way in which adjectives have been used.

Automóviles y caminos inteligentes

Dentro de **veinte** o **treinta** años, guiar un vehículo por las **tentaculares** y **congestionadísimas** autopistas de Los Angeles será quizá una diversión, y quien vaya al volante leerá el diario, mirará la televisión o dormirá la siesta.

> El automovilista de la **mega** metrópoli **californiana** adquirirá **tanta** libertad,
> 5 gracias a vehículos y caminos **"inteligentes"** dirigidos por **omnipresentes** y
> **sofisticados** computadores.
>
> ¿Un sueño **futurista** en una ciudad inmersa en el gas de los tubos de escape,
> donde la bicicleta amenaza con convertirse en el medio de locomoción más **rápido**?
>
> No, ya existe en **gran** parte la tecnología **necesaria** para poner al **inmenso**
> 10 ejército de las **cuatro** ruedas en un maxi-sistema **"inteligente"** y para aumentar
> en un 50 por ciento el tránsito **caminero**, evitando los **graves** embotellamientos
> y reforzando los niveles de seguridad.
>
> Diario *El Universal*, Venezuela

Adjectives

1 AGREEMENT OF ADJECTIVES

a In Spanish, adjectives agree in number (singular and plural) and gender (masculine and feminine) with the noun they qualify, e.g. sacrificios **humanos** (m/pl) (T. 1, l. 3–4) *human sacrifice*, momias **embalsamadas** (f/pl) (T. 1, l. 1) *embalmed mummies*, **inmenso** ejército (m/sing) (T. 2, l. 9–10) *immense army*.

b If the adjective refers to more than one noun, one of them being masculine, you will need to use the masculine plural form of the adjective:

elementos y vestimentas **funerarios** (T. 1, l. 10) *funerary elements and clothing*.

If the nouns are all of the same gender, use the same gender for the adjective.

2 POSITION OF ADJECTIVES

a In Spanish, adjectives usually follow the noun:

pico **nevado** (T. 1, l. 1) *snow-capped mountain*, jóvenes **vírgenes** (T. 1, l. 5) *young virgins*, vehículos y caminos **"inteligentes"** (T. 2, l. 5), *'intelligent' vehicles and roads*.

This is the normal position for adjectives expressing some form of contrast, even when this contrast is only implied, e.g. **vehículos y caminos "inteligentes"** *'intelligent' vehicles and roads*, as opposed to ordinary ones.

b Among other adjectives which are normally placed after the noun, we find those referring to science and technology, nationality and origin, colour, shape, substance, religion:

investigación **científica** (T. 1, l. 2–3) *scientific research*, metrópoli **californiana** (T. 2, l. 4) *Californian metropolis*, cultura **inca** (T. 1, l. 12) *Inca culture*, una camisa **blanca** *a white shirt*, una caja **cuadrada** *a square box*, una sustancia **dura** *a hard substance*, la Iglesia **católica** *the Catholic Church.*

c Adjectives which express some form of subjective judgement are usually placed before the noun. This position is also used as a device for lending greater force to the meaning of the adjective:

este **sorprendente** descubrimiento (T. 1, l. 12) *this surprising discovery*, **graves** embotellamientos (T. 2, l. 11) *serious traffic jams*, las **tentaculares** y **congestionadísimas** autopistas (T. 2, l. 1–2) *tentacular and congested motorways.*

d Among other adjectives which are placed before the noun we find those for cardinal and ordinal numbers and some common words such as **mucho, poco, otro, tanto, ambos**:

tres momias (T. 1, l. 1) *three mummies*, **primeras** indagaciones (T. 1, l. 7) *first investigations*, **tanta** libertad (T. 2, l. 4) *so much freedom.*

e Some adjectives change their meaning depending on whether they precede or follow the noun. Note the meaning of **único** in **la única civilización** (T. 1, l. 13) *the only civilisation*, as opposed to **una civilización única** *a unique civilisation*, and of **gran** in **en gran parte** (T. 2, l. 9) *to a great extent*, as opposed to **una parte grande** *a big part*, denoting size. Amongst other words of this kind we find the following ones:

	Preceding	*Following*
antiguo	*former*	*old*
diferentes	*several*	*different*
mismo	*same*	*self*
nuevo	*new, another*	*brand new*
pobre	*poor, miserable*	*poor, impecunious*

3 FEMININE FORMS

a Adjectives ending in **-o** change **-o** to **-a**:

profundo – profunda (T. 1, l. 2) *deep*, **científico – científica** (T. 1, l. 3) *scientific*, **primero – primera** (T. 1, l. 7) *first.*

Those ending in a vowel other than **-o** keep the same form, e.g. **reciente** (T. 1, l. 1) *recent*, **sorprendente** (T. 1, l. 12) *surprising.*

b Adjectives of nationality or origin form the feminine with **-a**:

andino – andina (T. 1, l. 2), **peruano – peruana** (T. 1, l. 2), **español – española** *Spanish*, **inglés – inglesa** *English.*

Those ending in **-a, -i, -e** remain unchanged:

el imperio **inca** *the Inca empire*, la cultura **inca** (T. 1, l. 12) *Inca culture*, **marroquí** (m/f) *Moroccan*, **costarricense** (m/f) *Costa Rican.*

c Adjectives ending in a consonant, with the exception of those referring to nationality or origin (see **b** above), do not change for the feminine.
Note the phrase **jóvenes vírgenes** (T. 1, l. 5) *young virgins*, where **virgen** can refer to a masculine or a feminine noun.

d Adjectives ending in **-án, -ón, -ín** and **-or** add **-a**:

> **holgazán – holgazana** *lazy*, **dormilón – dormilona** *sleepyhead*, **parlanchín – parlanchina** *chatty*, **seductor – seductora** *seductive*.

Comparative forms remain unchanged, e.g. **mayor** (m/f) *greater*.

e Some adjectives may be joined by a hyphen, in which case only the second one will change for gender and/or number, e.g. **rituales mágico-religiosos** (T. 1, l. 14) *magic-religious rituals*.

4 SHORT FORMS

Grande becomes **gran** before singular masculine and feminine nouns, e.g. **en gran parte** (T. 2, l. 9) *to a large extent*, but **grandes ciudades** *large cities*.
Malo, bueno, primero, tercero, alguno and **ninguno** lose the final **-o** before a singular masculine noun, e.g. un **mal/buen día** *a bad/good day*, **algún/ningún problema** *some/no problem*.

5 PLURAL FORMS

a Adjectives that end in an ustressed vowel add **-s**. Most of the adjectives in the texts fall within this category:

> momias **embalsamadas** (T. 1, l. 1) *embalmed mummies*, sacrificios **humanos** (T. 1, l. 3–4) *human sacrifices*, caminos **inteligentes** (T. 2, l. 5) *intelligent roads*.

b Adjectives that end in a consonant or a stressed vowel add **-es**:

> jóvenes **vírgenes** (T. 1, l. 5) *young virgins*, **tentaculares** … autopistas (T. 2, l. 1) *tentacular motorways*, inmigrantes **marroquíes** *Moroccan immigrants*.

Note that adjectives ending in **-z**, e.g. **feliz** *happy*, change this to **-c** to form the plural.

> días **felices**   *happy days*

6 INVARIABLE ADJECTIVES

Adjectives which are originally names of things do not change for gender and number:

> paredes **naranja** *orange walls*, pantalones **violeta** *violet trousers*

Other points to note in the text

- *Por* and *para*: Text 1: *para evitar* (l. 8), *cubiertos por elementos* (l. 10), *para realizar* (l. 14). Text 2: *por las … autopistas* (l. 1–2), *dirigidos por …* (l. 5), *para poner* (l. 9), *para aumentar* (l. 10) (see Chapter 28)

- Future tense: Text 2: *será* (l. 2), *leerá* (l. 3), *mirará* (l. 3), *dormirá* (l. 3), *adquirirá* (l. 4) (see Chapter 6)
- Ser and *estar*: Text 1: *habrían sido* (l. 5), *eran sacrificadas* (l. 8), *están momificados* (l. 9), *fue la única civilización* (l. 12–13) (see Chapter 13)

See for further information:	Batchelor and Pountain, pp. 128–33
	Butt, pp. 127–37
	Butt and Benjamin, pp. 51–71
	Kattán-Ibarra and Pountain, pp. 26–31
	Muñoz and Thacker, pp. 22–32, 192–6

EXERCISES

1 Complete the text by putting the appropriate ending to the adjectives.

Hay restos incaic____ en todos los países andin____ de Sudamérica. Muchos se preguntan cómo fue posible fundar una civilización tan avanzad____ en una región tan montaños____ e inhóspit____. Pero civilizaciones anterior____ a la incaic____ también tenían culturas ric____ e interesante____.

En los Andes las comunicaciones parecen imposible____ pero en los tiempos incaic____ existían dos carreteras principal____ muy buen____ que enlazaban el extrem____ norte del imperio con las regiones sureñ____.

En los templos de Cuzco, la capital del imperio, había adornos y estatuas cubiert____ de oro. Después de su larg____ y peligros____ periplo, los conquistadores español____ llegaron a Cuzco cansad____, hambrient____, y temeros____. Cuando vieron los suntuos____ templos y palacios de los Incas, se quedaron totalmente pasmad____.

2 Make the adjective in brackets agree with the noun. You may want to refer to Chapter 18 (**Articles**, 'Usage') before you begin.

a La compañía se llama Aguas (Cordobés) _____.
b El águila (pescador) _____ es un ave (protegido) _____.
c El ala (izquierdo) _____ del partido está en decadencia.
d Tengo un hambre (tremendo) _____.
e Hoy tenemos la clase en el aula (pequeño) _____.
f Vuestra hija es un hada (encantador) _____.

3 Complete the sentences, changing the adjective to agree with the new subject.

a Julio es muy trabajador. Julia es _____.
b El niño es dormilón. Las niñas son _____.
c Es una revista juvenil. Son revistas _____.

d Pepe es parlanchín. Susana es _____.

e María es bastante holgazana. Juanito es _____.

f Feliz cumpleaños. _____ fiestas.

g La profesora es burlona. El profesor es _____.

h Es mi hermano mayor. Son mis hermanos _____.

i Lleva un pantalón azul. Lleva un pantalón y una chaqueta _____.

j Mi amigo es alemán. Mi amiga es _____.

k Lee una novela rosa. Lee novelas _____.

l Compró un libro español. Compró un libro y una revista _____.

4 Cross out the incorrect part of the sentence.

a Fuimos a comer a un <u>italiano restaurante/restaurante italiano</u>.

b El hostal estaba en <u>el tercer/tercero piso</u>.

c Carlos es un muy <u>bueno/buen amigo</u>.

d Si ustedes tienen <u>algún/alguno</u> problema, no dejen de ponerse en contacto con nosotros.

e Viven en <u>una grande casa/una casa grande</u> con <u>playa privada/privada playa</u>.

f Mariano fue <u>el primer/primero</u> en llegar.

g No seas tan <u>mal/mala</u>.

h El diccionario me costó <u>la tercer/tercera</u> parte de mi sueldo.

i <u>Alguno/algún</u> día vendrá a visitarme.

j Nueva York es <u>una grande/gran ciudad</u> cosmopólita.

k El imponente <u>palacio real/real palacio</u> fue obra de Churriaga.

l El <u>primer/primero</u> día no hicimos nada especial.

5 The following is an extract from a longer magazine article called "Retrato del nuevo español" about the changing lifestyle of the Spanish male. Fill in each blank with an adjective from the list below.

algunos	**nuevo**	**guapo**	**revolucionario**	**solos**
muchas	**español**	**jóvenes**	**machistas**	**viejos**
nuevo	**mayor**	**buena**	**libre**	

Y por si fuera poco, ha surgido un competidor *con faldas.* La incorporación de la mujer a la actividad fuera de casa ha sido otro elemento ____(a)____ para el varón ____(b)____ [...] El español en fase de adaptación tiene que tomar conciencia de que es muy difícil mantener ____(c)____ comportamientos ____(d)____, tanto en casa como en el trabajo. [...] Afortunadamente el ____(e)____ español también dispone de ____(f)____ ratos de ocio. Una ____(g)____ parte del tiempo ____(h)____ [...] lo invierte en su cuerpo. El ____(i)____ español quiere estar ____(j)____ [...]. Otra novedad: los hombres suelen ir ahora ____(k)____ a comprar su ropa [...]. Hoy en ____(l)____ casas de matrimonios ____(m)____ el vestuario de él ocupa ____(n)____ espacio que el de ella.

Revista *Tiempo*, España

6 Use adjectives to answer these questions.

    a ¿Cómo es tu mejor amigo/a?

    b En tu opinión, ¿cómo es el español/hispanoamericano típico?

    c ¿Cómo sería tu casa ideal?

    d ¿Cómo será el coche del futuro?

21 | Adverbs

Text

The problem of unemployment among young Spanish people is illustrated below through a personal story. The grammar in the text focuses on the use of adverbs, words which provide more information about verbs, adjectives or other adverbs.

Veintiocho años, y en paro

Jaime M. tiene veintiocho años, la carrera de Empresariales, un "master" realizado en una universidad británica, habla y escribe **perfectamente** inglés, habla y escribe **menos perfectamente** francés. Extrovertido, simpático, **últimamente ya** no lo es **tanto**. **Nunca** ha conseguido un empleo. No sabe lo
5 que es trabajar en una oficina, en un despacho, tener un jefe o un compañero con el que compartir problemas. No encuentra empleo, **ni siquiera** a tiempo parcial. En unos sitios le exigen experiencia; en otros, creen que con sus títulos merece **más** de lo que le pueden dar, y Jaime M. está desesperado, **total** y **absolutamente** desesperado. Sus padres, que le han apoyado, empiezan a
10 agobiarse al verle en casa. Y aunque otros amigos suyos están **también** sin trabajo y viven **todavía** en la casa familiar porque no encuentran salida profesional de ningún tipo, **al cabo del tiempo hasta** los padres de Jaime, **siempre tan** comprensivos, **siempre tan** dispuestos a animarle, **siempre tan** cariñosos, comienzan a mostrarse incómodos por su presencia permanente.
15 Jaime M. no es una excepción. Con título y sin título, las cifras oficiales confirman que el veinte por ciento de los parados son jóvenes que no han conseguido **jamás** un empleo. Si triste es el caso del padre de familia que en la cuarentena se queda en la calle con escasas posibilidades de volver a encontrar un trabajo, tremendo es **también** que nuestros jóvenes no consigan acceder a un
20 empleo y se les venga el tiempo **encima** sin haber conocido lo que es un horario, una mesa de despacho, un taller o un balance. La Formación Profesional ha dado salida a bastantes jóvenes y se ha demostrado una fórmula **bastante** aceptable de colocación, pero no cubre las expectativas de aquéllos que desean acceder a unas profesiones de carácter universitario, ni **tampoco** ofrecen la posibilidad de
25 trabajo seguro.

Jaime M., por si les interesa, se encuentra bajo tratamiento psiquiátrico. Sus padres pueden pagarlo. Otros, sin embargo, no saben qué hacer para luchar contra la depresión de los hijos que viven con la obsesión de conseguir un primer empleo, tener su casa, formar su familia y, **especialmente**, vivir su propia vida.

Revista *Blanco y Negro*, Diario *ABC*, España

Adverbs

Adverbs are words that add information about verbs, adjectives or other adverbs.

Habla y escribe **perfectamente** inglés … (l. 2)   *He speaks and writes English perfectly …*
… **total** y **absolutamente** desesperado. (l. 8–9)   *… totally and absolutely desperate.*
Habla y escribe **menos** perfectamente francés. (l. 3)   He *speaks and writes French less perfectly.*

There are many different types and categories of adverbs, as you will see from the notes below, which also cover their use.

1 ADVERBS ENDING IN *-MENTE*

Adverbs can be formed by adding the suffix -**mente** to the feminine singular form of the adjective, for example **perfecto** (masculine singular adjective), **perfecta** (feminine singular adjective), **perfectamente** (adverb) (l. 2, 3) *perfectly.* Adjectives without a special feminine form simply add -**mente** to the singular form, for example **especial** (adjective), **especialmente** (adverb) (l. 29) *especially.* Note that the suffix -**mente** corresponds to the English ending -**ly**.

Adverbs ending in -**mente** keep the written accent of the adjective, e.g. **fácil** (adjective), **fácilmente** (adverb) *easily,* **económica** (adjective), **económicamente** (adverb), *economically.*

In a sequence of two or more adverbs of this kind, joined by a conjunction, only the last one carries the ending -**mente**, e.g. **total** y **absolutamente** (l. 8–9) *totally and absolutely.*

2 ADVERBIAL PHRASES

Overuse of adverbs in -**mente** is considered clumsy in Spanish. In order to avoid this, use adverbial phrases like the following, all of them followed by an adjective:

de manera (feminine) **rápida** (for **rápidamente**) *rapidly*
de forma (feminine) **lenta** (for **lentamente**) *slowly*
de modo (masculine) **silencioso** (for **silenciosamente**) *silently, quietly*

Note also the use of the preposition **con** followed by a noun:

> **con tranquilidad** (for **tranquilamente**) *quietly*
> **con astucia** (for **astutamente**) *cleverly, astutely*

There are a large number of adverbial phrases in Spanish, not all related to adjectives, for example **a escondidas** *secretly*, **a la fuerza** *by force*, **a oscuras** *in the dark*, **con cautela** *cautiously*, **de costumbre** *usually*, **de memoria** *by heart*, **en cambio** *on the other hand*, **sin cuidado** *carelessly*.

3 SINGLE-WORD INVARIABLE ADVERBS

A large number of adverbs in Spanish are single invariable words unrelated to adjectives, for example **luego** *later on, then*, **dentro** *inside*, **igual** *the same*. For further examples see "Categories of adverbs" below.

4 ADJECTIVES USED AS ADVERBS

A small number of adjectives can also function as adverbs, e.g. **rápido**, **duro**, **barato**.

> Conduce muy **rápido**.   *He/she drives very quickly.*
> Trabajaron **duro**.   *They worked hard.*
> Me lo vendió muy **barato**.   *He/she sold it to me very cheaply.*

5 CATEGORIES OF ADVERBS

Adverbs and adverbial phrases can be grouped according to their meaning or the kind of information they provide about the word they modify. Among the different categories we find the following ones. The examples here include mostly single-word invariable adverbs.

a Adverbs of *time*, for example **ahora** *now*, **antes** *before*, **después** *after*, **siempre** (l. 13) *always*, **nunca** (l. 4), **jamás** (l. 17) *never*, **hoy** *today*, **mañana** *tomorrow*, **ayer** *yesterday*, **aún**, **todavía** (l. 11) *still, yet*, **recientemente** *recently*, **últimamente** (l. 4) *lately, recently*, **ya** *already*, **ya no** (l. 4) *no longer, not … anymore*, **a menudo** *often*, **a tiempo** *in time*.

b Adverbs of *manner*, such as **así** *this way, thus*, **casi** *almost*, **bien** *well*, **mal** *badly*, **despacio** *slowly*. Among these we also find a number of adverbs ending in -**mente**, for example **perfectamente** (l. 2–3) *perfectly*, **totalmente** (l. 8–9) *totally*, **absolutamente** (l. 9) *absolutely*. Note also, adverbial phrases such as **a mano** *by hand*, **con soltura** *with ease*.

c Adverbs of *degree*, for example **bastante** (l. 22) *quite, enough*, **demasiado** *too (much)*, **más** (l. 8) *more*, **menos** (l. 3) *less*, **mucho** *(very) much*, **muy** *very*, **tan** (l. 13) *so*, **tanto** (l. 4) *so much, as much*.

d Adverbs of *place*, among them **abajo** *down, below*, **debajo** *underneath*, **arriba** *above*, **encima** *above, on top*, **aquí** *here*, **ahí** *there*, **allí** *there*, **acá** *here*, **allá** *there*, **adelante** *forward(s)*, **delante** *in front*, **atrás** *back(wards)*, **detrás** *behind*, **cerca** *near(by)*, **lejos** *far*.

e Adverbs of **affirmation**, **negation** and **doubt**, for example **sí** *yes*, **claro** *certainly*, **también** (l. 10, 19) *also*, **no** (l. 4, 6 …), **nada** *nothing*, **tampoco** (l. 24) *neither, not … either*, **a lo mejor**, **quizá(s)**, **tal vez** *perhaps*.

6 POSITION OF ADVERBS

Adverbs normally adjoin the word they modify, either preceding or following this. With verbs the usual position is after it, but for emphasis an adverb may come before the verb. Compare:

Nunca ha conseguido un empleo. (l. 4–5)   *He's never got a job.*
No han conseguido **jamás** un empleo. (l. 16–17)   *They've never got a job.*

Note that in the previous English sentences the adverb, *never*, comes between the auxiliary verb *to have* and the participle. In Spanish, an adverb must not split up an auxiliary from a participle or an infinitive. So, a sentence such as *We´re certainly going to do it*, translates in two possible ways: **Por supuesto** que vamos a hacerlo, or Vamos a hacerlo **por supuesto**.

For comparison of adverbs see Chapter 22.

Other points to note in the text

- Negation: *ya no* (l. 4), *nunca* (l. 4), *no sabe* (l. 4), *ni siquiera* (l. 6), *de ningún tipo* (l. 12), *incómodos* (l. 14), *no han conseguido jamás* (l. 16–17), *ni tampoco* (l. 24), etc. (see Chapter 27)
- Direct and indirect object pronouns: There are a number of examples of third person object pronouns in the text, among these *no lo es* (l. 4), *le exigen* (l. 7), *le pueden dar* (1. 8), etc. (see Chapter 25)
- *Ser* and *estar*: *ya no lo es* (l. 4), *no sabe lo que es* (l. 4–5), *está desesperado* (l. 8), *están … sin trabajo* (l. 10–11), etc. (see Chapter 13)
- Perfect tense: *nunca ha conseguido* (l. 4), *le han apoyado* (l. 9), *no han conseguido jamás* (l. 16–17), etc. (see Chapter 4)

See for further information:	Butt. pp. 148–53
	Butt and Benjamin, pp. 412–30
	Kattán-Ibarra and Pountain, pp. 59–60
	Muñoz and Thacker, pp. 151–5, 258–9

EXERCISES

1 Correct the sentence by forming an adverb with **-mente** from the word in italics.

a Saben *perfecto* _____ que no podemos alcanzarlos.
b Salimos *inmediato* _____ después de ustedes.
c Si te niegas a someterte a la prueba, quedas *automático* _____ descalificado.
d Se espolvorean las fresas *ligero* _____ de azúcar.

    e Cómprame un litro de leche *preferente* _____ desnatada.

    f No podía quejarse de él; habló *cortés* _____ y se portó *correcto* _____.

2 Link the adverb to the adverbial phrase with the same meaning.

a	obviamente	de costumbre
b	tristemente	por último
c	finalmente	por lo general
d	ciertamente	en efecto
e	difícilmente	en secreto
f	indudablemente	con tristeza
g	habitualmente	con dificultad
h	efectivamente	por supuesto
i	secretamente	sin duda
j	generalmente	por cierto

3 Complete the sentences with one of the adverbs of place given on p. 122.

    a – ¿Dónde están los servicios?

       – Para las señoras, _____. Suba por esas escaleras. Los de los señores, están _____, en el sótano.

    b Es curioso pero si a ti no te gustan los gatos, ellos lo saben y siempre se te sientan _____.

    c En el coche los padres viajan _____ y los niños _____.

    d – ¡Adelante! – gritó el sargento a los reclutas – el cuartel no está _____, está _____, a la vuelta de la esquina.

    e – ¿Está el señor García?

       – No. Esta semana no está, está _____.

    f – ¿Dónde has puesto las macetas que estaban en la terraza?

       – _____. Ahora están en el garaje.

    g – ¿Quieres que ponga las bolsas _____ en esta mesa?

       – No. Ponlas _____ en el rincón.

    h – Apártense ustedes. Desde _____ no se aprecia el estilo del pintor. Más _____ se ve mucho mejor el cuadro.

    i – ¿Los Blanco viven cerca?

       – ¡Qué va! Viven _____, muy _____ de _____.

    j – ¡Qué bien se ven las estrellas esta noche! Mira, ¿ves _____ la Cruz del Sur?

4 Complete the sentences with one of the adverbs of time on p. 122.

_____ Julio estaba desempleado pero _____ trabaja en una hamburguesería. Con todos los estudios que ha hecho _____ pensó que llegaría a esto. _____ pensaba que con los títulos conseguiría un buen empleo, un empleo bien pagado. Pero no está desanimado. _____ le queda la esperanza de que algo mejor le pueda salir y _____ va a mandar su currículo a algunas empresas. Cosa que hizo _____, y que hará _____ también.

5 Complete the sentences with one of the adverbs of degree on p. 122.

a – Otilia, aprendes portugués ¿verdad? ¿Qué tal lo hablas?

– _____ _____ ya que en realidad no estudio _____. Debo esforzarme _____, la verdad.

b El recuerdo que tengo de María es de cuanto comía. Comía _____ que pensaba que iba a reventarse.

c – ¡Cómo trabaja Consuelo!

– Sí, es verdad. Trabaja _____. De todos nuestros empleados es la que _____ trabaja.

– ¿No cree que trabaja _____?

d – ¿Te acuerdas del profesor de literatura? Hablaba mucho ¿verdad?

– Pues no, no hablaba _____.

– Sí, hombre, sí. Hablaba _____, _____.

e No se puede negar que los jóvenes viven _____.

– Bueno, algunos _____ y otros no _____ bien.

For exercises with adverbs expressing affirmation and negation, see Chapter 27; for adverbs expressing possibility, see Chapter 14.

Text 1, an extract from an article in a Spanish magazine, looks at the Mediterranean diet.
The grammar here focuses on the use of comparative forms.

> ### La dieta mediterránea
>
> La llamada dieta mediterránea está de moda, aunque hasta hace poco no gozaba
> de muy buena reputación. Los médicos y nutriólogos han descubierto que en los
> países mediterráneos la incidencia de enfermedades **es** mucho **menor que** en
> tierra adentro.
> 5   En Madrid convergen todas las dietas autonómicas de España. La dieta de los
> madrileños es equilibrada y saludable, y **es mejor que** la del resto de capitales
> comunitarias. No obstante, los madrileños **toman menos** verduras **de** las
> necesarias y demasiadas proteínas y sal. Como complemento, hay que decir que
> en Madrid **se come menos** pan y patatas y **más** fruta y pescados **que** en
> 10 otras partes de España.
>   Los desayunos que se toman los madrileños **son más ligeros** y se advierte una
> tendencia a no cocinar por la noche en casa. Uno de cada cinco escolares no
> desayuna y muchos de los que lo hacen **consumen menos** calorías **de** las
> aconsejables. Esto acarrea una **menor** capacidad de retentiva y **mayor**
> 15 dificultad de atención entre los estudiantes.
>
> Revista *Cambio 16*, España

Text 2 considers the results of a world-wide survey of people's attitudes towards subjects such as
sex, racism, religion, food. The article looks specifically at Latin Americans. Note the use of
superlative forms in this text.

> ### Los más apasionados y belicosos del mundo
>
> Los latinoamericanos se consideran felices, caritativos y apasionados, según
> **la** encuesta interactiva **más grande** que se ha realizado en el mundo, en el

sitio web *planetproject.com*. El sondeo lo contestaron 600.000 personas de
231 países del mundo. En América Latina unas 50.000 personas respondieron
5 la encuesta.

Los datos todavía son preliminares, pero ya muestran tendencias.
En América Latina, por ejemplo, los peruanos **son los más tradicionalistas**,
con **el** porcentaje **más alto** de la región que piensa que el objetivo del sexo
es la procreación. Puerto Rico **es el** país **menos racista**, de acuerdo a su
10 respuesta a la pregunta de si adoptaría un niño de otra raza. El 94 por ciento
de los encuestados afirmó que sí.

En religión, los latinoamericanos **son los más creyentes**, siendo Colombia
el país del área donde más gente contestó que cree que existe un Ser Superior,
seguido de Brasil y México.
15 En salud hay una diferencia marcada con los asiáticos. Los latinoamericanos
piensan que la alimentación **es lo más importante** para la salud, mientras que
los asiáticos consideran que es lo espiritual.

Aparte de las diferencias regionales, están las de género. Los hombres piensan
en el dinero el doble que las mujeres, pero la mayoría de éstas piensa en el
20 peso corporal diariamente mucho **más que** los hombres. Los hombres **son**
más tolerantes con las relaciones sexuales extramatrimoniales **que** las
mujeres.

Diario *El Mercurio*, Valparaíso, Chile

Comparison

The word "comparison" in this context is used with reference to forms such as *(tall)er, more/less …*
than, as … as, not so … as, all of which serve to compare people or things in terms of a specific
quality. Expressions such as these, known as *comparative* forms, focus on the degree to which
the people or things being compared share that quality, e.g. *Maria is tall, Ana is also tall, but*
*Ana is **taller than** Maria.*

To say that the noun being referred to possesses a specific quality in its highest degree,
English uses forms such as *the (tall)est, the most …,* which are known as *superlative* forms.
The notes below explain how to use these constructions.

1 COMPARATIVE FORMS OF ADJECTIVES

a Comparisons of inequality
Regular forms
Comparisons of inequality, such as *bigger than, more comfortable than, less expensive than* are
normally expressed in Spanish with **más** *more,* and **menos** *less,* followed by an adjective and

que *than*. **Que** *than* and the second element being compared may be omitted when the context is clear.

> Son **más** ligeros … (T. 1, l. 11)   *They are lighter …*
> Son **más** tolerantes … **que**.… (T. 2, l.20–1)   *They are more tolerant than …*

The two examples above, with **más** *more*, indicate superiority. Inferiority is shown by using **menos** *less*.

> Es **menos** interesante **que** el otro.   *It is less interesting than the other one.*

Comparisons of inequality can also be expressed with the construction **no tan … como** *not as … as*, or simply **no tan** followed by the adjective if the context is clear.

> **No** es **tan** bueno **como** el tuyo.   *It is not as good as yours.*
> **No** son **tan** sabrosos.   *They are not as tasty.*

Note also the use of **no tanto como** *not as much as.*

> Es eficiente, pero **no tanto como** Andrés.   *He/she is efficient, but not as much as Andrés.*

Irregular forms
Some adjectives have irregular comparative forms:

bueno *good*	**mejor** *better*
malo *bad*	**peor** *worse*
grande *big*	**mayor** *older, bigger, greater* (also **más grande**)
pequeño *small*	**menor** *younger, smaller* (also **más pequeño**)

> … es … **menor que** … (T. 1, l. 3)   *… it is smaller than …*
> … es **mejor que** … (T. 1, l. 6)   *… it is better than …*
> Javier es **mayor que** Alvaro.   *Javier is older than Alvaro.*
> Cristina es **menor**.   *Cristina is younger.*

Mayor and **menor** are not normally used with reference to size.

b Comparisons of equality
Comparisons of equality are expressed with the construction **tan … como** *as … as*.

> Es **tan** delgado **como** ella.   *He is as slim as her.*
> Son **tan** grandes **como** los de José.   *They are as big as José's.*

2 COMPARISON INVOLVING NOUNS, NUMBERS AND CLAUSES

For comparisons involving nouns, use **más … que** and **menos … que** for inequality and **tanto/a/os/as … como** for equality.

> Se come **menos** pan y patatas y **más** fruta y pescados **que** … (T. 1, l. 9)   *They eat less bread and potatoes and more fruit and fish than …*
> Gana **tanto** dinero **como** ella.   *He earns as much money as her.*

Before a word indicating quantity or a number, use **más/menos de** instead of **que**.

menos verduras **de** las necesarias (T. 1, l. 7–8)   *fewer vegetables than necessary*
menos calorías **de** las aconsejables (T. 1, l. 13–14)   *fewer calories than is advisable*
más de una docena   *more than a dozen*

Before a clause containing a noun, use **más del/de la/de los/de las que**, depending on the gender of the noun. If there is no noun, use **de lo que**.

Había **más** comida **de la que** esperábamos.   *There was more food than we expected.*
Es **más** difícil **de lo que** parecía.   *It is more difficult than it seemed.*

3 SUPERLATIVE FORMS

a To convey ideas such as *the biggest, the most conservative, the least racist,* use the definite article (**el, la, los** or **las**, or the neuter form **lo**) followed by **más** *most* or **menos** *least* and the corresponding adjective.

… **la** … **más** grande … (T. 2, l. 2)   … *the biggest* …
… son **los más** tradicionalistas … (T. 2, l. 7)   … *they are the most conservative* …
… es **el** … **menos** racista (T. 2, l. 9)   … *it is the least racist* …
… es **lo más** importante … (T. 2, l. 16)   … *it is the most important thing* …

b Another form of the superlative is that formed with the suffix **-ísimo/-ísima** added to the adjective, with the final vowel being removed.

Es **dificilísimo**.   *It is very/extremely difficult.*
Es **carísima**.   *It is very/extremely expensive.*

Note spelling changes with adjectives ending in **-co**, **-go**, or **-z**:

seco *dry*   **sequísimo** *extremely dry*
largo *long*   **larguísimo** *very long*
feliz *happy*   **felicísimo** *very happy*

c There are also some special superlative forms:

pobre *poor*   **paupérrimo** *extremely poor*
antiguo *old, ancient*   **antiquísimo** *very old*

4 COMPARATIVE FORMS OF ADVERBS

Adverbs are compared in much the same way as adjectives. Note the following examples:

Habló **más claramente que** nunca.   *He/she spoke more clearly than ever.*
Me trataron **menos amablemente**.   *They treated me less kindly.*
Corre **más rápido/rápidamente**.   *He/she runs faster.*
No actúa **tan bien como** ella.   *He doesn't act as well as her.*
Ahora viene **más a menudo**.   *Now he/she comes more often.*

The comparative forms of **bien** *well* and **mal** *badly* are **mejor** *better* and **peor** *worse*.

Pepe se comporta **mejor que** Inés.   *Pepe behaves better than Inés.*

Other points to note in the text

- *Ser* and *estar*: Text 1: *está de moda* (l. 1), *es mucho menor* (l. 3), *es equilibrada* (l. 6), *es mejor* (l. 6), *son más ligeros* (l. 11). Text 2: *son preliminares* (l. 6), *son los más tradicionalistas* (l. 7) *es la procreación* (l. 9), etc. (see Chapter 13)
- Impersonal sentences: Text 1: *se come* (l. 9), *se advierte* (l. 11) (see Chapter 11)
- Neuter *lo*: Text 2: *lo más importante* (l. 16), *lo espiritual* (l. 17) (see Chapter 18)
- Definite article used with a possessive value, meaning "the ones belonging to": Text 1: *es mejor que la del resto de capitales comunitarias* (l. 6–7). Text 2: *aparte de las diferencias regionales, están las de género* (l. 18) (see Chapter 18)
- Definite article used with a demonstrative value: Text 1: *muchos de los (aquellos) que lo hacen* (l. 13) (see Chapter 18)

See for further information:	Batchelor and Pountain, pp. 294–6
	Butt, pp. 132–5, 151
	Butt and Benjamin, pp. 72–81
	Kattán-Ibarra and Pountain, pp. 30–1, 234–40
	Muñoz and Thacker, pp. 27–32, 197–9

EXERCISES

1 Make comparisons of inequality with the following elements. Use **más … que** and **menos … que**.

a La cocina francesa	la cocina alemana	sabroso
b El Hotel Crillón	el Ritz	bueno
c Los peruanos	los portorriqueños	racista
d Las mujeres	los hombres	pensar en el dinero
e Los estadounidenses	los españoles	comer pescado
f La sed	el hambre	malo

2 **Que** or **de**? Complete the sentences, adding other elements where necessary.

a Hay que comer más _____ cinco porciones de fruta por día.

b Anoche David comió más _____ quince albóndigas.

c Las fresas de nuestra tierra son menos grandes pero mucho más dulces _____ las de Huelva.

d Pasamos más tiempo en el pueblo _____ queríamos.

e Roberto gasta más dinero _____ gana.

f Si esta camisa vale más _____ 15 dólares, no me la compro.

g La religión es menos importante para los europeos ____ para los americanos.

h La diferencia entre las dietas era mayor ____ se esperaba.

i Era más viejo ____ parecía.

j Trajo mucho más vino ____ podíamos beber.

k El pobre Ernesto gana mucho menos ____ los que viven con él.

l No quiero comprar más fruta ____ me hace falta.

m Hay un mayor índice de obesidad entre los que no desayunan ____ entre los que desayunan.

n Había menos gente ____ esperaban.

o Comían mucho más ____ lo debido.

3 Translate the bracketed elements into Spanish.

a Comer en una cafetería es (as expensive as) _____ comer en un restaurante.

b Esta fruta es (as good as) _____ parece.

c Ahora los ingleses beben (as much coffee as) _____té.

d No comemos (as many greens as) _____ debemos.

e Todavía la mujer no tiene (as many opportunities as) _____ el hombre.

f No tienen (as much experience as) _____ ellos.

g Pero el hombre no trabaja (as much as) _____ la mujer en la casa.

h Pedro y Pablo no son (as ambitious as) _____ sus padres.

i Mariana no habla portugués (as well as) _____ su hermana.

j No vamos al cine (as often as) _____ antes.

4 Answer these questions using the superlative formed with the suffix **-ísimo**.

a ¿Son dulces esas naranjas?

b ¿Es rica la paella?

c ¿Es caro ese restaurante?

d ¿Es largo el viaje en autocar?

e ¿Estas joyas son antiguas?

5 Translate the bracketed English into Spanish.

a Hay quienes dicen que la dieta mediterránea es (the best) _____ del mundo.

b Las patatas aportan (the greatest amount) _____ de calorías.

c Según una investigación, los norteamericanos son (the fattest) _____ del mundo.

d El desayuno es (the most important meal) _____ del día.

e Una antigua esclava brasileña es (the oldest woman) _____ del mundo.

6 Use comparisons of equality and inequality, and superlatives to form sentences about:

a Madrid   Buenos Aires   Ciudad de México

b fútbol   baloncesto   tenis

c Mercedes   Ferrari   Porsche

d tren   coche   autobús

23 | Demonstratives

In an interview, the Colombian writer García Márquez talked about his work. As you read the text, study the way in which demonstratives, the Spanish for words like *this*, *that*, have been used.

El amor es mi único discurso

– *Usted pertenece a la generación que ha usado todo tipo de herramientas para escribir, desde el lápiz al procesador de texto, pasando por la máquina de escribir.*

– Sí, pero no pienso que el ideal del escritor haya variado mucho por **eso**. Tuve
5   suerte de conseguir un procesador de palabras en una época en que estaba a punto
de perder el control de mi trabajo creativo. Justo al final de su vida Evelyn Waugh
temía que nunca podría volver a escribir una novela porque no podía recordar
cada palabra contenida en el manuscrito que estaba escribiendo o la relación
entre **esa** palabra y las otras en la novela. No puedo soportar usar el mismo
10 adjetivo dos veces en el mismo libro. El procesador de palabras es muy útil para
resolver **ese** tipo de problemas. Pero no puede arreglar la memoria de la
narración, **eso** es labor del novelista.

En *El amor y otros demonios* había originalmente un marqués que vuelve a
ver a su mujer. Abandoné el personaje, pero el disco duro de mi computador
15 mantuvo cuatro líneas sobre él y **éstas** aparecieron en la versión en español del
libro. En otras palabras, dejé un personaje volando en el aire hasta que un lector
me lo contó. He corregido personalmente las otras versiones, pero no me percaté
de **este** error cuando estaba leyendo las pruebas. Mi memoria como novelista
está empezando a fallar.

20 – *Todo su trabajo ficcional, aparte de una docena de historias breves, está
situado en el Caribe.*

– ¿Y por qué ponerlas en algún otro lugar? El Caribe ofrece de todo. Para darle
una idea de mis sentimientos acerca de **éste**, puedo contarle un incidente de mi
infancia, cuando la gente de mi pueblo estaba buscando el cuerpo de un
25 hombre que se había ahogado. Tomaron una calabaza, le pusieron una vela y la
colocaron en el río. Me acuerdo perfectamente de **aquella** escena. La vela fue

llevada por la corriente, pero de pronto se detuvo y empezó a dar vueltas en
círculo: allí estaba el cuerpo del ahogado. Creo que hoy el Caribe es un poco
como el lugar donde **aquella** vela se detuvo después de recorrer todo el lugar.
30 Ofrece de todo.

   – ... *Y epidemias también, dice usted.*
   – Siempre me han encantado las epidemias. Es verdad: está la epidemia del
   olvido en *Cien años de Soledad*, la plaga en *La mala hora*, el cólera. Lo que
   debería decirme a mí mismo es, no más epidemias.
35   – *¿Y no más amor tampoco?*
   – Oh, no, no me canso nunca del amor. **Éste** es la fuerza motriz detrás de mis
   libros, mi único argumento, mi única ideología. Yo creo firmemente que el amor
   es el único discurso en mis libros.

Diario *La Nación*, Chile

Demonstratives

1 USAGE

Demonstratives are words like *this*, *that*, *these*, *those*, which are used to identify things and to
avoid repeating words and ideas already mentioned or understood. In his replies, García
Márquez uses this device a number of times. The following notes contain more information
about their use:

a As in English, demonstratives can function as adjectives, with an accompanying noun,
for example, **esa** palabra (l. 9) *that word*, **ese** tipo (l. 11) *that type*, **este** error (l. 18)
this mistake.

b Demonstratives may also be used to refer to a noun without mentioning it specifically, just like
this (one)/that (one) in English, in which case they act as pronouns. Demonstrative pronouns
in Spanish are normally written with an accent.

   Mantuvo cuatro líneas ... y **éstas** aparecieron ... (l. 15)   *It kept four lines and these*
   appeared ...
   No me canso nunca del amor. **Éste** es la fuerza motriz ... (l. 36)   *I never tire of love.*
   This is the driving force ...

c Spanish has a set of neuter pronouns which do not refer back to a specific noun. English
uses the same forms as for adjectives and pronouns. Consider the use of the neuter form
eso (l. 4, 12) *that*, in the text. In line 4 this refers back to the idea that, in his writing, García
Márquez has used different tools, "ha usado todo tipo de herramientas para escribir".

2 FORMS

In Spanish, there are three types of demonstratives, with forms which agree in gender and number with the noun they qualify or refer to.

	masculine	feminine	
singular	**este**	**esta**	this, this one
plural	**estos**	**estas**	these, these ones
singular	**ese**	**esa**	that, that one
plural	**esos**	**esas**	those, those ones
singular	**aquel**	**aquella**	that, that one (distant)
plural	**aquellos**	**aquellas**	those, those ones (distant)

Most educated speakers will use an accent when writing the above words when they are used as pronouns, although the Spanish Academy has ruled that this is not required unless there is ground for ambiguity.

Neuter and invariable forms are: **esto** *this*, **eso** *that*, **aquello** *that* (distant)

Aquel, **aquella**, etc. are used to refer to things which are far from the speaker, whether in space or time, for example **aquella escena** (l. 26) *that scene*, **aquella vela** (l. 29) *that candle*. Here, García Márquez is remembering his childhood, so these demonstratives help to establish that distance between the present and a remote past.

Other points to note in the text

- *Por* and *para*: *para escribir* (l. 2), *pasando por* (l. 2), *por eso* (l. 4), *para resolver* (l. 10–11), *para darle una idea* (l. 22–3), *fue llevada por la corriente* (l. 26–7) (see Chapter 28)
- Preterite tense: *tuve* (l. 4), *abandoné* (l. 14), *mantuvo* (l. 15), *aparecieron* (l. 15), etc. (see Chapter 2)
- Gerund: *escribiendo* (l. 8), *volando* (l. 16), *leyendo* (l. 18), *buscando* (l. 24) (see Chapter 9)
- Direct and indirect object pronouns: *me lo contó* (l. 17), *ponerlas* (l. 22), *darle* (l. 22), *contarle* (l. 23), *le pusieron* (l. 25), *la colocaron* (l. 25–6) (see Chapter 25)

See for further information:	Butt, pp. 138–40
	Butt and Benjamin, pp. 82–7
	Kattán-Ibarra and Pountain, pp. 43–4, 224–5
	Muñoz and Thacker, pp. 48–52, 202–3

✎ EXERCISES

1 Replace the underlined definite article with the correct form of the demonstrative adjective for *this/these*.

a Merece la pena leer <u>la</u> novela.

b ¿Por qué no escribís con <u>los</u> lápices?

c Has usado dos veces <u>el</u> adjetivo en <u>la</u> oración.

d <u>La</u> señora es la esposa del doctor.

e <u>El</u> vino no es muy bueno.

f No nos gustan <u>las</u> flores.

g <u>Los</u> timbales son de Amadito ¿verdad?

h <u>El</u> periodista escribe artículos llenos de humor.

2 Complete the sentences, using the correct form of the demonstrative pronoun **ése/ésa/ésos/ésas**.

a Este ordenador* ya está viejo; _____ es más moderno.

b Estos vasos están sucios; _____ están limpios.

c No me gustan estas botas; prefiero _____.

d – ¿Este autobús va a Ribadeo?

   – No, el autobús que va a Ribadeo es _____.

e ¿Va a comprar estas manzanas o _____?

f No se siente en esta silla; siéntese en _____.

g _____ melocotones están verdes.

h ¿Vas a comprarte esta camisa o _____?

* *In Latin-American Spanish: **computador** (a).*

3 Complete the sentences with **aquel/aquella/aquellos/aquellas**.

a _____ días fueron los mejores de mi vida.

b ¿Cuál prefieres: este vestido azul o _____ blanco?

c _____ chicas están riéndose de mí.

d _____ noche no salimos.

e Creo que los López viven en _____ casa.

f No sé cómo soportasteis _____ ruido.

g En _____ tiempos no había agua corriente ni electricidad en el pueblo.

h No compre estas naranjas; _____ son más dulces.

4 Relating **aquí** *(here)* with **este/a/os/as**

   ahí *(there)* with **ese/a/os/as**

and **allí** *(over there)* with **aquel/aquella/os/as**

Complete the questions with the appropriate demonstrative.

Example: **Ahí** hay un abrigo. ¿De quién es **ese** abrigo?

a Aquí hay un bolígrafo. ¿Es _____ tu bolígrafo?

b Ahí hay un libro. ¿Es _____ tu libro?

c Allí hay unos jardines. ¿Son bonitos _____ jardines?

d Ahí hay una chaqueta. ¿Es tuya _____ chaqueta?

   e Aquí hay una carta. ¿Para quién es _____ carta?

   f Ahí hay dos chicos. ¿Conoces a _____ chicos?

   g Tienes muchos libros aquí. ¿Vas a leer todos _____ libros?

   h Allí hay una mesa. ¿Está ocupada _____ mesa?

5 Translate into Spanish.

   a This is not difficult.

   b I have read this book before.

   c Can I try on these shoes?

   d At that precise moment there was no one at home.

   e I don't like this at all.

   f Those biros write better than these.

   g I remember those times perfectly. Those were happy times.

   h Why have you left all this here?

24 | Possessives

In an interview, the Spanish soprano Montserrat Caballé talked about herself and her family. As you read the text, focus attention on the Spanish equivalent of words such as *my*, *mine*, *your*, *yours*, which are known as possessives.

Entrevista: Montserrat Caballé

– ¿Cómo es **su** vida familiar? ¿Cómo ha podido compaginarla con **su** profesión?
– Creo que ha sido paciencia y mucho amor de **mi** familia. Primero con **mis** padres y **mi** hermano antes de casarme. Me ayudaron muchísimo. **Mi** hermano empezó siendo secretario **mío**, después **mi** "manager". Yo siempre decía "**Mi**
5 barco es un barco que no encontrará puerto," porque nunca llegaba esa función que yo soñaba. **Mi** hermano me dijo: "Durante un año voy a trabajar para ti, y si no consigo llevar a cabo este deseo **tuyo** serás libre de hacer lo que quieras." **Mi** hermano supo desde el principio tener ese sexto sentido para guiar **mi** carrera y así lo hizo. Y así fue también cuando conocí a **mi** esposo, que me enamoré mucho
10 de él, y **mi** hermano me dijo: "Me gustaría tanto verte casada, pero es tan difícil encontrar un buen hombre en la vida. Creo que Bernabé es un hombre muy bueno. No sé si pasarán dos Bernabés por **tu** vida." Yo no tenía dudas, lo que sí tenía era miedo a la responsabilidad y pensar si Bernabé realmente quería casarse conmigo. Me parecía mentira que me quisiera. Aquello me animó mucho y nunca
15 se lo agradeceré bastante. Y Bernabé fue algo maravilloso en **mi** vida. Y es. [. . .] Hemos tenido la suerte de tener dos hijos [. . .]. Yo siempre deseé que se parecieran a **su** padre, que es algo muy especial, y verdaderamente se parecen mucho a él. Ése es el gran triunfo de **mi** vida.

Revista *Blanco y Negro*, Diario *ABC*, España

Possessives

1 USAGE

Words like **mi** *my*, **tu** *your* (familiar), **mío** *mine*, **tuyo** *yours* (familiar) are called possessives. Spanish possessives can be grouped into two main categories: ***short forms*** and ***long forms***.

a Short forms can only function as **adjectives**, always preceding the noun or noun phrase, e.g. **mi** familia *my family* (l. 2).

b Long forms can function as **adjectives**, as the equivalent of English '*of mine/yours/his ...*':

este deseo **tuyo** (l. 7)   *this wish of yours,*

or as **pronouns**, normally preceded by the definite article:

¿Me puedes prestar tu teléfono móvil? He dejado **el mío** en casa.   *May I borrow your mobile phone? I've left mine at home.*

Teléfono is a masculine noun, hence the use of **el mío**.

c No definite article is needed when the possessive is preceded by the verb **ser** *to be*:

Estas gafas no son **mías**.   *These glasses are not mine.*

But note the use of the article in:

Estas gafas no son **las mías**, son **las tuyas**.   *These glasses are not mine, they are yours.*

in which the possessive serves to establish a distinction.

2 FORMS

a Short forms

Short forms always agree in number (singular or plural) with the noun they refer to, not with the owner. The first person plural and the second person plural familiar also agree in gender (masculine or feminine).

Singular		Plural		
Masc	*Fem*	*Masc*	*Fem*	
mi	**mi**	**mis**	**mis**	*my*
tu	**tu**	**tus**	**tus**	*your* (of **tú**)
su	**su**	**sus**	**sus**	*his, her, its, your* (of **Vd.**)
nuestro	**nuestra**	**nuestros**	**nuestras**	*our*
vuestro	**vuestra**	**vuestros**	**vuestras**	*your* (of **vosotros/as**)
su	**su**	**sus**	**sus**	*their, your* (of **Vds.**)

Except for **mío** *mine* (l. 4) and **tuyo** *yours* (l. 7), all the examples in the text correspond to short forms, that is, to adjectives, e.g. **su vida familiar** (l. 1) *your family life*, **mis padres** (l. 2–3) *my parents*, **mi hermano** (l. 3, 6, 10) *my brother*, **tu vida** (l. 12) *your life*.

De + subject pronoun to avoid ambiguity

If you need to avoid ambiguity when using **su/sus**, which can mean *his, her, your, their*, you can use forms such as **de él, de ella, de Vd**, e.g. **el libro de él** *his book*.

Definite article for possessive

When the relationship between the possessor and the thing possessed is clear, as in **Ricardo vendió el apartamento** *Ricardo sold **his** apartment*, Spanish uses the definite article instead of a possessive adjective.

The possessive adjective is also replaced by the definite article when the possessive relationship is already established by a pronoun:

Clara se lavó **las** manos.   *Clara washed **her** hands.*
Se me quebraron **las** gafas.   *I broke **my** glasses.*

b Long forms

Long forms agree in number and gender with the noun they refer to.

Singular		Plural		
Masc	Fem	Masc	Fem	
mío	**mía**	**míos**	**mías**	*mine*
tuyo	**tuya**	**tuyos**	**tuyas**	*yours* (of **tú**)
suyo	**suya**	**suyos**	**suyas**	*his, hers, its, yours* (of **Vd.**)
nuestro	**nuestra**	**nuestros**	**nuestras**	*ours*
vuestro	**vuestra**	**vuestros**	**vuestras**	*yours* (of **vosotros/as**)
suyo	**suya**	**suyos**	**suyas**	*theirs, yours* (of **Vds.**)

There are only two examples of long forms in the text, both functioning as adjectives:

Empezó siendo secretario **mío**. (l. 4)   *He started by being my secretary.*
Si no consigo llevar a cabo este deseo **tuyo** … (l. 6–7)   *If I can't manage to fulfil this dream of yours.*

De + subject pronoun to avoid ambiguity

To avoid the ambiguity of **suyo** use the construction **de** + subject pronoun:

un amigo **de él**   *a friend of his*,
instead of
un amigo **suyo**   *a friend of his/hers/yours/theirs*.

LATIN AMERICAN USAGE

The familiar form **vuestro** is not used in Latin America, where the short form **su** and the long form **suyo** are used in both formal and familiar address. The use of long forms after prepositional phrases such as **detrás** *behind*, **delante** *in front*, **enfrente** *opposite*, is common in spoken Latin American Spanish, e.g. **detrás mío** *behind me*, instead of **detrás de mí**, **delante nuestro** *in front of us*, instead of **delante de nosotros**.

Other points to note in the text

- Imperfect subjunctive: *me parecía mentira que me quisiera* (l. 14), *yo siempre deseé que se parecieran a su padre* (l. 16–17) (see Chapter 15)

- Demonstratives: *esa función* (l. 5), *este deseo* (l. 7), *ese sexto sentido* (l. 8), *ése es el gran triunfo* (l. 18) (see Chapter 23)
- Direct and indirect object pronouns: *compaginarla* (l. 1), *me ayudaron* (l. 3), *me dijo* (l. 6), *lo hizo* (l. 9), *me gustaría . . . verte* (l. 10), *se lo agradeceré* (l. 15), etc. (see Chapter 25)

See for further information:	Butt, pp. 141–4
	Butt and Benjamin, pp. 94–101
	Kattán-Ibarra and Pountain, pp. 45–7, 252–7
	Muñoz and Thacker, pp. 53–6, 204–5

✎ **EXERCISES**

1 Rewrite the sentence as in the example, using a possessive adjective.

Example: Tengo una habitación grande. Mi habitación es grande.

  a Tengo un escritorio muy viejo.
  b Carmen tiene una hermana que es médica.
  c Tienes unos amigos muy simpáticos.
  d Usted tiene una habitación reservada.
  e Tenemos una casa muy moderna.
  f Ustedes tienen los billetes en la mesa.
  g Tenéis un coche muy cómodo.
  h Los estudiantes tienen unas ideas muy buenas.
  i Tenemos libros muy interesantes.
  j Ustedes tienen una opinión muy mala de Gonzalo.

2 Complete the sentences using the possessive pronoun.

  a Estos son tus regalos. Estos regalos son _____.
  b Este bolso es de Miguel. Es _____.
  c Estas son nuestras revistas. Estas revistas son _____.
  d Estos son mis pañuelos. Estos pañuelos son _____.
  e Aquella maleta es de los señores. Aquella maleta es _____.
  f Estos son nuestros juguetes. Estos juguetes son _____.
  g Estas son vuestras corbatas. Estas corbatas son _____.
  h Este es mi diccionario. Este diccionario es _____.

3 Translate the bracketed English to complete the sentences.

  a Yo vendo mi apartamento y él vende (his) _____.
  b Pedro va en su coche y yo voy en (mine) _____.
  c Tu casa es grande pero prefiero (ours) _____.
  d Este libro no es de Antonia; (hers) _____ está allí.

e La camiseta de Rosario es verde; (mine) _____ es azul.

f Aquí está mi paraguas. ¿Saben ustedes dónde están (yours) _____?

g Paco, pon tu plato aquí y Marta y Teresa, poned (yours) _____ allí.

h Tus fotos han salido muy bien; (mine) _____ no tan bien.

i Mientras tú vas preparando tus cosas, nosotros vamos preparando (ours) _____.

j Como no tenemos coche y vosotros sí, ¿podemos ir en (yours) _____?

4 Possessive or definite article? Translate the following sentences into Spanish.

a She took off her coat and put on her jacket.

b Where have I put my passport?

c Would you give me your telephone number? (**usted**)

d He took his money out of his pocket.

e My stomach aches.

f I liked their flat.

g We talked about our children.

h Have you cut your finger?

5 Complete the following texts.

a Anoche fui a una función pero como _____ coche estaba estropeado, Ricardo me dejó_____. _____ coche es un BMW deportivo que _____ padre le compró para _____ cumpleaños. Desde luego yo no tengo tanta suerte. _____ padre está en paro y yo y _____ hermanos tenemos que trabajar mucho para mantener a _____ padres.

b – María, hija ¿quieres poner _____ zapatos debajo de _____ cama?

   – No son _____ zapatos. _____ ya están debajo de _____ cama. Esos zapatos son de Antonio.

   – No, no son _____. _____ son marrones y éstos son negros. María ¿de quién serán si no son _____?

c Acabamos de volver de la boda de _____ hija. ¿Quieres ver _____ fotos? Aquí estamos mi esposo y yo con uno de _____ hijos. Y ésta es una foto de _____ hija con _____ esposo y unos amigos _____. Y ésta es una foto de otra hija _____ con _____ novio.

25 | Personal pronouns

Text

The following passage is from the novel *Arráncame la vida* by the Mexican writer Ángeles Mastretta. In the grammar notes you will find information on how to use the Spanish equivalent of words such as *I/me*, *he/him*, *she/her*, etc.

Arráncame la vida

– ¿Quién **te** dijo a **ti** que las tierras de Alchichica eran de esa mujer? – preguntó Andrés cuando cerramos la puerta.
– **Ella** – **le** contesté. **Me** vino a ver hace como un mes. Quería que **yo te** hablara, que **te** convenciera de que su padre **las** heredó de su padre y que por muchos
5 años **ellos las** cultivaron, hasta que De Velasco **se las** quitó a la mala y ahora que está en quiebra se **le** hace muy fácil vender**le** a Heiss lo que no es suyo. Y Heiss compra barato con el pretexto de que hay riesgo de invasión. ¡Qué bárbaros, Andrés!
– ¿Qué dijiste? – preguntó.
10 – ¿Qué **le** iba **yo** a decir? Que buscara otro camino, que **yo** a **ti** no **te** podía hablar de eso, que no **me** oías. ¿Qué importa lo que **le** dije? No **la** ayudé. Sentí vergüenza cuando se levantó y dio la vuelta para irse a la calle sin dar**me** la mano.

From *Arráncame la vida*, © Ángeles Mastretta

Subject pronouns

1 USAGE

Words such as **yo** *I*, **tú** *you* (familar), **usted** *you* (formal), **él** *he*, etc., are known as subject pronouns. Subject pronouns are not normally needed in Spanish, as the verb ending is usually sufficient to indicate the person this refers to. But there are cases in which these are used:

a For emphasis.

Quería que **yo** te hablara. (l. 3)   *She wanted me to speak to you.*

¿Qué le iba **yo** a decir? (l. 10)   *What was I going to say?*

The use of **yo** *I* in these sentences is emphatic, as the context in which they occur leaves no doubt as to the person the verbs refer to, even when the same verb forms (the imperfect subjunctive in the first sentence, and the imperfect indicative in the other) also stand for **usted**, **él** and **ella**. Also emphatic is the use of **ellos** in:

... por muchos años **ellos** las cultivaron ... (l. 4–5)   ... *they cultivated them for many years* ...

b To avoid ambiguity.

..., que **yo** a ti no te podía hablar de eso ... (l. 10–11)   ..., *that I couldn't speak to you about that* ...

The presence of **yo** in this line has a double purpose. It is emphatic, stressing the *I* as opposed to another person, but it also serves to avoid ambiguity, as the first and third person singular of the imperfect indicative have similar forms. Without it, there would be a slight ambiguity, as the narrator might be referring to **ella**, the person being discussed in these lines. The context, again, helps to makes things clear.

Ambiguity in the following example can only be prevented by the use of a subject pronoun, **usted**, **él** or **ella**, as verb forms for **usted** are the same as for **él** and **ella**, as also happens in the third person plural, where **ustedes**, **ellos**, and **ellas** share similar forms.

¿Vive en México?   *Do you/does he/she live in México?*

c On its own, without an accompanying verb.

Ella – le contesté. (l. 3)   *'She did,' I replied.*

d As a way of establishing a contrast or comparison.

Yo tengo 30 años. ¿Qué edad tienes **tú**?   *I'm 30 years old. How old are you?*

e For politeness.

Usted (usually abbreviated **Vd.** or **Ud.**) *you* (formal, sing.) and **ustedes** (usually abbreviated **Vds.** or **Uds.**) *you* (formal, pl.) are often used for politeness, even when they are not needed.

2 FORMS

	singular	*plural*
1st person	**yo** *I*	**nosotros/as** *we*
2nd person	**tú** *you* (familiar)	**vosotros/as** *you* (familiar)
3rd person	**usted** *you* (formal)	**ustedes** *you* (formal)
	él *he*, **ella** *she*	**ellos/ellas** *they* (masc./fem.)

¿*Tú* or *usted*?
Generally speaking, the formal forms **usted** and **ustedes** (and all forms related to these) are used to address people one doesn't know, as well as the elderly and one's superiors.

The familiar forms **tú** and **vosotros/as** are used among friends, equals (for example colleagues), and generally among younger people, even if they haven't met before. Within the family, the standard form is the familiar one. In Latin America, the familiar form is less prevalent than in Spain.

LATIN AMERICAN USAGE

Latin Americans do not use **vosotros/as** and the forms related to this, e.g. **os** (see direct and indirect object pronouns below). **Ustedes** is used in both formal and familiar address.

In certain regions of Latin America, the **tú** form is replaced by **vos**, a system known as *voseo*. This is the norm in the Río de la Plata area (Argentina and Uruguay), but it is also common, but less extensive, in areas such as Central America and Colombia. It is also heard in Chile, normally among uneducated speakers.

In the Río de la Plata area **vos** takes a special form of the verb in the present tense indicative, the present subjunctive and the imperative (e.g. **vos hablás**, **vos comés**, **vos vivís**, instead of **tú hablas**, **tú comes**, **tú vives**). See also Chapters 1, 14 and 17.

Direct object pronouns

1 USAGE

a A direct object is that part of the sentence – a noun or a pronoun – which undergoes the action of the verb in a direct way:

Cerramos **la puerta**. (l. 2)   *We closed the door.*
Ellos **las** cultivaron. (l. 5)   *They cultivated them.*

The direct objects in these sentences are **la puerta** *the door* and **las** *them*, both affected directly by the action of the verb.

b Direct object pronouns stand for a person:

Me vino a ver. (l. 3)   *She came to see me.*
No **la** ayudé. (l. 11)   *I didn't help her.*

or a thing:

Se **las** quitó. (l. 5)   *He took them away from her.*

Las *them* in this sentence stands for **las tierras** *land*, already mentioned in line 1.

c **Lo** *you, him, it*, sometimes refers to an idea, but it is not always translated:

¿Sabe ella dónde viven? – No **lo** sabe.   *Does she know where they live? – She doesn't know.*
No sé qué pasó. – Simplemente no **lo** entiendo.   *I don't know what happened – I just don't understand.*

2 FORMS

	singular	*plural*
1st person	**me** *me*	**nos** *us*
2nd person	**te** *you* (for **tú**)	**os** *you* (for **vosotros/as**)
3rd person (masc.)	**lo** *you* (for **Vd.**), *him, it*	**los** *you* (for **Vds.**), *them*
(fem.)	**la** *you* (for **Vd.**), *her, it*	**las** *you* (for **Vds.**), *them*

REGIONAL VARIATIONS

There are some important regional variations in the use of 3rd person direct object pronouns, especially in the masculine forms. The use of **le** instead of **lo** for human males is common in Spain today, in speech as well as in writing, particularly in Central and Northern Spain, with **lo** being used for things:

Le llevé a casa *I took him home*, **Lo** llevé a casa *I took it home.*

While this variation is considered correct, the use of the plural **les** for **los**, also common in the same areas, is sometimes frowned upon by educated speakers, even though its use is becoming more widespread. Most other regions, including Latin America, use **lo** and **los** for human males and for things. Variations in the use of the feminine forms **la** and **las** are less extensive and are generally considered unacceptable.

Note that the plural familiar **os** form is replaced by **los** (masc.) or **las** (fem.) throughout Latin America.

A + él/ella/usted

The ambiguity in a sentence such as **Lo llamaré esta tarde** *I'll call him/you this afternoon*, can be avoided by the use **a** + **él/usted**: **Lo llamaré a él/Vd. esta tarde.**

Indirect object pronouns

1 USAGE

a In a sentence such as **Le compraré la casa** *I'll buy him/her the house*, the house, which is the thing bought, is the direct object. **Le** *him/her*, which stands for the person for whom you bought it (also affected by the action of the verb, but in an indirect way), is the indirect object. Similarly, in **sin darme** la mano (l. 12) *without shaking hands with me*, the indirect object is **me**. Note also the use of the indirect object pronouns **te** and **le** in:

¿Quién **te** dijo … ? (l. 1)   *Who told you … ?*
Ella – **le** contesté. (l. 3)   *'She did,' I replied (to him).*
¿Qué importa lo que **le** dije? (l. 11)   *What does it matter what I said to her?*

b In a sentence with two object pronouns, one direct and the other indirect, the indirect object pronoun must come first, e.g. **Me las** quitó *He/she took them away from me.*

c **Le** and **les** become **se** before **lo/la/los/las**, e.g. **Se las** quitó (l. 5) *He took them away from her.*

REDUNDANT PRONOUNS

In a sentence such as **Se le hace muy fácil venderle a Heiss** (l. 6) *It is very easy for him to sell to Heiss*, the second **le**, coming before the indirect object **a Heiss**, is redundant. This kind of redundancy is a common feature of Spanish, and it also occurs with direct object pronouns, as in **Las manzanas las compré yo** *I bought the apples*. In the second example, however, in which the object has been highlighted by being placed before the verb, the redundant pronoun cannot be omitted.

2 FORMS

	singular	**plural**
1st person	**me** *(to) me*	**nos** *(to) us*
2nd person	**te** *(to) you* (for **tú**)	**os** *(to) you* (for **vosotros/as**)
3rd person	**le** *(to) you* (for **Vd.**),	**les** *(to) you* (for **Vds.**),
	(to) him, her, it	*(to) them*

REGIONAL VARIATIONS

The use of third person indirect object pronouns presents little variation throughout the Spanish-speaking world. A notable exception is the use of **la** for **le**, in the feminine, in central Spain, especially in Madrid, e.g. **la dije** for **le dije** *I told her*. This usage is considered incorrect by most educated speakers.

Note that the **os** form is replaced by **les** (plural, familiar and formal) throughout Latin America.

POSITION OF DIRECT AND INDIRECT OBJECT PRONOUNS

Direct and indirect object pronouns are normally placed before the verb:

¿Qué importa lo que **le** dije? No **la** ayudé. (l. 11)   *What difference does it make what I said to her? I didn't help her.*

But in a construction using a finite verb + infinitive/gerund, the object pronoun may be placed before the finite verb or it may be added to the infinitive or gerund:

Me vino a ver (l. 3) *or* Vino a ver**me**.   *He came to see me.*
Te está mirando *or* Está mirándo**te**.   *He/she is looking at you.*

If there is no finite verb, the pronoun must be added to the infinitive or gerund:

Se le hace muy fácil vender**le** a Heiss. (l. 6)   *It's very easy for him to sell to Heiss.*

Object pronouns are also added to positive imperatives, e.g. **Dámelo** *Give it to me*.

PREPOSITIONAL FORMS

a Pronouns which follow prepositions are the same as the subject pronouns, except for **mí** *me* and **ti** *you* (sing.):

¿Quién te dijo a **ti** que ... ? (l. 1) *Who told you that ... ?*

... que yo a **ti** no te podía hablar de eso ... (l. 10–11) *... that I couldn't talk to you about that ...*

¿Esto es para **mí**? *Is this for me?*

Note that the function of **a ti** in the first two sentences is purely emphatic, as the use of **te** makes this redundant.

b **Con** + **mí/ti/sí** results in the following forms: **conmigo** *with me*, **contigo** *with you* (familiar, sing.), **consigo** *with himself/herself*, etc. But **con él/ella/vd.**, etc. *with him/her/you*.

¿Quieres venir **conmigo**? *Do you want to come with me?*

La vi **contigo**. *I saw her with you.*

c **Yo** and **tú** rather than **mí** and **ti** are used after **entre** *between*, **hasta**, **incluso** *even*, **excepto**, **menos**, **salvo** *except*, **según**, *according to*.

entre tú y yo *between you and me*

hasta tú lo podrías hacer *even you could do it*

todos excepto yo *everyone except me*

según tú *according to you*

Other points to note in the text

- Preterite and imperfect tenses: *dijo* (l. 1), *eran* (l. 1), *preguntó* (l. 2), *cerramos* (l. 2), *contesté* (l. 3), *vino* (l. 3), *quería* (l. 3), etc. (see Chapters 2 and 3)
- Imperfect subjunctive: *Quería que yo te hablara, que te convenciera ...* (l. 3–4), *que buscara otro camino* (l. 10) (see Chapter 15)
- Definite article with possessive value: *sin darme la mano* (l. 12) (see Chapter 18)
- Infinitive: *me vino a ver* (l. 3), *se le hace muy fácil venderle* (l. 6), *¿qué le iba yo a decir?* (l. 10), *no te podía hablar* (l. 10–11), *para irse* (l. 12) (see Chapter 8)

See for further information:	Batchelor and Pountain, pp. 280–5
	Butt, pp. 104–18
	Butt and Benjamin, pp. 127–48
	Kattán-Ibarra and Pountain, pp. 36–42, 252–6
	Muñoz and Thacker, pp. 40–7

✎ EXERCISES

1 Fill the gap with a subject pronoun.

  a ¿_____ vas a hablar con la directora o soy _____ la que tiene que hablar con _____?

  b ¿Cuándo vais _____ a Suiza?

c A él le ha gustado esa película mexicana pero a ____ no nos ha gustado nada.

d ¿La tortilla es para ____, señor o es para la señora?

e No sé lo que vamos a hacer porque si ____ no quieren ir, y ____ no podemos, pues, no hay nadie más.

f Señores ¿han dejado todos ____ las llaves en recepción?

2 Answer the questions using the information provided.

Example: ¿Dónde compró Raúl el poncho? / Argentina
       Lo compró en Argentina.

a ¿Cuándo escribió Marta la carta? / viernes

b ¿Viste a los señores Gil? / el lunes pasado

c ¿Dónde compras las flores? / en el mercado

d ¿Conoces al tío de Silvia? / No

e ¿Vendieron las tierras? / Sí

f ¿Llamaste a tu madre? / ayer

g ¿Dónde has puesto mi libro? / en el estante

h ¿Habéis probado la tarta? / todavía no

3 Rewrite these sentences, replacing the bracketed words with the appropriate pronoun.

a Montse regaló un collar (a su madre).

b La señora no dio ninguna respuesta (a mí).

c He preparado un café (para tí).

d Nuestro padre mandó una carta (a tí y a tu hermano).

e El jefe ha explicado el problema (a ustedes).

f Ellos no querían vender las tierras (a nosotros).

g Yo siempre digo la verdad (a usted).

h Tenemos que dar los libros (a los alumnos).

4 Rewrite these sentences, replacing the words in italics with appropriate pronouns.

a No me dio *la mano.*

b Marta nos mostró *las fotos.*

c Roberto no os ha hecho *la reserva* ¿verdad?

d No te puedo contar *mis problemas.*

e Me entregaron *el premio.*

f Pepe no quiere darme *las joyas.*

g ¿Por qué no os quiso comprar *las revistas*?

h Federico va a leernos *los poemas.*

5 Replace the words in italics with appropriate pronouns.

a El guía explicó *la historia a los turistas.*

b La señora no quería vender *las tierras a Andrés y su mujer.*

c Recomendé *el libro a los estudiantes*.

d Carlos va a pedir *las notas a Enrique*.

e No pensaba devolver *el dinero a Rosario*.

f ¿Pasaste *los trabajos a Pedro*?

6 Complete the text with the appropriate pronoun.

Ramoncito encontró el CD en el rastrillo y ____ compró sin pensar____ más porque sabía que era mi cumpleaños y ____ compró para ____. Nada más comprar ____, vino acá para regalar ____ de modo que llegó tarde a casa y su padre se enfadó con ____ y ____ castigó.

Cuando me enteré, ____ dije al padre que no debería haber ____ hecho porque Ramoncito estaba pensando en ____ y quien tenía la culpa era ____. Pero el padre ____ dijo que no tenía por qué meter ____ en asuntos ajenos y si ____ quería castigar a su hijo, ____ haría.

Volví a casa furiosa y cuando vi que mis hijas estaban en el salón escuchando mi disco, ____ grité:

– ¿Quién ____ ha dado permiso para escuchar esto?

– Calma ____, mamá, – ____ contestaron, – Es una música preciosa. ____ encanta. Siénta ____ y escucha ____. Y otra cosa, ____ hemos preparado la cena así que ____ a descansar.

7 Translate into Spanish.

a Who gave you this watch? Nobody gave it to me; I found it.

b I can't give her the money today, I'll give it to her tomorrow.

c Have you visited them before? Between you and me, they are not very friendly.

d Everybody has given you something except her.

e Children, I'll give you your gloves and you can put them on to go out.

f Sir, Madam, how can I help you?

g Her husband listened to her while she served him his dinner.

h "I'll invite you for a coffee" is what Ricardo said to us.

Text 1

Like many illegal migrants today, who cross the Straits of Gibraltar from North Africa into Europe in improvised **balsas** *rafts*, prehistoric man may have made a similar crossing a million and a half years ago. This is the subject of the first text, which, like the one below, focuses on the use of relative pronouns.

El homo erectus, el primer "balsero" del estrecho de Gibraltar

Los africanos **que** ahora se juegan la vida para venir a Europa en embarcaciones precarias no son los primeros **que** han hecho ese viaje. Hace cientos de miles de años, otros africanos, **quienes** son nuestros antecesores, hicieron ese mismo camino y colonizaron Europa, según las teorías de algunos de los paleontólogos

5 **que** han estudiado el tema. Parece probado que los primeros humanos nacieron en Africa, en las fértiles praderas del oriente, desde **las que** se expandieron por Asia y Europa en diferentes oleadas. La mayoría de los paleontólogos ha estado siempre de acuerdo en que esa migración se produjo por Oriente Próximo, exactamente por el valle del Jordán. Pero, el paleontólogo surafricano Phillip

10 Tobias explicó una nueva hipótesis: los homínidos **que** llegaron a Europa no lo habrían hecho por Oriente Próximo sino cruzando el estrecho de Gibraltar, a través **del cual** se adentraron en la Península Ibérica, un viaje **que** habría tenido lugar entre 1,5 y 1,6 millones de años atrás.

Revista *Tiempo*, España

Text 2

Text 2 looks at Internet addiction through a personal story.

Esclavos de la tecnología

He conocido a Willy G. en un *chat* (ya sabéis, uno de esos sitios **que** hay en Internet, desde **los que** puedes comunicarte con otros usuarios de la Red en

tiempo real; la única cosa **que** tienes que hacer es escribir con tu teclado el
mensaje **que** quieres emitir, e instantáneamente aparecerá en los monitores
5 de todos los participantes **que** estén conectados a ese *chat*). Encuentro a Willy,
mi nuevo amigo virtual, en uno **que** se relaciona con amistad. Willy, **que** es
estudiante, tiene veintiún años, y hace dos no podía pasar ni un solo día sin
conectarse a Internet. "Mi adicción era tal que chatear me era tan imprescindible
como puede serlo cualquier otra droga," escribe Willy. Y lo que comenzó como
10 un juego divertido pronto dejó de serlo y su novia terminó dejándole: "Cuando
me dejó, comprendí que tenía que superar mi adicción." Hoy en día Willy, **quien**
se sigue conectando, pero mucho menos que antes, me cuenta que procura
relacionarse más con sus amigos no virtuales. "No existe realidad más agradable
que **la que** tenemos ante nuestros ojos todos los días, y no necesariamente
15 delante de un ordenador."

Revista *DT*, España

Relative pronouns

1 GENERAL USAGE

a Relative pronouns are words like **que** *who, whom, that, which,* **el/la que, el/la cual** *that, whom, which,* **cuyo/a** *whose,* which introduce relative clauses. A relative clause is a group of words which refers back to something previously mentioned in the sentence, a noun or a pronoun, known as the ***antecedent***. In Text 1, line 10, for example, the relative pronoun **que** links the noun **Los homínidos** ... (the antecedent) to the relative clause **llegaron a Europa** ... *The hominids who arrived in Europe ...*

b A relative pronoun can be the ***subject*** or ***object*** of the relative clause. In Text 1, line 1, **Los africanos que ahora se juegan la vida** ... *The Africans who now risk their lives ...* **que** is functioning as the subject of the relative clause, which refers back to **los africanos**. In Text 2, lines 3–4, ... **el mensaje que quieres emitir** ... *the message (that/which) you want to send ...* **que** is the object, a direct object in this case, referring back to **el mensaje**. In English, the relative pronoun can be omitted when this is the direct object of a relative clause. In Spanish, this cannot be done.

2 QUE *WHO, WHOM, WHICH, THAT*

Que is the most common relative pronoun in Spanish, in the spoken and the written language. It is invariable, and it can refer to people and to things.

... los paleontólogos **que** han estudiado ... (T. 1, l. 4–5)   ... *paleontologists who have studied ...*
... la única cosa **que** tienes que hacer ... (T. 2, l. 3)   ... *the only thing (that/which) you need to do ...*
Willy, **que** es estudiante, tiene veintún años. (T. 2, l. 6–7)   ... *Willy, who is a student, is twenty-one years old.*

In the first and second examples, **que** introduces a ***restrictive clause***, one which restricts the scope of the antecedent. No comma or pause is used between the relative pronoun and the antecedent. In the last example, the clause is ***non-restrictive***. It is there simply to provide more information about the antecedent, so a comma is needed in writing, and a pause in speech. As part of a non-restrictive clause, **que**, in this example, can be replaced by **quien** or **el cual**,

> Willy, **quien/el cual** es estudiante, tiene ...

Que is often used with short prepositions such as **a**, **con**, **de**, **en**, with reference to a non-human antecedent.

> el dinero **con que** lo compré   *the money I bought it with*
> la casa **en que** viví   *the house I lived in*

Note that the preposition must come before the relative pronoun, never at the end of the clause, as it can do in English.

3 EL/LA QUE, LOS/LAS QUE, EL/LA CUAL, LOS/LAS CUALES *WHOM, WHICH, THAT*

El/la que is less formal and more frequently used than **el/la cual**.
These forms are often used following prepositions. In Text 1, for example, note **desde las que** (l. 6) *from which*, and **a través del cual** (l. 11–12) *across which*.
They are also used when there is a pause in speech, or a comma in writing, between the antecedent and the relative clause.

> Llamamos a la policía, **la que** lo arrestó.   *We called the police, who arrested him.*

El que, **los que**, etc. can also mean *he/those who, the one(s) who/which, etc.*
Some proverbs are expressed with this construction.

> **El que** termine primero, puede irse.   *He who finishes first, can leave.*
> **Los que** hablan español tendrán más posibilidades.   *Those who speak Spanish will have a better chance.*
> **El que** a hierro mata, a hierro muere. (proverb)   *He who lives by the sword, dies by the sword.*
> **El que** ríe último ríe mejor. (proverb)   *He who laughs last laughs longest.*

4 LO QUE, LO CUAL *WHAT, WHICH*

These are neuter forms, which refer back to an idea, never to a specific noun.

> Me escribió Antonio, **lo que** me alegró muchísimo.   *Antonio wrote to me, which made me very happy.*

5 QUIEN, QUIENES *WHO, WHOM*

Quien, and its plural form **quienes**, can only refer to people, and its use does not differ much from that of **el que/cual** above. It can function as a subject or as an object pronoun, and it can also follow a preposition.

> ... otros africanos, **quienes** son nuestros antecesores, ... (subject, T. 1, l. 3)   *... other Africans, who are our ancestors, ...*

Elena, a **quien** admiro mucho, ganó el premio. (object)   *Elena, whom I admire very much, won the prize.*

Luis, para **quien** nada es difícil, lo solucionó.   *Luis, for whom nothing is difficult, solved it.*

Like **el que**, etc., **quien** and **quienes** are used in initial position to translate expressions like *he who, the one(s) who, those who.*

Quienes están listos pueden comenzar.   *Those who are ready can start.*

6 CUYO *WHOSE*

Cuyo can refer to people or things and it must agree in gender (masculine or feminine) and number (singular or plural) with the noun that follows it.

Una situación **cuyas** consecuencias pueden ser desastrosas   *A situation whose consequences can be disastrous*

La persona en **cuya** casa vivíamos   *The person in whose house we lived*

Other points to note in the text

- Preterite tense: Text 1: *hicieron* (l. 3), *colonizaron* (l. 4), *nacieron* (l. 5), *se expandieron* (l. 6), etc. Text 2: *comenzó* (l. 9), *terminó* (l. 10), *dejó* (l. 11), etc. (see Chapter 2)
- *Por* and *para*: Text 1: *para venir* (l. 1), *por Asia* (l. 6–7), *por Oriente Próximo* (l. 8), *por el Valle del Jordán* (l. 9) (see Chapter 28)
- Personal *a*: Text 2: *He conocido a Willy* (l. 1), *Encuentro a Willy* (l. 5) (see Chapter 28)
- Negation: Text 1: *no son* (l. 2), *no . . . sino* (l. 10–11). Text 2: *no podía pasar ni un solo día* (l. 7), *imprescindible* (l. 8), *amigos no virtuales* (l. 13), *no necesariamente* (l. 14).

See for further information: Butt, pp. 124–6

Butt and Benjamin, pp. 494–504

Kattán-Ibarra and Pountain, pp. 48–50

Muñoz and Thacker, pp. 57–60, 206–8

✎ EXERCISES

1 Use a relative pronoun to make one sentence out of two.

a El castillo está en el puerto. Data del siglo XVI.

b Encontramos una pensión. Nos hizo recordar Santo Domingo.

c Una camarera nos sirvió. Era muy antipática.

d Un hombre contestó al teléfono. Me dijo que estabas fuera.

e Te dejé prestada la grabadora. Devuélvemela.

f En octubre te llevé a un restaurante. Ahora está cerrado.

g Aquéllos son los vecinos. Me quejo de ellos.

h Me escribió una carta. En la carta me explicó todo.

2 Complete the sentences with **que** or **quien**.

   a Rosario, a _____ todo el mundo quería, murió el mes pasado.

   b Las recepcionistas _____ trabajan en ese hotel son todas muy amables.

   c Fue Susana _____ perdió la llave, no yo.

   d Las flores _____ mejor crecen aquí son los cardos.

   e Han detenido al hombre _____ te dio la paliza.

   f El periódico _____ prefiero leer es *El Mundo*.

   g El hombre con _____ estabas hablando es el presidente de la junta.

   h La chica _____ estuvo conmigo en París se hizo modelo.

3 Complete the sentences with one of the following prepositions and a relative pronoun.

de	debajo de	en	encima de
enfrente de	entre	para	por

   a La casa _____ se construye un casino pertenece al Doctor Clarín.

   b Si quieres, te dejo el video _____ te hablé anoche.

   c Los soportales _____ siempre hay tenderetes son una característica de la ciudad.

   d Los pueblos _____ hemos pasado doblan sus poblaciones en verano.

   e Esa caja _____ guardo mis cositas me la hizo Rafa.

   f En el salón hay un sofá _____ cuelga uno de los primeros cuadros de Miró.

   g La compañía _____ trabajé tantos años está en quiebra.

   h En la plaza tocaban varios músicos _____ reconoció a su primo Jacobo.

4 Complete the sentences with **que** or **lo que**.

   a Todo _____ has hecho está bien.

   b Cálmate; no es _____ te imaginas.

   c El problema _____ nos enfrentaba no tenía solución.

   d Cesar dijo exactamente _____ pensaba, _____ me pareció fatal.

   e La señora _____ acaba de salir es la persona _____ hace las esculturas.

   f Nico pasó horas y horas chateando, _____ le costó su trabajo.

   g La página web _____ creó Marco tiene mil visitantes por día.

   h Muchos académicos utilizan la red para acceder a bibliotecas en el extranjero _____ facilita mucho sus investigaciones.

5 Complete the sentences with the correct form of the relative pronoun **cuyo**.

   a Hoy he hablado con Valentina _____ hermanos acaban de volver del Perú.

   b El estudiante _____ madre está enferma no ha venido a clase hoy.

   c Ven, quiero presentarte a Teresa _____ padre es el pintor que tanto te gusta.

   d Por fin llegamos a conocer al chico _____ bromas nos han divertido tanto.

   e ¿Cómo se llama la mujer en _____ casa nos alojamos?

   f Un huérfano es un niño _____ padres han muerto.

g Por esta calle hay una casa _____ balcones están siempre repletos de flores.

h "En un lugar de La Mancha, de _____ nombre no quiero acordarme ..." es la famosísima primera frase de *El Quijote* de Cervantes.

6 Rewrite these sentences as one, using an appropriate relative pronoun.

a La excavación por paleontólogos y arqueólogos de Atapuerca empezó en los años 70 del siglo XX. Atapuerca está en la sierra de Burgos.

b En Atapuerca se han descubierto fósiles humanos. Los fósiles pertenecen a seis individuos diferentes.

c Los seis individuos podrían haber sido los europeos más antiguos. Sus restos tienen unos 800.000 años de antigüedad.

d No se parecen a otros fósiles humanos encontrados en Europa. Este hecho revoluciona las teorías convencionales sobre la evolución de *Homo sapiens.*

e El equipo investigador le puso a esta nueva especie el nombre de *Homo antecessor.* El significado del nombre en latín es pionero.

f Han usado técnicas geofísicas avanzadas. Estas técnicas han permitido una datación precisa del yacimiento de los fósiles.

g En los huesos de *Homo antecessor* hay marcas. Por estas marcas sabemos que era caníbal.

h Los jóvenes arqueólogos han hecho las tesis. Necesitan ayuda económica para poder seguir trabajando. Su labor es de sumo interés general.

27 | Negation

Text 1

An increasing number of couples are turning to antenatal tests to ensure that they have a healthy child, but medical advance and ethics, once again, seem to clash. This is the main subject of this text, which, like Text 2 below, illustrates *negation* in Spanish.

Si usted quiere un hijo perfecto ...

Recuerdo perfectamente el caso de una chica de 21 años que **no** se hizo **ningún** tipo de prueba porque **no** estaba en el segmento de riesgo y tuvo un niño con síndrome de Down. Pues bien, **no** quisieron **ni** conocerlo. Tanto ella como su compañero, también muy joven, decidieron en veinticuatro horas darlo en

5 adopción. Es cruel, sin duda, pero pasa. Ello pone de relieve el creciente rechazo de las parejas más jóvenes a tener niños con malformaciones.

Los futuros padres desean tener el mayor grado de seguridad con respecto a la salud de sus futuros hijos. Esta tendencia se inscribe dentro de una sociedad muy competitiva, en donde **no** se aceptan las debilidades **ni** las imperfecciones **ni** las

10 dificultades. Todo debe regirse en torno al éxito. Y este factor también ha llegado a la hora de tomar la decisión de tener un hijo.

Las parejas que se consideran sin riesgo para engendrar son aquéllas cuyos integrantes **no** alcanzan los treinta años, están sanos, **no** son drogadictos **ni** alcohólicos **ni** padecen alguna enfermedad congénita y llevan un régimen

15 alimenticio equilibrado. Pero aún así, en este fragmento de parejas se están dando casos de niños con malformaciones graves. La ciencia todavía **no** puede explicar por qué.

La información adecuada es vital en cualquier prueba de este tipo porque un feto puede tener una dolencia que, operada tras su nacimiento, se supera sin

20 dificultad. Lo que pasa es que **no** siempre los padres reciben la información adecuada o **no** van al centro adecuado. Sí existe una presión social por saber cómo está el feto, pero **no** sólo de los futuros padres **sino** de toda la familia.

Revista *Tiempo*, España

Text 2

Forest fires are turning large areas of the Iberian Peninsula into barren land. The following text gives some practical advice on how to prevent them. As you read the text, note the use of negative forms.

Consejos para evitar incendios

- En verano **no** hacer **ningún** tipo de fuego en el bosque, **ni siquiera** en las áreas habilitadas para ello.
- **No** fumar en el monte. Las cerillas y colillas, aun cuando se piense que están apagadas, constituyen un grave peligro de incendios.
5 - **No** dejar basuras, ya que pueden convertirse en combustible fácilmente inflamable.
- Si se encuentra una hoguera, **no** abandonarla hasta cerciorarse de que está completamente apagada.
- **No** abandonar **tampoco** botellas o trozos de vidrio que, por refracción, pueden
10 originar un foco calorífico.
- Cuando se viaja por ferrocarril o por carretera **no** se deben arrojar **nunca** cerillas **ni** colillas encendidas por la ventana.

Revista *Tribuna*, España

Negation

1 NEGATIVE WORDS

Negation in Spanish is expressed through the following words:

no	*no, not*	**ni**	*nor, not even*
nada	*nothing*	**ni ... ni ...**	*neither ... nor ...*
nadie	*nobody, no-one, not anybody*	**ni siquiera**	*not even*
nunca	*never*	**tampoco**	*neither, not either*
jamás	*never*	**apenas**	*hardly, scarcely*
ninguno	*no, not any, none*		

Other negative expressions

de ninguna manera	*by no means*	**por nada del mundo**	*for all the world*
en absoluto	*not at all*	**¡qué va!**	*not at all, quite the opposite,*
en mi vida	*never in my life*		*of course not!*
en ninguna parte	*nowhere*	**todavía no**	*not yet*
nunca jamás or **jamás de los jamases**	*never ever*	**ya no**	*not any more/longer*

2 USING NEGATIVE WORDS

a *No*

No is the most commonly used negative word.

> **No** quisieron ... (T. 1, l. 3)   *They didn't want ...*
> **No** alcanzan los 30 años ... (T. 1, l. 13)   *They are not yet 30 ...*
> **No** fumar ... (T. 2, l. 3)   *Do not smoke ...*

See also Text 2, lines 5 and 9.

b Double negative

Negative words such as **nunca**, **nadie**, **ninguno**, **tampoco**, may follow the verb, in which case another negative word must precede it, resulting in a double negative construction.

> **No** se hizo **ningún** tipo de prueba ... (T. 1, l. 1–2)   *She didn't undergo any kind of test ...*
> **No** se deben arrojar **nunca** cerillas ... (T. 2, l. 11–12)   *You must never throw matches ...*
> **No** abandonar **tampoco** botellas ... (T. 2, l. 9)   *Do not leave bottles either ...*

More emphasis can be achieved by placing such words before the verb, in a single negative construction.

> **Ningún** tipo de prueba se hizo ...
> **Nunca** se deben arrojar cerillas ...
> **Tampoco** (se deben) abandonar botellas ...

c *Ninguno*

Ninguno can function as an adjective and as a pronoun, agreeing in number and gender with the noun it qualifies or refers to. Its plural form, however, is rarely used nowadays. Before a masculine singular noun, **ninguno** becomes **ningún**, as in **ningún tipo** in text 1, lines 1–2, and text 2, line 1, where it is functioning as an adjective. Here are some further examples:

> No tienen **ninguna** posibilidad. (adjective)   *They haven't any chance.*
> ¿Te gusta alguno? – No, **ninguno**. (pronoun)   *Do you like any? – No, none.*

d *Alguno* for *ninguno*

Alguno may be used as an adjective, after a noun, with the same meaning as **ninguno**, a construction which is more formal and emphatic.

> **No** vemos solución **alguna**.   *We don't see any solution.*

e Negative words in comparison

In comparative sentences, words like **nadie**, **nada**, **nunca**, etc. translate *anyone*, *anything*, *ever*, etc.

> Él lo sabe mejor que **nadie**.   *He knows it better than anyone.*
> Nunca he visto **nada** más absurdo.   *I've never seen anything more absurd.*
> Llovió más que **nunca**.   *It rained more than ever.*

f *Sin/sin que* + negative word

In these constructions with **sin** *without*, negative words such as **nada**, **nadie**, **nunca**, etc., translate *anything*, *anyone*, *ever*, etc.

Sin nada que hacer   *Without anything to do*
Sin que nadie lo supiera   *Without anyone knowing*
Sin quejarse **nunca**   *Without ever complaining*

g *Ni, ni siquiera*

Ni has different meanings. In Text 1, line 3, it is the equivalent of **ni siquiera** *not ... even*.

... no quisieron **ni** conocerlo.   *... they didn't even want to know him.*
(**Ni siquiera** quisieron conocerlo.)

Note also **ni siquiera** in Text 2, line 1.

... **ni siquiera** en las áreas ...   *... not even in the areas ...*

In Text 1, lines 9–10, it translates *or*.

No se aceptan las debilidades **ni** las imperfecciones **ni** las dificultades.   *Weaknesses or imperfections or difficulties are not accepted.*

In Text 1, lines 13–14, **no ... ni** corresponds to the English construction *neither ... nor*.

No son drogadictos **ni** alcohólicos **ni** padecen ...   *They are neither drug addicts nor alcoholic, nor do they suffer from ...*

h *No ... sino/no sólo ... sino (también)*

These constructions with **sino** *but* are used to indicate contradiction or correction.

No este año **sino** el próximo.   *Not this year but the next one.*
No sólo de los futuros padres **sino** de toda la familia. (T. 1, l. 22)   *Not only from the future parents but from all the family.*

i *Tampoco*

Tampoco is used in negative sentences with the meaning of *not ... either, neither ...*

No abandonar **tampoco** botellas ... (T. 2, l. 9)   *Do not leave bottles either ...*
No lo sé – Yo **tampoco**.   *I don't know – Neither do I.*

3 NEGATION OF ADJECTIVES

Adjectives may be negated by means of prefixes such as **an-, a-, des-, de-, i-, in-** (**im-** before **b** or **p**).

anormal *abnormal*	**decrecer** *decrease*
analfabeto *illiterate*	**ilegal** *illegal*
desordenado *untidy*	**incapaz** *incapable*

Adjectives may also be negated by means of words such as **no, poco, nada**.

países **no desarrollados**   *underdeveloped countries*
objetos voladores **no identificados**   *unidentified flying objects*
poco atractivo   *not very attractive, unattractive*
poco eficaz   *not very efficient, inefficient*
nada claro/caro   *not at all clear/expensive*

4 MAKING NOUNS NEGATIVE

A few nouns accept the word **no** before them to negate their meaning.

no fumadores   *non-smokers*
la **no violencia**   *non-violence*
la **no intervención**   *non-intervention*

Other points to note in the text

- *Ser* and *estar*: Text 1: *estaba en el segmento* (l. 2), *es cruel* (l. 5), *son aquéllas* (l. 12), *están sanos* (l. 13), etc. Text 2: *están apagadas* (l. 3–4), *está . . . apagada* (l. 7–8) (see Chapter 13)
- Reflexive verbs: Text 1: *no se hizo* (l. 1), *se inscribe* (l. 8), *regirse* (l. 10). Text 2: *convertirse* (l. 5), *cerciorarse* (l. 7) (see Chapter 12)
- Passive and impersonal *se*: Text 1: *no se aceptan las debilidades* (l. 9), *se consideran* (l. 12). Text 2: *aun cuando se piense* (l. 3), *si se encuentra una hoguera* (l. 7), *cuando se viaja* (l. 11), *no se deben arrojar nunca cerillas* (l. 11–12) (see Chapter 11)

See for further information: Batchelor and Pountain, pp. 231–3
Butt, pp. 154–6
Butt and Benjamin, pp. 328–38
Kattán-Ibarra and Pountain, pp. 61–3
Muñoz and Thacker, pp. 147–50, 256–7

✎ EXERCISES

1 Give negative answers to these questions.

    a ¿Hay alguien aquí?
    b ¿Tenéis algo que hacer?
    c ¿Habéis ido alguna vez a Acapulco?
    d No voy al cine esta noche. ¿Y tú?
    e ¿Has visto a alguno de mis compañeros?
    f ¿Vas a enseñarme alguno de tus cuadros?
    g ¿Quieres té o café?
    h ¿Ya tenéis los resultados?

2 Rewrite these sentences in a different way.

    a No tenía dinero nunca.
    b No acompañaba nadie al concejal.
    c En esa tienda no vendían ni bolígrafos.
    d No me ayudaron tampoco.
    e No viene nunca nadie.

f Federica no entiende nada nunca.

g Yo no entiendo nunca nada tampoco.

h No te lo podría explicar ningún científico.

3 Complete the sentences using a negative from the list below.

nada	**nadie**	**ni**	**ninguno**
no	**nunca**	**sino**	

a No queremos hablar con _____.

b Salió de allí sin decir _____.

c Todavía _____ se ha presentado _____ oportunidad para decírselo.

d Pepe tiene cara de tonto pero _____ es _____ tonto.

e Porfidio _____ explicó _____ de sus acciones.

f La culpa _____ es del niño _____ de los padres.

g Los chistes de Juanjo _____ tienen _____ de gracia.

h _____ queremos _____ disculpas _____ excusas.

i _____ buscamos la juerga _____ la tranquilidad.

j _____ he visto _____ tan espectacular como los fuegos artificiales de Las Fallas.

4 Unjumble the words to make meaningful sentences.

a nada • en • nadie • monte • el • dejó

b desviamos • no • del • nos • sendero • nunca

c fumadores • grupo • había • el • no fumadores • en • y

d tiramos • no • ni • ni • sin • colillas • cerillas • apagar

e encendimos • tampoco • hogueras • no

f ningún • del • no • área • fuego • de • hicimos • fuera • indicada • tipo

g el • sabía • fogón • nadie • utilizar • el • en • grupo

h nadie • pasamos • sin • a • el • ver • día

5 Translate into Spanish.

a I spent the whole day at home doing nothing.

b Pablito never understands anything.

c He hasn't given me any kind of help.

d What you have written isn't at all clear.

e They don't read the papers or listen to the news on the radio.

f I haven't got the results yet and Jorge hasn't either.

g He went off without saying anything to anyone.

h She did it without any difficulty.

Text

The following extract from an article by Greenpeace looks at genetically modified crops. As you read the text, note the use of words such as **por**, **para**, **en**, **con**, **de**, known as prepositions.

Ingeniería genética: Frankenstein o el moderno Prometeo

La ingeniería genética está dejando **de** ser – **a** una velocidad alarmante – una técnica **de** laboratorio **para** convertirse **en** un proceso comercial. **En** este proceso, el material genético puede ser transferido **entre** organismos **de** especies no relacionadas, una habilidad que ha sido apropiada **por** la industria, como
5 un método **para** introducir nuevas características **en** las plantas, animales y microorganismos. Se pretende que muchos **de** ellos sean producidos comercialmente **a** gran escala, originando la liberación **al** ambiente **de** organismos vivientes "diseñados".

Esta tecnología ha despertado preocupación **desde** el punto **de** vista
10 científico, socioeconómico y ético. **Por** ejemplo, es posible que se produzcan nuevas plagas y, dado que se trata de organismos vivientes, será imposible hacerlos volver **al** laboratorio. Está surgiendo así una nueva manera **de** contaminación: la contaminación genética.

Los impulsores **de** la ingeniería genética, **sin** embargo, están ansiosos **por**
15 convencer **a** la gente **de** que estas preocupaciones son equivocadas y **de** que la tecnología genética resolverá el problema **del** hambre mundial, revolucionando la agricultura **por** ejemplo.

Uno **de** los desarrollos más comunes es la producción **de** plantas resistentes **a** herbicidas. **Sin** duda, esto conducirá **a** un mayor uso **de** herbicidas **en** la
20 agricultura, ya que podrán ser aplicados **en** dosis mayores, concentraciones más altas y **con** más frecuencia **sobre** los cultivos modificados genéticamente, puesto que éstos no serían dañados. Asimismo, se está utilizando la ingeniería genética **para** desarrollar resistencia **a** insectos y enfermedades.

Frecuentemente, las corporaciones transnacionales consiguen la protección **de**
25 patentes **para** las plantas modificadas **por** ingeniería genética y **para** los métodos utilizados, **para** producirlas **en** países que no son miembros de la OCDE, generando una forma **de** colonialismo genético. Las patentes se utilizan

> **para** asegurar monopolios **de** importación y **para** controlar la producción
> local **de** los países **en** desarrollo. Asimismo, numerosas empresas **del** Norte
> 30 parecen estar usando **a** los países menos desarrollados como campos **de**
> prueba **para** los cultivos diseñados **con** el fin **de** satisfacer **a** sus mercados
> **del** Norte.
>
> Greenpeace, Revista *Este país*, México

Prepositions

Only basic meanings of prepositions are given here. For further information on the use of single and compound prepositions see the references at the end of this section.

A

A is one of the most common prepositions in Spanish and has a number of uses and meanings:

a In grammatical constructions:

 i Before a direct object denoting people (*personal* **a**) including proper names and pronouns (e.g. **alguien** *someone*), and known animals. This rule also applies to personified nouns as well as collective nouns referring to people.

   Note the following examples from the text:

   Están ansiosos por convencer **a** la gente ... (l. 14–15)   *They are anxious to convince people ...*
   Parecen estar usando **a** los países menos desarrollados ... (l. 30)   *They seem to be using the less developed countries ...*

   The following contrastive examples may help to understand the use of *personal* **a** more clearly:

   Conozco muy bien la ciudad/**a** María.   *I know the city/Maria very well.*
   Vimos la procesión/**a** un amigo.   *We saw the procession/a friend.*

 ii Before an indirect object.

   Le di el dinero **a** Carlos.   *I gave the money to Carlos.*
   A Raquel le gusta el tenis.   *Raquel likes tennis.*

 iii In the construction **al** + infinitive.

   Al salir del cine vi a José.   *On leaving the cinema I saw José.*

 iv With a number of verbs, for example **asistir a** *to attend*, **empezar/comenzar a** *to begin*, **ayudar a** *to help*, **jugar a** *to play*.

   Empezó a llover.   *It started to rain.*

b To indicate direction and motion.

> ... volver **al** laboratorio. (l. 12)   ... *come back **to** the laboratory.*
> ... la liberación **al** ambiente ... (l. 7)   ... *the release **into** the atmosphere*
> Llegaron **a** Madrid.   *They arrived **in** Madrid.*
> Doble **a** la izquierda.   *Turn left.*

Note that **al** is the combination of **a** + **el**.

c To indicate rate.

> ... **a** una velocidad ... (l. 1)   ... ***at** a speed ...*
> ... **a** gran escala ... (l. 7)   ... ***on** a large scale ...*

d To express position or location and distance.

> Está **a** la derecha.   *It is **on** the right.*
> Sentarse **a** la mesa.   *To sit **at** the table.*
> Sentarse **al** sol/**a** la sombra.   *To sit **in** the sun/shade.*
> **A** unos minutos/metros de aquí.   *A few minutes/metres from here.*

e To express time and frequency.

> **A** las seis y media.   ***At** half past six.*
> Estamos **a** 20 de enero.   *It's January the 20th.*
> **A** la semana siguiente.   *The following week.*
> **A** mediados/finales de julio.   ***In** mid-July/**At** the end of July.*
> Dos veces **al** día.   *Twice a day.*

f To indicate means and manner.

> **A** mano.   ***By** hand.*
> **A** pie.   ***On** foot.*
> Pescado **a** la plancha/**al** vapor.   *Grilled/steamed fish.*

g To indicate price or value

> Está **a** dos euros la docena/el kilo.   *It costs two euros the dozen/kilo.*

Ante

Ante usually translates *before* or *faced with.*

> Compareció **ante** el juez.   *He/she appeared before the judge.*
> **Ante** una situación así, no sabría qué hacer.   *Faced with a situation like this, I wouldn't know what to do.*
> **Ante** el descalabro económico, el presidente renunció.   *In view of the economic disaster, the president resigned.*

Antes de means *before* in relation to time.

> **Antes de** las seis.   *Before six.*

Bajo, debajo de

Bajo and **debajo de** mean *under*, but the first tends to be used more in a figurative sense and in set phrases, while **debajo de** is normally used in a literal sense.

Las llaves estaban **debajo de** la cama.   *The keys were under the bed.*

Bajo ninguna circunstancia.   *Under no circumstance.*

Con

The basic meaning of **con** is *with*.

Con más frecuencia. (l. 21)   *More frequently.*

Con el fin de ... (l. 31)   *In order to ...*

Contra

Contra normally translates *against*.

Se estrelló **contra** un muro.   *He/she crashed against a wall.*

De

De is another very frequent preposition in Spanish, and it has a wide range of uses and meanings, amongst them *of*, *in*, *from*, *about*. Only the most common meanings are given here. For other uses of **de** consult the references at the end of this section.

a As an equivalent of the English construction noun + noun.

Una técnica **de** laboratorio (l. 1–2)   *A laboratory technique*

Monopolios **de** importación (l. 28)   *Import monopolies*

b With a number of verbs, for example **dejar de** *to stop, cease*, **terminar de** *to finish*, **depender de** *to depend on.*

Está **dejando de** ser ... (l. 1)   *It is ceasing to be ...*

c Indicating position.

... sus mercados **del** Norte ... (l. 31–2)   *... its markets **in** the North ...*

d Expressing the idea of possession or belonging to.

... la producción local **de** los países en desarrollo ... (l. 28–9)   *... local production **of** developing countries ...*

e After a noun signalling an agent or an action.

Los impulsores **de** la ingeniería genética ... (l. 14)   *The promoters **of** genetic engineering ...*

La liberación ... **de** organismos vivientes (l. 7–8)   *The release **of** living organisms*

f Expressing origin.

Son **de** Córdoba.   *They are **from** Cordoba.*

g In time expressions.

De lunes/nueve a viernes/cinco.   *From Monday/nine to Friday/five.*

h Indicating the material something is made of.

Una taza **de** porcelana   *A porcelain cup*

i Meaning *about*.

Hablamos **de** muchas cosas.   *We spoke **about** many things.*

Desde

Desde usually translates *from* as well as *since* and *for* in time phrases.

Desde el punto de vista científico ... (l. 9–10)   ***From** a scientific point of view ...*
Desde ayer.   ***Since** yesterday.*
Desde hace muchos años.   ***For** many years.*

En

En is used:

a As the Spanish equivalent of *in, on, at*, to indicate position.

... **en** las plantas ... (l. 5)   *... **in** plants ...*
... **en** países ... (l. 26)   *... **in** countries ...*
En la mesa/casa.   ***On** the table/**At** home.*

b In expressions of time.

En diciembre/el año 2003/primavera.   ***In** December/the year 2003/spring.*

c Means of transport.

En avión/tren/bicicleta.   ***By** plane/train/**by** bike/**on** a bicycle.*

d To indicate value.

Lo compré **en** doscientos euros.   *I bought it **for** two hundred euros.*

e With a number of verbs, amongst them **entrar en** (Latin Americans use **entrar a**) *to go into*, **pensar en** *to think of*, **confiar en** (alguien) *to trust (someone)*.

Entre

The basic meanings of **entre** are *between* and *among*.

... **entre** organismos ... (l. 3)   *... **between** organisms ...*
Estaba **entre** tus cosas.   *It was **among** your things.*

Excepto

Excepto is used in similar contexts to *except* in English.

Fueron todos, **excepto** tú.   *They all went, **except** you.*

Hacia

Hacia normally translates *towards*, in sentences like the following:

Iban **hacia** el norte.   *They were heading north**wards**/**towards** the north.*
Hacia las tres de la tarde.   ***Towards** three o'clock in the afternoon.*

Hasta

Hasta indicates limit, both in time, meaning *until*, and space, translating *as far as*.

Hasta las nueve.   *Until nine.*
Hasta el final de la calle.   *As far as the end of the street.*

Para

Para and **por** (below) can be difficult for English speakers, as both can mean *for*, although they have clearly distinctive uses. As a general guideline, it may be useful to remember that **para** can indicate purpose, destination and movement towards, while **por** often expresses cause or reason. The following are more specific uses of **para**:

a To express movement towards.

... **para** convertirse ... (l. 2)   *... **in order to** become ...*

b To express purpose.

... **para** introducir nuevas características ... (l. 5)   *... **in order to** introduce new characteristics ...*
... **para** producirlas ...... (l. 26)   *... **in order to** produce them ...*

c To express destination.

... protección ... **para** las plantas ... (l. 24–5)   *... protection **for** plants ...*
... **para** los métodos utilizados ... (l. 25–6)   *... **for** the methods used ...*
Son **para** ti.   *They are **for** you.*

d To indicate direction.

Salieron **para** Cuba.   *They left **for** Cuba.*

e With expressions of time indicating limit, deadline and duration.

Lo quiero **para** mañana/el lunes.   *I want it **for** tomorrow/Monday.*
Queremos una habitación **para** una semana.   *We want a room **for** a week.*

(Most Latin Americans will use **por** in the second example.)

f To express a comparative notion.

Para ser extranjero habla bien.   *He/she speaks well **for** a foreigner.*

Por

Por is used:

a To introduce an agent, e.g. in passive sentences.

Ha sido apropiada **por** la industria. (l. 4)   *It has been used **by** industry.*
... modificadas **por** ingeniería genética (l. 25)   *... modified **by** genetic engineering*

b To indicate cause or reason.

Lo hice **por** ellos.   *I did it **because of** them/for their **sake**.*
Por la lluvia no pudimos salir.   *We couldn't go out **because of** the rain.*

c With expressions of time.

> Se fueron **por** la mañana/noche.   *They left **in** the morning/**at** night.*

d To indicate movement *through* or *along*.

> Pasamos **por** Madrid.   *We passed **through** Madrid.*
> Paseamos **por** el río.   *We took a walk **along** the river.*

e To express cost or value.

> ¿Cuánto pagaste **por** él?   *How much did you pay **for** it?*

f To express means.

> **Por** fax/correo electrónico.   ***By** fax/electronic mail.*

g To indicate rate.

> **Por** hora/día.   ***Per** hour/day.*

Según

Según normally translates *according to* and *depending on.*

> **Según** Aurora, no es verdad.   ***According to** Aurora, it is not true.*
> **Según** el tiempo que haga.   ***Depending on** what sort of weather we have.*

Sin

Sin means *without.*

> **Sin** duda. (l. 19)   ***Without** a doubt.*

Sobre

Sobre is used to indicate

a Position, with or without actual contact.

> **sobre** los cultivos (l. 21)   ***over** the crops*
> **sobre** la cómoda   ***on** the chest of drawers*

b Approximation in time and space (especially Spain).

> **sobre** las dos/20 kilos   ***about/around** two o'clock/20 kilos*

c Subject or topic.

> un libro **sobre** la guerra   *a book **about** the war*

Tras

Tras *after*, corresponds to a very formal, literary style. In colloquial language, it is replaced by **después de**, with reference to time, and **detrás de**, to refer to space.

> **tras** (**después de**) haber cenado ...   ***after** having dinner ...*
> **tras** (**detrás de**) la montaña   ***behind** the mountain*

Other points to note in the text:

- Gerund: *dejando* (l. 1), *surgiendo* (l. 12), *revolucionando* (l. 16), *utilizando* (l. 22), *generando* (l. 27), *usando* (l. 30) (see Chapter 9)
- Passive with *ser* + past participle: *puede ser transferido* (l. 3), *ha sido apropiada* (l. 4), *que ... sean producidos* (l. 6), *podrán ser aplicados* (l. 20), *no serían dañados* (l. 22) (see Chapter 11)
- Passive *se*: *se está utilizando la ingeniería* (l. 22), *las patentes se utilizan* (l. 27) (see Chapter 11)
- Present subjunctive: *se pretende que ... sean* (l. 6), *es posible que se produzcan* (l. 10) (see Chapter 14)

See for further information: Batchelor and Pountain, pp. 178–228

Butt, pp. 159–86

Butt and Benjamin, pp. 461–93

Kattán-Ibarra and Pountain, pp. 127–42

Muñoz and Thacker, pp. 156–68, 260–3

✎ EXERCISES

1 Insert the preposition **a** where necessary.

  a Hoy no he visto Juan.

  b Sólo tengo un hermano.

  c Mi madre no le gusta que visite la tía.

  d Buscan una secretaria que sepa italiano.

  e No oí el profesor.

  f Mis tíos les gusta ver sus hijos progresar.

  g Pablo quiere mucho Isabel.

  h Requieren una chica en la peluquería.

2 Complete the following sentences using one of these prepositions: **de**; **a**; **hasta**; **desde**.

  a Salieron _____ casa _____ las ocho _____ la mañana con rumbo _____ Santiago pero no llegaron _____ muy entrada la noche.

  b Llamé _____ Perú para decirle que no volvería _____ diciembre.

  c El museo quedó cerrado _____ octubre _____ principios _____ mayo.

  d Allí venden jamón _____ Teruel _____ 22 euros el kilo. Lo traen _____ las serranías _____ Albarracín.

  e Escribió un libro _____ poesías, durmiendo _____ día y escribiendo _____ noche _____ terminarlo.

  f _____ tiempo inmemorial _____ la muerte de Patricio, la familia fue _____ ese pueblo _____ veranear.

3 Complete the following sentences using one of these prepositions: **con**; **sin**; **contra**; **según**; **hacia**.

   a Te lo haré _____ mucho gusto.

   b _____ fuentes oficiales, el choque del avión _____ la torre fue un accidente.

   c _____ gran sorpresa mía y _____ la ayuda de nadie, gané el premio.

   d Hay que luchar _____ la discriminación para poder mirar _____ el futuro _____ sosiego.

   e _____ Pablo, la playa aquí está contaminada; hay que ir más _____ el norte.

   f Como ese día no hacía tanto frío, salió _____ sombrero, _____ guantes, _____ nada.

4 Complete the following sentences with one of these prepositions: **sobre**; **en**; **entre**.

   a Alfonso os ha hablado _____ el tema ¿verdad?

   b Hubo un incidente _____ el Paseo de la Castellana _____ las cuatro de la tarde.

   c No veo ninguna diferencia _____ este bolso y el otro menos _____ el precio.

   d _____ Salamanca, el viejo puente _____ el río data de los tiempos romanos.

   e ¿Tiene alguna información _____ vuelos a Madrid?

   f ¿Quieres poner este cenicero _____ la mesita que está _____ los dos sillones?

5 Underline the correct preposition.

   a Los revolucionarios lucharon *por/para* la igualdad.

   b La ley fue aprobada *por/para* el Senado.

   c El avión se retrasó dos horas *por/para* la niebla.

   d *Por/para* relajarme, doy largos paseos *por/para* la playa.

   e Pagó muy poco *por/para* el coche que compró *por/para* su hijo.

   f Van a Bolivia *por/para* unos tres meses pero esperan estar de regreso *por/para* Navidad.

   g Pili no consiguió el puesto *por/para* no tener conocimientos de inglés.

   h Mañana *por/para* la mañana pasaremos *por/para* tu casa *por/para* recogerte.

   i Hemos perdido el tren *por/para* tu culpa.

   j ¿*Por/para* qué sirve esto? ¿*Por/para* hacer agujeros?

   k Acababa de pasar *por/para* debajo del puente cuando la policía lo pilló.

   l Me tomaron *por/para* tonto y no querían escucharme.

6 Complete the texts with suitable prepositions.

   1 Agustín es ___(a)___ Madrid pero ___(b)___ septiembre vive ___(c)___ Castellón donde estudia ___(d)___ ser farmacéutico. Comparte un apartamento ___(e)___ Benicasim ___(f)___ su amigo Eduardo. Como Benicasim está ___(g)___ unos 4 kilómetros ___(h)___ la universidad, los dos chicos van ___(i)___ la Facultad ___(j)___ autobús. Sólo tienen clases ___(k)___ la mañana. Dos tardes ___(l)___ semana entrenan ___(m)___ un equipo ___(n)___ baloncesto y los domingos juegan ___(o)___ otro equipo. ___(p)___ su madre, Agustín es un chico muy listo, pero no creo que tome sus estudios muy ___(q)___ serio.

   2 ___(a)___ un reportaje del diario *Noticias de China*, la República China apuesta ___(b)___ la ingeniería genética ___(c)___ alimentar al pueblo. Es, ___(d)___ ellos, la única forma ___(e)___ terminar ___(f)___ siempre ___(g)___ el hambre que aflige ___(h)___ millones ___(i)___ sus habitantes.

Un equipo ___(j)___ médicos mandado ___(k)___ el gobierno ___(l)___ zonas rurales ha descubierto un alto porcentaje ___(m)___ niños ___(n)___ enfermedades debilitantes.

___(o)___ el fin de erradicar estas enfermedades, el gobierno ha puesto en marcha un programa que insiste ___(p)___ la producción ___(q)___ la seguridad. ___(r)___ muchas regiones ya se venden las semillas transgénicas ___(s)___ control y muchas veces producidas ___(t)___ compañías estatales.

Text

The Spanish writer Ana María Matute remembers her first days at school. Read the text and, as you do so, note the use of the words in bold, which are known as **conjunctions**.

Lo que aprendí en la escuela

"Las niñas del colegio eran unas brujas asquerosas"

Hasta la primera comunión fui al colegio de monjas San Josep Cluny. Entonces tenía cinco años; recuerdo **que** la monja se quedó estupefacta **porque** yo ya sabía el alfabeto. Me pusieron una medalla de aluminio con un lacito amarillo. ¡Fue la primera **y** última condecoración que me dieron! Yo sabía leer **y** enlazar

5 palabras, era muy tranquila, **pero** hacía preguntas improcedentes; en realidad, era incómoda, **pero** no revoltosa. Siempre última de la clase, no me interesaba estudiar **y** aquellas señoras me parecían unas estúpidas inmensas; cuando un niño se da cuenta de **que** una persona mayor es idiota . . . ¡No hay manera, no les crees! No creía nada de lo que me decían aquellas imbéciles.

10 Además, no tenía amigos, era tartamuda. ¡Me lo pasé muy mal! Las niñas del colegio eran unas brujas asquerosas. **No obstante** había aspectos en el colegio que sí me gustaban **y** en los cuales despuntaba. Por ejemplo: la geografía **o** la gramática. Odiaba las matemáticas, **pero** es algo que ahora lamento mucho **porque** sé que si me hubieran enseñado bien la aritmética – **porque** entonces no

15 eran matemáticas, **sino** aritmética – a mí me hubiesen encantado. Me acuerdo **que** yo era muy chiquitina, y todavía llevábamos pizarras en las que hacíamos las cuentas. Recuerdo **que** con las lágrimas borraba la pizarrita. ¡**Ni** me lo explicaban bien, **ni** podía resolverlas!

El País Semanal, España

Conjunctions

Conjunctions are words such as **y** *and*, **pero** *but*, **porque** *because*, whose function is to link words, groups of words or whole ideas. There are two main types of conjunctions: *co-ordinating* and *subordinating* conjunctions.

1 CO-ORDINATING CONJUNCTIONS

Their function is to link words, phrases or clauses of a similar kind. In this group we find **o** (**u** before **o**- and **ho**-) *or*, **y** (**e** before **i**- and **hi**-) *and*, **ni** *neither, nor*, **pero** and **sino** *but*.

a Co-ordinating conjunctions in the text

... la geografía **o** la gramática ... (l. 12–13)   ... *geography or grammar* ...

¡Fue la primera **y** última condecoración! (l. 4)   *It was the first and last medal!*

¡**Ni** me lo explicaban bien, **ni** podía resolverlas! (l. 17–18)   *They neither explained it well nor could I solve them!*

Era muy tranquila, **pero** hacía preguntas improcedentes ... (l. 5)   *I was very quiet, but I used to ask improper questions* ...

Entonces no eran matemáticas, **sino** aritmética ... (l. 14–15)   *They weren't called mathematics then, but arithmetic* ...

b Using *pero* and *sino*

Note that **pero** and **sino** both translate *but*, but their uses are different. **Sino** is used in a construction with two contrasting elements which are mutually exclusive, the first one negative, the second one positive. The English word *but* translates **sino** in the constructions *not ... but*, and *not only ... but also*. Most other uses of *but* in English correspond to **pero** (see also Chapter 27).

No esta semana **sino** la que viene.   *Not this week but the next one.*

No sólo aquí **sino también** en España.   *Not only here but also in Spain.*

2 SUBORDINATING CONJUNCTIONS

These introduce a subordinate clause, i.e., a group of words containing a subject and a verb which is part of a sentence and is dependent on the main clause.

a Subordinating conjunctions in the text

In the text we find: **que**, the most common subordinating conjunction, which, unlike *that* in English, cannot normally be omitted; **porque**, also common, and used in the expression of cause; and **no obstante**, a much less frequent one expressing concession and usually found in literary registers. Note how they have been used:

Recuerdo **que** la monja se quedó estupefacta. (l. 2)   *I remember that the nun was astonished.*

Me acuerdo **que** yo era muy chiquitina. (l. 15–16)   *I remember that I was very little.*

... un niño se da cuenta de **que** una persona mayor es idiota ... (l. 7–8)   ... *a child realises that an adult is an idiot* ...

Se quedó estupefacta **porque** yo ya sabía el alfabeto. (l. 2–3)   *She was astonished because I already knew the alphabet.*

Es algo que ahora lamento mucho **porque** sé que ... (l. 13–14)   *It is something I regret very much because I know that* ...

No obstante había aspectos en el colegio que sí me gustaban. (l. 11–12)   *Nevertheless, there were things at school which I did like.*

b *Que* in subordinate clauses with a verb in the subjunctive

Que is also the common conjunction in subordinate clauses containing a subjunctive verb (see Chapters 14–16).

Le pedí a Carlos **que** me ayudara.   *I asked Carlos to help me.*

For other uses of **que** see **Comparison**, Chapter 22, and **Relative pronouns**, Chapter 26.

c Other common subordinating conjunctions

Here is a list of common subordinating conjunctions, grouped according to usage.

Cause

como *as, since,* **pues** *because, since, for,* **puesto que, ya que** *because, since.*

Time

antes/despues (de) que *before/after,* **cuando** *when,* **hasta que** *until,* **mientras (que)** *while.*

Condition

a menos que, a no ser que *unless,* **con tal de que, siempre que** *provided that,* **(en el) caso de que** *in case.*

Purpose

para que, *in order that,* **de manera/modo/forma que** *so that,* **a fin de que** *so that.*

Concession

aunque *although,* **a pesar de que** *although,* **sin embargo** *however, nevertheless.*

Consequence

de manera/modo que *so that.*

A number of these conjunctions, among them those expressing purpose and condition, require the subjunctive. For more information on this see Chapters 14 and 15.

Other points to note in the text

- Imperfect and preterite tenses: *fui* (l. 1), *tenía* (l. 2), *se quedó* (l. 2), *sabía* (l. 3), *pusieron* (l. 3), etc. (see Chapters 2 and 3)
- Adverbs: *entonces* (l. 1), *ya* (l. 2), *siempre* (l. 6), *ahora* (l. 13), *bien* (l. 14), *todavía* (l. 16), etc. (see Chapter 21)
- Pluperfect subjunctive: *si me hubieran enseñado* (l. 14), *me hubiesen encantado* (l. 15) (see Chapter 16)

See for further information: Butt, pp. 187–90

Butt and Benjamin, pp. 444–60

Kattán-Ibarra and Pountain: pp. 155–8

Muñoz and Thacker, pp. 169–74, 264–8

✎ **EXERCISES**

1 Insert a co-ordinating conjunction into the appropriate places in these sentences.

    a Jorge Javier han montado su propia compañía.

    b ¿Cuál quieres: el negro el azul?

    c Los Reyes Católicos se llamaban Fernando Isabel.

    d Yo quería que vinieran Cecilia Ignacio no pudieron.

    e No vi a Paco a Alejandro.

    f Llamé siete ocho veces no había contestación.

    g Exportan sus productos a Alemania Italia.

    h No sólo vinieron españoles sudamericanos también.

2 Link an element in Column A with one in Column B to form a sentence.

A	B
a Como es tu cumpleaños	**1** podemos divertirnos.
b La maestra la castigó	**2** pues hace frío.
c Adoptemos el otro plan	**3** no le he dado la noticia.
d Estudiaba contabilidad	**4** pues hay trabajo para todos.
e Puesto que no hay otra	**5** puesto que le encantaban los números.
f Como no me escribe	**6** porque no está dispuesto a trabajar.
g Ya que se ha ido Alvaro	**7** tendremos que seguir esta ruta.
h Ponte el abrigo	**8** te he hecho una tarta.
i Bonifacio no conseguirá nada	**9** ya que han surgido problemas con éste.
j Venid	**10** porque había peleado con Victor.

3 Turn the two sentences into one, using one of the following conjunctions of time and making any adjustments necessary.

    mientras   **antes de (que)**   **cuando**   **hasta que**   **después de (que)**

    a Leía el periódico. Desayunaba.

    b Estamos de vacaciones. Nos gusta hacer algo cultural.

    c Tenemos que tener esto terminado. Vuelve el jefe.

    d No volveremos al trabajo. El dinero se nos acaba.

    e Nos iremos al teatro. Llegan los abuelos.

    f No adelgazarás. Sigues tan golosa.

    g Hay que pintar la casa. Viene el mal tiempo.

    h No me muevo de aquí. Sale Rodrigo Montalbán.

    i Nos acostamos. Cenamos.

    j Hay que sacar las entradas. Las han vendido todas.

4 Complete the sentences using **a pesar de** or **aunque**.

    a Lo pasamos bien _____ el mal tiempo.

    b Seguimos tomando baños de sol _____ somos conscientes de los riesgos.

c En estas tierras sales _____ llueva.

d Mantuvo la misma postura _____ todo lo que le habían dicho.

e No lo van a contratar _____ sea la persona más idónea.

f Es fuerte _____ ser bajito.

5 Translate the words in italics into Spanish.

  a Arreglaré el cuarto *in case he comes.*

  b Sus cuadros eran buenos *so she sold them all.*

  c *Provided that everything is in order,* podéis marcharos.

  d Aquí tiene mi teléfono *in case you need it.*

  e No iré a la fiesta *unless they send me an invitation.*

  f Le mandaron a Sigüenza *so that he would meet Josefa.*

  g Sus padres estaban contentos *provided she made progress.*

  h Nos explicó el proceso *in such a way that we understood it all.*

  i Los juegos se celebrarán el sábado *unless it rains.*

  j Os he traído a este museo *so that you see Picasso's "Guernica".*

6 Complete the following extracts (**a**) from this chapter's text, and (**b**) from the text of Chapter 1 (from line 15), using the conjunctions given in bold. Check your work against the originals when you have finished.

> **ni   pero   porque   que   y   ya que   sino**

a Recuerdo _____ la monja se quedó estupefacta _____ yo ya sabía el alfabeto. [...] Yo sabía leer _____ enlazar palabras, era muy tranquila, _____ hacía preguntas improcedentes; en realidad, era incómoda _____ no revoltosa. Siempre última de la clase, no me interesaba estudiar _____ aquellas señoras me parecían unas estúpidas inmensas. [...] Odiaba las matemáticas, _____ es algo que ahora lamento mucho _____ sé que si me hubieran enseñado bien la aritmética – _____ entonces no eran matemáticas, _____ aritmética – a mí me hubiesen encantado. [...] ¡ _____ me lo explicaban bien, _____ podía resolverlas!

b En días normales duermo como ocho horas [...] _____ después de una presentación, me es muy difícil. Hoy eran las cinco _____ todavía no podía conciliar el sueño. _____ te quedas excitado, no sólo en el papel, _____ que por la función misma. (*Hablando de donde veranea*) vamos a la playa la mayoría de veces, _____ hemos tratado de que las últimas vacaciones sean siempre en México, _____ mi madre vive allí.

30 | Word order

The threat of a large meteorite falling on Earth and the actions being taken to prevent a disaster are the subject of this text. The grammar focuses on word order.

A la caza del meteorito

El impacto contra la superficie terrestre de un solo meteorito de un kilómetro de diámetro sería suficiente para devastar el planeta. Científicos de todo el mundo buscan soluciones para prevenir una catástrofe como la que según diversos indicios pudo acabar con el reino de los dinosaurios.

5 **¿Existe alguna probabilidad** de que esto ocurra? Los científicos creen que sí, que más que una hipótesis es una amenaza real para la que hay que estar prevenido. Gran Bretaña ha tomado la delantera en la detección de asteroides, pero la NASA no se quiere quedar atrás. **Empieza la caza** del meteorito.

La posibilidad de que un gran cometa o asteroide impacte contra la Tierra dejó
10 de ser ciencia-ficción cuando, en 1994, uno de estos cuerpos chocó contra Júpiter. **¿Por qué en nuestro planeta no puede pasar otro tanto?** Mejor dicho, ya ocurrió. Fue hace 65 millones de años con la caída de un gran cuerpo celeste en la península mexicana de Yucatán, que acabó con la vida de los dinosaurios.

¿Podrá volver a ocurrir algo parecido? El responsable del proyecto de
15 observación de NEOS – objetos celestes cercanos a la Tierra – en el Instituto Astrofísico de Canarias asegura que **la hipótesis en absoluto es desechable**. Y **prevenido quiere ser el Gobierno británico**, que ha apoyado un proyecto científico para la detección de meteoritos. El objetivo: salvar al mundo.

"El problema – explica el encargado de NEOS – es que **no sabemos cuál**
20 **es el problema**. Sabemos que pueden chocar contra la Tierra, pero no sabemos con qué frecuencia ni en qué probabilidad." **Responder estas preguntas es, precisamente, lo que pretenden los científicos ingleses**.

Diario *16*, España

♀ **Word order**

1 STATEMENTS

a Spanish is much more flexible than English with regard to word order in sentences. Although by and large the verb usually follows the subject, as it does in English, for emphasis or focus different elements within the sentence can be placed in initial position. This includes the verb, which can precede the subject. Most sentences in the text follow the pattern **subject + verb**, but note the following ones where the verb comes first.

> Empieza la caza del meteorito. (l. 8)   *The hunt for the meteorite starts.*
> Prevenido quiere ser el Gobierno británico ... (l. 17)   *The British Government wants to be prepared ...*

Both examples above could be rewritten following the pattern **subject + verb**, e.g. **La caza del meteorito empieza**, but the emphasis achieved by having the verb in initial position is somewhat lost, at least in writing.

b With short sentences, the tendency is to place the verb before the subject.

> Llegó Tomás.   *Tomás arrived.*
> Murió su madre.   *His/her mother died.*

c If the subject is much longer than the verb, again the tendency is to have the verb in initial position.

> Respondieron Carmen y su marido, y un par de personas más.   *Carmen and her husband, and a couple of other people replied.*

d Within a clause, the verb is normally put before the subject.

> ... lo que pretenden los científicos ingleses. (l. 22)   *... what English scientists intend to do.*

e In statements focusing on more than one element, for example the theme or topic of a conversation and another element one wishes to highlight, the latter may go in final position. Note the following example, in which the object of the sentence (**the topic**) has been placed before the verb, with the final position being reserved for the element we want to emphasise.

> La cena (object) la preparó (verb) Raquel. (subject)   *It was Raquel who prepared dinner.*

Note the redundant pronoun **la** in *la cena **la** preparó* ... This redundancy is obligatory when the object is placed before the verb. (see **Redundant pronouns** in Chapter 25.)

f Adjectives and participles used as adjectives can also be placed, for emphasis, at the beginning of the sentence, as in:

> Y **prevenido** quiere ser el Gobierno británico ... (l. 17) instead of
> El Gobierno británico quiere ser **prevenido** ...

which would be a more neutral position.

g Adverbial phrases can be highlighted by placing them before the verb, as in:

¿Por qué **en nuestro planeta** no puede pasar otro tanto? (l. 11), instead of

¿Por qué no puede pasar otro tanto **en nuestro planeta**?　*Why could the same not happen again on our planet?*

a more likely position for a longer phrase. Note also the position of **en absoluto** *by no means* in:

Asegura que la hipótesis **en absoluto** es desechable. (l. 16)

h Relative clauses introduced by **lo que** are usually placed, in the spoken language, in initial position:

Lo que más me gusta es ...　*What I like most is ...*
Lo que pasa es que ...　*What's happening is that ...*

In line 22 of the text,

Lo que pretenden los científicos ingleses ...　*What English scientists are endeavouring (to do) ...*

has been placed in final position, in order to highlight the centre of interest, in this case the clause **Responder estas preguntas es** ...　*Answering these questions is ...*

2　QUESTIONS

a In direct questions the verb usually precedes the subject.

¿Existe alguna probabilidad ...? (l. 5)　*Is there any probability ...?*
¿Podrá volver a ocurrir algo parecido? (l. 14)　*Could something similar happen again?*

Note also the question introduced by **¿por qué?** in line 11.

b In speech, questions are often signalled through intonation, word order being that of a normal statement.

¿El problema está resuelto?　*Is the problem solved?*

c In indirect questions the verb comes before the subject.

No sabemos cuál es el problema. (l. 19–20)　*We don't know what the problem is.*

For the position of other grammatical elements such as adjectives, adverbs, object pronouns, see the relevant chapters.

Other points to note in the text

- Present subjunctive: *¿Existe alguna probabilidad de que esto ocurra?* (l. 5), *la posibilidad de que ... impacte* (l. 9) (see Chapter 14)
- Prepositions: *para* (lines 2, 3, 6, 18). There are numerous other prepositions in the text.
- Modal verbs: *pudo acabar* (l. 4), *hay que estar* (l. 6), *no se quiere quedar* (l. 8), *no puede pasar* (l. 11), *podrá volver* (l. 14), *pueden chocar* (l. 20)

- *Ser* and *estar*: *sería suficiente* (l. 2), *es una amenaza* (l. 6), *estar prevenido* (l. 6–7), *dejó de ser* (l. 9–10), etc. (see Chapter 13)

See for further information: Batchelor and Pountain, pp. 172–7

Butt, pp. 211–13

Butt and Benjamin, pp. 513–24

Kattán-Ibarra and Pountain, pp. 159–60

Muñoz and Thacker, pp. 177–80, 269–70

EXERCISES

1 Rewrite these sentences, beginning with the underlined word.

  a Los tíos, los primos y alguna otra persona más <u>vinieron</u>.

  b Susana <u>te</u> ha llamado.

  c El castillo de Medina del Campo se encuentra <u>a</u> unos dos kilómetros del pueblo.

  d Tomar el sol es <u>lo</u> que más les gusta hacer.

  e La fresa es la fruta que más se cultiva <u>aquí</u>.

  f Nos pusimos en camino <u>al</u> salir el sol.

  g Tuve experiencias únicas <u>dando</u> la vuelta al mundo.

  h Dice <u>lo</u> mismo hoy que dirá mañana.

2 Rewrite these sentences, starting with the underlined object of the verb. Include the necessary object pronoun(s) and make any other changes to the word order that might seem appropriate.

  a Sabes muy bien <u>la respuesta</u>.

  b Tú dirás <u>la verdad</u>.

  c Compré <u>estos libros</u> en el Rastro.

  d Os darán <u>el dinero</u> el lunes.

  e Dieron el primer premio <u>a Conchita</u>.

  f Dio ayuda <u>a los que la necesitaban</u>.

  g Le entregué <u>el paquete</u> al policía.

  h No lo hemos dado <u>a nadie</u>.

3 Translate these sentences into Spanish, thinking about a possible word order different from the English.

  a María is going to the concert as well.

  b They have always come here.

  c We have to think about the future now and again.

  d Finish your work quickly.

  e One doesn't do something like that every day.

  f It would be difficult to tell the truth here.

4 Read this text, which is about one of the possible reasons for the extinction of dinosaurs, and identify where you could improve the word order.

La extinción en masa se produjo hace millones de años de la mayoría de los dinosaurios que poblaban nuestro planeta. El fenómeno ha siempre fascinado a los científicos y varias hipótesis existen sobre su extinción de las que tres tienen una base en la realidad. La más popular es la hipótesis de la caída de un meteorito. Un meteorito de hecho cayó a una velocidad de hasta 250.000 kilómetros por hora hace unos 65 millones de años y chocó contra la costa del golfo de México. Ocasionó terremotos y maremotos de gran magnitud, lanzando una nube inmensa de polvo y fragmentos de roca a la atmósfera. La materia sólida incandescente provocó graves incendios al volver a la tierra y el polvo impidió la penetración de rayos solares durante meses. Las consecuencias fueron graves para las plantas y los animales. Algunas especies sin embargo sobrevivieron como las aves y los reptiles.

Consolidation exercises

364 días en automóvil

Es de justicia comenzar declarando que el automóvil es una cosa estupenda. Lo
malo es que los demás también lo tienen. Y resulta que en una ciudad, por más
túneles que se hagan, los automóviles de los demás no caben en las calles.

5 La dura realidad es que la densidad de población hace físicamente imposible que
los desplazamientos se efectúen en automóvil privado. Y aún más imposible que
una buena parte de los ciudadanos vivan fuera y entren cada día en su coche
privado. Es imprescindible que en toda área urbana haya un sistema de movilidad
planificado de forma integral, que permita los desplazamientos en un tiempo,
coste y comodidad razonables.

10 En el fondo de todo automovilista hay un usuario potencial del transporte
público, esperando que alguien lo saque a la luz.

Brindo dos posibles medidas en favor del transporte público:

a Que cada automovilista lleve visible en el parabrisas su abono de transporte
público (lo que permitiría reducir el precio del abono y, a lo mejor, ya que lo
15 han comprado, que prueben a usarlo).

b Que todos los alcaldes y concejales usen siempre el transporte público para sus
desplazamientos y hagan ostentación de ello con cara de satisfacción y
continuas manifestaciones de alegría.

Sé que se trata de unas modestísimas contribuciones, pero por algo concreto hay
20 que empezar.

Diario *El País*, España

ANALYSIS

1 As you read the text, identify the verbs which are in the subjunctive mood, and account for
their use. (Chapter 14)

2 What is the rule for the formation of the present subjunctive? Of the verbs in subjunctive
which you have identified, which one is irregular and what is its infinitive form?

3 Why is the adjective *razonables* (l. 9) plural? (Chapter 20)

4 *Lo malo es que los demás también lo tienen* (l. 1–2). Account for the different uses of *lo* in this sentence. (Chapters 18 and 25)

5 Identify other examples of *lo* as direct object pronoun in the text and say in each case what *lo* refers to.

6 State the function of *se* in *se hagan* (l. 3) and *se efectúen* (l. 5). (Chapter 11)

Text 2

In this interview Mario Molina, Nobel Prize winner for chemistry (1995), talks about the ozone layer.

¿Cuál es el principal problema que plantea la capa de ozono?
La capa de ozono protege la superficie terrestre de radiación ultravioleta. Esta radiación afecta de manera importante a diversos sistemas biológicos, sobre todo a los menos protegidos. Por otra parte, la estructura de la atmósfera depende de
5 la existencia del ozono; por eso nos preocupa que pueda ser dañada.

¿Cree que la sociedad en general es consciente del problema?
Cada vez más, pero hay que seguir trabajando porque la capa de ozono se está convirtiendo en un queso gruyere. El papel de los periodistas es muy importante para dar cuenta a la sociedad de todos estos factores que poco a poco destruyen
10 el medio ambiente.

¿Hay una solución factible?
Eliminar la emisión de los compuestos que afectan la capa de ozono – que se usan en refrigeración o en latas de aerosol – y que se pueden sustituir por otros compuestos. Ya se han llevado a cabo diversos acuerdos internacionales para que
15 la producción de estos compuestos nocivos termine. Actualmente, sólo los países en vías de desarrollo continúan produciendo estas sustancias, aunque lo hacen en pequeñas cantidades.

¿Cómo afecta el ozono a un ciudadano normal y corriente?
Los efectos más directos son las quemaduras y cáncer de piel por exposición al sol.
20 Pero existen también efectos indirectos como los cambios climáticos.

¿Qué consejos daría usted a la gente para evitar en lo posible los efectos del ozono?
Primero hay que seleccionar lo que se compra, pero sobre todo hacer presión sobre los diferentes gobiernos. Hay que tener conciencia ecológica para que el gobierno se dé cuenta de que es un tema que le importa a la gente y tome
25 medidas.

> *¿Cuál es su previsión para los próximos años?*
>
> El tema del ozono parece que poco a poco se va resolviendo, pero hay otros problemas muy graves de contaminación global. Uno de ellos es la superpoblación del planeta. Cuando los países desarrollados incrementen sus
> 30 economías, los cambios serán muy fuertes. Hay demasiada gente e inevitablemente cambiará la manera de vivir. Habrá que conservar energía, por ejemplo, y tomar muchas otras medidas.
>
> Revista *Cambio16*, España

ANALYSIS

1 What Spanish phrase does Mario Molina use to say what must be done to protect the ozone layer? How many times does he use this phrase in his discourse? (Chapter 10)

2 Identify the examples of the gerund in the text and translate them into English. (Chapter 9)

3 *termine* (l. 15) What verb form is this and why is it being used here? Find the other example in the text of the same use of this verb form. (Chapter 14)

4 Why *incrementen* in line 29? (Chapter 14)

5 **a** Why *pueda* in line 5? (Chapter 14)
  b What type of construction is *ser dañada* (l. 5) and why is the past participle in the feminine form? (Chapter 11)

6 Find the seven occurrences of *se* in the text and account for their use. (Chapters 11 and 12)

7 What is the function of **lo** in … *aunque lo hacen en pequeñas cantidades* (l. 16–17)? (Chapter 25)

8 The text has examples of the infinitive used with modal auxiliary verbs. Find where else the infinitive is used in the text and explain its use. (Chapter 8)

9 Identify the nouns in the text which end in -*a* but are masculine. (Chapter 19)

Text 3

> Margarita lloraba con el rostro oculto entre las manos: lloraba sin gemir, pero las lágrimas corrían silenciosas a lo largo de sus mejillas, deslizándose por entre sus dedos para caer en la tierra, hacia la que había doblado su frente.
>   Junto a Margarita estaba Pedro, quien levantaba de cuando en cuando
> 5 los ojos para mirarla, y viéndola llorar, tornaba a bajarlos, guardando a su vez un silencio profundo.

Y todo callaba alrededor y parecía respetar su pena. Los rumores del campo se apagaban; el viento de la tarde dormía y las sombras comenzaban a envolver los espesos árboles del soto.

10 Así transcurrieron algunos minutos, durante los cuales se acabó de borrar el rastro de luz que el sol se había dejado al morir en el horizonte; la luna comenzó a dibujarse vagamente sobre el fondo violado del cielo del crepúsculo y unas tras otras fueron apareciendo las mayores estrellas.

Pedro rompió al fin aquel silencio angustioso, exclamando con voz sorda
15 y entrecortada, como si hablase consigo mismo:

– ¡Es imposible …, imposible!

Gustavo Adolfo Bécquer: *La Promesa*

ANALYSIS

1 Comment on the main verb tenses used in the passage. (Chapters 2 and 3)

2 Identify the examples of the pluperfect in the text. (Chapter 5)

3 *Junto a Margarita estaba Pedro* (l. 4). Why is the verb *estar* used here? (Chapter 13)

4 If a verb follows a preposition, what form must it take? Find examples in the passage. (Chapter 8)

5 Comment on the function of *se* where it occurs in the passage. (Chapter 12)

6 Find a verb in the subjunctive. What tense is it and why? (Chapter 15)

7 *para mirarla, y viéndola llorar* (l. 5). Justify the position of the object pronouns. (Chapter 25)

8 Comment on the word order of *se acabó de borrar el rastro de luz* (l. 10–11) and *unas tras otras fueron apareciendo las mayores estrellas* (l. 12–13). (Chapter 30)

9 Explain the form of the relative pronoun in *hacia la que había doblado su frente* (l. 3) and *durante los cuales* (l. 10). (Chapter 26)

Text 4

Juan cogió a su mujer como si fuera una muñeca, y le dijo:

– Alma mía, tus sentimientos son de ángel, pero tu razón, allá por esas nubes, se deja alucinar. Te han engañado; te han dado un soberbio timo.

– Por Dios, no me digas eso – murmuró Jacinta, después de una pausa en que
5 quiso hablar y no pudo.

– Si desde el principio hubieras hablado conmigo – añadió el Delfín muy cariñoso – pero aquí tienes el resultado de tus tapujos … ¡Ah, las mujeres! Todas ellas tienen una novela en la cabeza, y cuando lo que imaginan no aparece en la vida, que es lo más común, sacan su composicioncita … […]

10   Jacinta, anonadada, quería defender su tema a todo trance.

– Juanín es tu hijo, no me lo niegues – replicó llorando.

– Te juro que no … ¿Cómo quieres que te lo jure? … ¡Ay, Dios mío! Ahora se me está ocurriendo que ese pobre niño es el hijo de la hijastra de Izquierdo. ¡Pobre Nicolasa! Se murió de sobreparto. Era una excelente chica. Su niño tiene, con 15 diferencia de tres meses, la misma edad que tendría el mío si viviese.

Benito Pérez Galdós: *Fortunata y Jacinta*

ANALYSIS

1 Account for the preposition *a* in the first line. (Chapter 28)

2 Find the negative commands in the passage and explain the construction. (Chapter 17)

3 Find in the text where Spanish uses the definite article and English does not. (Chapter 18)

4 Account for the use of the subjunctive in *¿Cómo quieres que te lo jure?* (l. 12). (Chapter 14)

5 *Se murió de sobreparto* (l. 14). What tense is this? In what way is it irregular? Which other common verb is similarly irregular? (Chapter 2)

6 *Te han engañado; te han dado un soberbio timo* (l. 3). Explain why the third person plural is used here and translate the sentence into English. (Chapter 11)

7 *el mío* (l. 15). To what is Juan referring here? (Chapter 24)

8 Find the superlative expression in the text. (Chapter 22)

9 Apart from *como si fuera* (l. 1), find the two "if" clauses in the text and explain the constructions. (Chapters 15 and 16)

Keys

Where not stated in the exercises, *you* will be rendered as **tú**.

● Key 1: The present tense

1 **a** saco; llamo **b** estudias; aprendes **c** visitan; vive **d** escribe **e** bailamos; bebemos **f** reciben **g** hablan **h** subís **i** vivimos **j** intentan.

2 **a** dice; conduzco **b** conoces; conozco **c** empieza **d** pensáis **e** oigo; leo; salgo **f** quieres; tienes **g** juega **h** sé; vuelvo **i** dejas; tengo **j** calienta; fríe; añade **k** llueve **l** vienen; dicen; quieren **m** sabes; sigo **n** van; prefieren; piden.

3 **a** comen **b** pinta **c** nieva **d** pierdes **e** empiezan **f** duerme **g** son **h** va **i** sirve **j** conducen.

4 – El viernes nos despedimos de María. ¿Qué le regalamos?
   – Le gustan las joyas. ¿Le damos unos pendientes?
   – Sí, ¿por qué no? La llamo esta noche para decirle que el jueves por la noche hay una fiesta en mi casa.
   – ¿Y cuándo compramos los pendientes?
   – ¿Lo dejamos para/hasta el miércoles? Tengo que ir a París y no vuelvo hasta el martes.
   – Vale. ¿Dónde quedamos/nos encontramos? ¿Delante de la joyería?
   – Sí. Te veo allí a las diez.

6 – ¿A qué hora empieza a trabajar y a qué hora termina?
   – ¿Come con los actores?
   – Para relajarse ¿qué libros lee?
   – ¿Qué música escucha?
   – ¿Qué programas ve en la televisión?
   – ¿Qué deporte hace/practica para mantenerse en forma?

● Key 2: The preterite

1 **a** pasé; salí **b** estudiaste; leíste **c** preparó; bebió **d** entró; cogió **e** viajamos; salimos **f** mandasteis; recibisteis **g** llamaron; subieron **h** encontraron; volvieron.

2 **a** fui; fue **b** supo; hizo **c** anduvimos; anduvimos; pudimos **d** estuvisteis; vinisteis **e** sirvieron; fuimos; dijeron **f** tradujeron; estuvieron **g** compraste; compré; trajo **h** toqué; entré; puse; toqué **i** empecé; empezó; llegué; tomé; me puse; vino; tuve.

3 nació; decidieron; llegaron; fue; nació; adoptó; recibió; incorporó; se convirtió; escribió; salió; llegó; murió; se estrelló.

4 se despertó; quiso; dio; fue; se enfrió; tuvo; se durmió; durmió; se levantó.

5 **a** ¿Adónde fuiste de vacaciones?
   b ¿Cuánto tiempo estuviste allí?
   c ¿Viajaste solo?
   d ¿Cómo viajasteis?

e ¿Dónde os alojasteis?

f ¿Qué hicisteis el primer día?

g ¿Qué sitios visitasteis?

h ¿Salisteis por la noche?

i ¿Qué tiempo hizo?

j ¿Qué compraste?

k ¿Qué tal lo pasaste?

● Key 3: The imperfect

1 eran; vivían; tenía; cultivaba; se ocupaba; hacía; cargaba; se llamaba; iba; vendía; acompañaba; estaban; llevaban.

2 **a** hacía; daba **b** era; llevaba; tocaba **c** trabajaban; charlabas **d** estudiábamos **e** íbamos; llovía **f** veían; se acostaban **g** sabía; podíamos **h** era; dejaba; quería.

4 **a** La última vez que vi a Fernando, él estaba buscando trabajo.

b Entramos en el museo porque llovía.

c Cuando conocí a Isabel, tenía el pelo largo y rubio.

d Pedro y yo íbamos por la calle cuando nos topamos con Ana.

e Eran las once de la mañana cuando partieron para Santiago.

5 **a** En aquellos tiempos las chicas no salían después de las diez.

b Mientras esperaba charlaba conmigo.

c Estábamos muy cansados cuando llegamos.

d No me di cuenta de que estaba enfermo.

e Vivíamos en un pueblo pequeño donde todo el mundo se conocía.

f Todo iba bien hasta que empezó a llover.

● Key 4: The perfect

1 **a** hemos entendido **b** han visto **c** ha visitado **d** ha llegado **e** han recibido **f** he podido.

2 **a** he aprendido **b** has ido **c** ha salido **d** hemos vendido **e** ha llamado **f** se me ha caído **g** han tenido **h** habéis entendido.

3 **a** Siempre hemos ido de vacaciones a España.

b No le han dicho nada a Pili porque no la han visto.

c ¿Por qué no has hecho esto?

d ¿Dónde han puesto las bolsas?

e Todavía no ha vuelto Gonzalo de París.

4 he hecho; he comprado; he escrito; he envuelto; he puesto; he cambiado; he leído; he podido; he dicho; he dado; he olvidado.

5 **a** has dormido **b** han comido **c** habéis visitado **d** ha ido **e** han pasado **f** ha abierto **g** ha hecho **h** ha llovido **i** he perdido.

● Key 5: The pluperfect

1 **a** habían invitado **b** habíamos repetido **c** habías echado **d** habíais salido **e** había dicho **f** había visto **g** había terminado **h** habían prometido.

2 **a** habían cerrado **b** había ido **c** habíamos visitado; habíamos visto **d** había dicho **e** habían entrado **f** habían robado **g** se había encontrado **h** habían dado.

3 a Estaba contenta porque Roberto me había dado un regalo.
  b Lo había envuelto y lo había dejado en mi asiento.
  c No le había dicho que era mi cumpleaños.
  d Más tarde me dijo que había comprado la pulsera porque le había gustado.
  e No había pensado en el precio.

● Key 6: The future

1 a Haré; será **b** acompañará; será **c** llevaremos; tendré; guiaré; sacará **d** nos alojaremos; intentaremos; bajaremos **e** haré; seguiré; iré; entraré; rezaré; subiré; abrazaré; golpearé; dará **f** volveremos; nos quedaremos; revelará; escribiré; publicaremos **g** saldrá; pondremos; gustará.

2 a ¿Cómo hará el Camino de Santiago?
  b ¿Quién lo acompañará?
  c ¿Qué llevarán en el globo?
  d ¿Dónde se alojarán?
  e ¿Qué hará en Santiago?
  f ¿Cuánto tiempo se quedarán en Santiago?
  g ¿Cuándo saldrá el libro?

3 *This is a model answer.*
El miércoles a las nueve de la mañana, **los estudiantes llegarán** al Instituto donde **los recibirá el director** y a continuación **visitarán** las instalaciones. A las once y cuarto **se presentará** el grupo de alumnos del Instituto y a las doce y media los estudiantes **saldrán** del centro para visitar el Ayuntamiento. **Comerán** en el Ayuntamiento.

El jueves **empezarán** a las ocho y media y **trabajarán** toda la mañana. A las doce menos cuarto el grupo de alumnos del Instituto **se reunirá** con ellos y **seguirán trabajando** hasta la hora del almuerzo. **Comerán** en la cantina y por la tarde **efectuarán** una visita turístico-cultural de la ciudad para conocer los principales monumentos.

Al día siguiente a partir de las diez de la mañana **revisarán** el proyecto. A las once y media **tomarán** café y a las doce **planificarán** las actividades que **tendrán** que realizar durante el resto del año hasta la próxima reunión. A las dos **comerán** y **tendrán** la tarde libre.

El sábado también lo **tendrán** libre para hacer visitas y realizar compras.

A las ocho y media del domingo **se dirigirán** al aeropuerto donde **tomarán** el vuelo de regreso.

● Key 7: The conditional

1 a podrías **b** podría **c** haría **d** importaría **e** podría **f** permitirían.

2 a serían **b** compraría **c** habría **d** serían **e** dolería.

3 a participarían; costaría **b** tomaría **c** mediría; sería; vivirían; trabajarían **d** pondría; encontraríamos.

4 a volvería **b** comprendería **c** se asombraría **d** sufriría **e** llegaría.

● Key 8: The infinitive

1 a Fueron a Salamanca para aprender español.
    They went to Salamanca to learn Spanish.
  b Estoy aquí sin hacer nada.
    I'm here doing nothing.
  c Al entrar en el salón encendió la luz.
    As s/he went into the living room, s/he turned on the light.

d Después de cenar salimos.
After dining, we went out.

e Al llegar, llamaron a sus amigos.
When they arrived, they called their friends.

f Se fue sin decir nada.
S/he went without saying anything.

g Antes de iniciar el programa acudieron al médico.
Before starting the programme, they went to the doctor's.

h Marta compró media docena de huevos para hacer una tortilla.
Marta bought half a dozen eggs to make an omelette.

i Después de visitar el castillo compraron recuerdos.
After visiting the castle, they bought some souvenirs.

j Antes de hablar con Juan leyó la carta.
Before speaking to Juan, s/he read the letter.

2 a Siento no poder ayudarte.
  b Espera ir a Madrid.
  c Inés no quiso seguir con los ejercicios.
  d Es muy importante hacer ejercicio.
  e Hay que escuchar para aprender.
  f No puedo ir al gimnasio porque tengo que trabajar.
  g Es imposible ponerse en forma sin hacer ejercicio.
  h Quieren comprar un coche para ir a España.

3 a Al entrar empezaron a cantar.
  b Los oí cantar.
  c Lo mejor de vivir aquí es poder ir al teatro.
  d Ir al gimnasio es una buena manera de ponerse en forma.
  e Es incapaz de dejar de fumar.
  f Niega haber ayudado a los ladrones.

4 a No fumar.
  b No usar.
  c No ducharse antes de las siete.
  d No dejar ropa en los vestuarios.
  e Apagar las luces antes de medianoche.
  f Quitar/recoger la mesa después de comer.
  g Fregar/lavar los platos.
  h Hacer la cama al llegar.

● Key 9: The gerund

1 a durmiendo **b** trabajando **c** corriendo **d** sustituyendo **e** usando.

2 a saludando **b** escribiéndome **c** ayudándonos **d** sabiendo **e** leyendo **f** descansando.

3 a Los agricultores llevan dos años plantando bosques.
The farmers have been planting trees for two years.

  b Sofía lleva seis meses yendo al trabajo en autobús.
Sofia has been going to work by bus for six months.

  c Los oficinistas llevan año y medio reciclando el papel.
The office workers have been recycling paper for a year and a half.

  d Nosotros llevamos mucho tiempo reduciendo nuestro consumo de electricidad.
We have been reducing our electricity consumption for a long time.

  e Los ecologistas llevan más de treinta años creando conciencia sobre los peligros que corre el planeta.
The Greens have been raising awarerness of the dangers facing the planet for more than thirty years.

4 a se está acumulando **b** va mejorando **c** venimos notando **d** acabará destruyendo
e viene contaminando **f** están instalando **g** seguirán apoyando **h** vamos cambiando.

5 a anda diciendo **b** vamos aprendiendo **c** sigues fumando **d** andan buscando **e** nos quedamos
charlando **f** voy conociendo **g** seguimos tirando **h** iba escribiendo.

6 a acabarán/terminarán derritiéndose **b** acusando a los ecologistas de sensacionalismo
c seguirán aumentando **d** depositando plásticos y latas en una bolsa y tirando las materias
orgánicas en otra bolsa **e** consumiendo sólo el agua y electricidad necesarias **f** reciclando el vidrio
g está amenazando a las poblaciones indígenas **h** llevan registrándose las temperaturas.

● Key 10: Modal verbs

1 a Quiero ir a México de vacaciones.
  b ¿Cuánto tiempo podemos quedarnos aquí?
  c Debéis hablar con Juan cuanto antes.
  d ¿Quieres venir conmigo?
  e Debemos tomar las cosas con calma.

2 a Suelo jugar un partido de ajedrez después de la cena.
  b Los abuelos solían echar la siesta después de comer.
  c No debes tomar el sol entre las dos y las seis.
  d Solemos ir a la piscina dos veces por semana.
  e Debéis pedir ayuda.
  f Debes tomar una aspirina si te duele la cabeza.
  g Solíamos tomar las vacaciones con los amigos.
  h Jorge no sale; debe (de) estar estudiando.

3 a tenía que **b** hay que **c** debe **d** tengo que **e** debe **f** hay que **g** debemos **h** tiene que; debe.

4 a ¿Sabes tocar la guitarra?
  b Solíamos pasar la mañana en la playa.
  c ¿Por qué tienes que marcharte?
  d Si quieres tomar el sol, debes usar un buen bronceador.
  e No hay que olvidar que los rayos solares pueden ser dañinos.
  f Solía trabajar diez horas diarias hasta que el médico le dijo que tenía que relajarse.
  g Para viajar en el AVE, hay que reservar los asientos con antelación.
  h Pepe, debes prestar más atención.
  i ¡Claro que sé cocinar!
  j Tendremos que madrugar mañana.

5 a quiero + infinitive **b** puedo + infinitive **c** suelo + infinitive **d** debo + infinitive **e** tengo
que + infinitive **f** hay que + infinitive.

● Key 11: Passive and impersonal sentences

1 a Leopoldo Alas escribió *La Regenta*.
  b El policía interrogó al camionero.
  c Los chicos rompieron los cristales.
  d Agustín ha desmontado el motor.
  e Tele-Mundo no emitirá el campeonato.
  f Mi padre construyó estas casas.
  g Mi hermano diseñará la casa de mis sueños.
  h Los agricultores han cortado los árboles.

2 a fueron excavados **b** han sido repoblados/serán repoblados **c** han sido analizados/fueron analizados
d fue invitada/ha sido invitada **e** son programados/serán programados **f** fue organizada.

3 **a** La catedral se construyó en el siglo XV.
  b Este libro no se ha traducido al inglés.
  c Las películas se conservarán en cajas metálicas.
  d Las estatuas se destruyeron en el bombardeo.
  e La noticia del accidente se difundió por televisión.

4 *Identify where in Text 2 these sentences have come from and check your translations.*

5 **a** No nos han pagado este mes. **b** Me han dado mucho apoyo. **c** No les ayudaron mucho.
  d Investigaron la causa del accidente. **e** Van a abrir un nuevo cine aquí. **f** Han arreglado el ascensor.

6 **a** El turrón se elabora/El turrón lo elaboran … **b** Se descubrirá/descubrirán … **c** Se fotocopian y
  piratean/fotocopian y piratean … **d** Se construirá/construirán … **e** Hospitalizaron al … /se
  hospitalizó al conductor … **f** Se bombardearon/bombardearon … **g** Se rescató al … /rescataron al
  alpinista …

● Key 12: The reflexive

1 **a** te **b** se **c** me; me **d** se **e** nos; nos; se **f** se; se **g** os; os **h** se.

2 **a** se parecen **b** levantarme **c** quejándose **d** nos aburrimos **e** te acostaste **f** se sientan **g** se preocupa
  h poneros.

3 **a** Me lo pasé fatal en la fiesta de Carlitos.
  b Primero me tomé un aperitivo con Juanjo en el Bar Florida.
  c Después, al llegar a la casa de Carlitos, me resbalé y me caí.
  d La madre de Carlitos me dio un coñac y aunque no me gusta, me lo bebí.
  e Bailé un rato y luego me dormí.
  f Cuando me desperté, Juanjo se había ido.

4 **a** reciprocal **b** reciprocal **c** reflexive **d** reflexive **e** reciprocal **f** reflexive **g** reciprocal **h** reciprocal;
  reflexive.

5 **a** Aquí se respira aire puro. **b** Se manda la factura a esta dirección. **c** Según lo que se dice,
  en Escocia se bebe mucho. **d** En España se cena tarde. **e** Se ha destruido el centro de la ciudad.
  f ¿Dónde se baja para la Plaza Mayor?

● Key 13: *Ser* and *estar*

1 **a** es; es **b** está; está **c** es; es; es; son **d** son; están **e** es **f** estamos **g** es; es **h** es; soy **i** es; está; está **j** están;
  están; están **k** es; es; está **l** están; es **m** estaba; estaba **n** es; es; está **o** es; está.

2 **a** está; es **b** es; está **c** ser; está **d** es; está **e** es; está **f** estar; es **g** está; está **h** está; es; es.

3 **a** El banco está abierto. **b** El gato está muerto. **c** La sopa está fría. **d** La llave está perdida.
  e La cena está servida.

4 *The correct verbs are*: era; era; estar; estaba; estaban; era; estuviera.

5 **c** Nuestro aniversario **es** en junio.
  d El dinero siempre **está** más seguro en el banco.
  f La sopa **estaba** muy sosa.
  h **Estoy** sin dinero …

6 **a** La casa estaba bastante lejos de la estación.
  b Era tarde y estábamos cansados cuando llegamos.
  c No vamos a salir porque está lloviendo.
  d Las calles están muy concurridas hoy.
  e El espejo está roto.

f ¿Te gusta este cuadro? No está mal ¿verdad?

g No es bueno/no está bien estar tan descontento.

h ¿A qué hora es el concierto? Es en el Ayuntamiento ¿verdad?

i El café estará frío y Marga estará de mal humor si no vienes ahora mismo.

j El hotel estaba completo lo que fue/era una pena.

● Key 14: The present subjunctive

1 **a** llames **b** jueguen **c** abra **d** escriba **e** prepare **f** hablemos **g** estudie; vea **h** dejéis **i** miremos **j** hablen **k** lleguen **l** cierres

2 **a** Siento mucho que Gloria no se encuentre bien.

b Nos extraña que mientan.

c ¿Os molesta que digamos la verdad?

d Temen que haya un accidente.

e Está muy contento de que nos conozcamos.

f No me sorprende que lo hayan pasado bien en México.

g Me alegro de que te den un aumento de sueldo.

h No creo que venga Pedro a la hora indicada.

i No le gusta que su hijo salga con Marta.

j No creo que este trabajo sea muy duro.

k Dudamos que sepan mucho sobre el incidente.

l Odio que la gente no diga la verdad.

3 *As there is no one correct way of linking the two parts of the sentence, only the subordinate clause introduced by* **que** *is given.*

que proponga nuevas ideas en el trabajo.

que aprenda o perfeccione un idioma.

que reconozca tanto sus puntos fuertes como sus puntos débiles.

que se esfuerce por hacer siempre bien el trabajo.

que acepte las críticas sin enfadarse.

que se desconecte del trabajo una vez en casa.

que no almuerce en el área de trabajo.

que acuda a cursillos de especialización.

que cuide su aspecto personal.

que diga "no" a un exceso de trabajo.

4 **a** 5 **b** 10 **c** 9 **d** 1 **e** 8 **f** 7 **g** 4 **h** 2 **i** 6 **j** 3.

5 **a** Tal vez no **tenga** todos los datos. **b** Quizás **venga** mañana. **c** Tal vez nos **inviten** a cenar. **d** Quizás no **esté** en casa. **e** Quizás me **llame** esta tarde.

6 **a** escriba **b** pueda **c** dé **d** sea **e** guste **f** pida.

7 **a** llegue **b** toque **c** apruebe **d** duerma **e** haya **f** tenga **g** paséis **h** vaya **i** seas **j** mejore

8 **a** Queremos que Eduardo **vaya** a Roma el jueves.

Verb expressing a wish; subject of the verb in the subordinate clause different from the main clause verb.

b Espero que **estén** ustedes bien.

Verb expressing emotion (hope); subject of the verb in the subordinate clause different from the main clause verb.

c Les rogamos a los señores pasajeros que **se abrochen** los cinturones de seguridad.

Verb expressing a request; subject of the verb in the subordinate clause different from the main clause verb.

d No conozco a nadie que **toque** el piano como tú.

Use of the subjunctive after the relative pronoun, which is referring back to someone unknown.

    e Me pide que le **dé** mis apuntes.
      Verb expressing a request; subject of the verb in the subordinate clause different from the main clause verb.

    f No le gusta a la gente que uno **tenga** éxito.
      Verb expressing an emotion; subject of the verb in the subordinate clause different from the main clause verb.

    g Es muy buena idea que **visiten** la destilería antes de marcharse.
      Subjunctive used after "es muy buena idea que".

    h No vamos a empezar hasta que **venga** Rodrigo.
      Subjunctive used after conjunction indicating time in relation to the future; subjects different in main and subordinate clauses.

    i No me extraña que a Paloma no le **guste** su trabajo.
      Verb expressing an emotion; subject of the verb in the subordinate clause different from the main clause verb.

    j Cuando **vaya** a Madrid ¿quieres que te **traiga** algo?
      Subjunctive used after conjunction indicating time in relation to the future. Verb expressing a wish; subject of the verb in the subordinate clause different from the main clause verb.

    k Es imposible que **vayan** ustedes antes de que **vuelva** mi jefe.
      Subjunctive after "es imposible que" and used after conjunction indicating time in relation to the future; subjects different in main and subordinate clauses.

9 **a** Siento que no estés bien; espero verte cuando estés mejor/te hayas mejorado.
    b No creo que haya alguien aquí que nos ayude.
    c No hace falta verlo pero es importante que sepamos cómo funciona.
    d Quizás pueda decirnos qué pasa antes de que vuelva Juan.
    e Aunque consiga un trabajo, Julio tendrá que seguir estudiando.
    f Puede que Samuel tenga más experiencia pero no es muy probable que haya estudiado tanto como tú.

● Key 15: The imperfect subjunctive

*Only the **-ra** form of the imperfect subjunctive is given in the answers.*

1 **a** escribiera **b** vieran **c** hiciéramos **d** hablara **e** fuera **f** pidiera **g** ayudara **h** se despidiera **i** supiéramos **j** salieran; lloviera.

2 **a** A Luis no le gustaba que Ana Luisa sacara mejores notas que él.
    b Ana Luisa no quería que su marido se sintiera inferior a ella.
    c Era importante que Luis reconociera los éxitos de su esposa.
    d Siendo macho, era lógico que Luis tuviera celos.
    e Alberto le prohibió a Lucía que trabajara fuera de casa.
    f Era una pena que los ingresos de Alberto no fueran suficientes para mantener a la familia.
    g A Luisa le dolía que su marido no le diera apoyo.
    h No estaba bien que Alberto no ayudara en casa.
    i Lucía le exigió a Alberto que contrataran una persona que hiciera las tareas domésticas.

4 **a** ¿Qué esperaba que hiciera su marido?
    b Le pidió que cuidara a los niños.
    c En aquel entonces no era normal que las mujeres trabajaran.
    d Muchas mujeres no comían para que sus hijos no pasaran hambre.
    e Vivían en esa casa sin que nadie supiera que existían.
    f Todo el mundo salió antes de que llegara Juan.
    g Sentimos mucho que no pudierais venir a la fiesta.

5 **a** acabaras **b** os quedarais **c** fuera **d** acompañaras **e** ganara **f** ofrecieran.

6 *The correct verbs are:* **a** tuviera **b** fumaras **c** pudiéramos **d** dijera **e** vinieran **f** pidiera

● Key 16: The pluperfect subjunctive and conditional perfect

Only the **-ra** *form of the pluperfect subjunctive is given in the answers.*

1 **a** hubieran dado **b** hubieran venido **c** hubiera comprado; hubiéramos vivido **d** hubiera heredado **e** hubieras traído **f** hubiéramos visto.

2 **a** Si hubiera sabido que llovía tanto, me habría/hubiera traído un impermeable.
   b Si me hubiera quedado, me habría/hubiera encontrado con el cineasta.
   c Si hubiera hecho buen tiempo, habríamos/hubiéramos salido de excursión.
   d Se lo habría/hubiera dicho si hubieran venido.
   e Habrían/hubieran acudido a la cita si alguien les hubiera avisado.
   f Te habría/hubiera salido bien si me hubieras hecho caso.

3 **a** De haberlo sabido **b** De haberlo hecho de otra forma **c** De habérmelo dicho **d** De haberse dado cuenta **e** de haberse consolidado el golpe de estado **f** De haber seguido mis instrucciones.

5 **a** Si tuviera tiempo, iría al cine.
   b Si hubiera tenido tiempo, habría/hubiera ido al cine.
   c Si lo hiciera, me arrepentiría.
   d Si lo hubiera hecho, me habría/hubiera arrepentido.
   e Si fuéramos ricos, te llevaríamos de viaje.
   f Si hubiéramos sido ricos, te habríamos/hubiéramos llevado de viaje.
   g Si leyeran más libros, entenderían más.
   h Si hubieran leído más libros, habrían/hubieran entendido mucho más.
   i Cuando lo vi, no hubiera creído que estaba enfermo.

● Key 17: The imperative

1 **a** pase/n; no pase/n **b** léalo/léanlo; no lo lea/n **c** oiga/n; no oiga/n **d** siéntese/siéntense; no se siente/n **e** tenga/n; no tenga/n **f** venga/n; no venga/n **g** pruébelo/pruébenlo; no lo pruebe/n **h** sea/n; no sea/n.

2 **a** mira; no mires **b** acuéstate; no te acuestes **c** apréndelo; no lo aprendas **d** dámela; no me la des **e** hazlo; no lo hagas **f** dinos; no nos digas **g** póntelos; no te los pongas **h** vete; no te vayas.

3 **a** mirad; no miréis **b** acostaos; no os acostéis **c** aprendedlo; no lo aprendáis **d** dádmela; no me la deis **e** hacedlo; no lo hagáis **f** decidnos; no nos digáis **g** ponéoslos; no os los pongáis **h** idos; no os vayáis.

4 **a** empecemos **b** nos enfademos **c** leamos **d** sentémonos **e** nos acostemos **f** sigamos

5 **a** Procura **b** Utiliza **c** No uses **d** Cuida **e** Destaca **f** No mientas **g** No lo escribas **h** No mandes **i** No incluyas **j** Recuerda firmarlo.

6 *These are the changes that you should have made to the text.*
   ● Viaje . . .
   ● Elija . . . le ayudarán . . .
   ● Pida . . . si prefiere . . . que le cobran . . . ir en taxi le puede. . . .
   ● . . . Si es un viajero . . . sabe moverse . . . no dude . . .
   ● Haga su reserva . . . contrate en la propia agencia . . .
   ● Aproveche . . . si tiene la suerte de no tener que ajustar sus vacaciones . . . Pero tenga en cuenta . . . difícilmente podrá elegir el destino que más le guste.
   ● Si quiere hacer un tour . . . siempre le saldrá . . .

7 **a** Cortad las patatas en láminas finas y freídlas en aceite.
   b Batid unos huevos y una vez cocidas las patatas, mezclad todo.
   c Ponedle la sal necesaria.
   d Calentad un poco de aceite en una sartén y cuando esté caliente, echad la mezcla.
   e Cuando la tortilla esté dorada por un lado, dadle la vuelta.

● Key 18: Articles

0 = no article, definite or indefinite, needed.

1 **a** los; la; la; 0 **b** la; los **c** la **d** del; el **e** la; la **f** 0 **g** el; la **h** la; el; 0 **i** los; la **j** el; el; la **k** el; las **l** la; el **m** los; el **n** el; el **o** la.

2 **a** El consumo de alcohol es frecuente entre la juventud de hoy.
   b Las mujeres también beben más que antes.
   c Más del cuarenta por ciento de los jóvenes bebe los fines de semana.
   d La cerveza es una bebida popular.
   e Ramón, el mejor amigo de José, empezó a beber a los doce años.
   f El doctor Justino León piensa que el paro causa muchos problemas.
   g Ahora las chicas beben tanto como los chicos.
   h Las estadísticas demuestran que el ciclismo y la natación son buenos para la salud.

3 **a** Lo importante . . . **b** . . . lo bonitos . . . **c** Lo mío es mío y lo suyo es suyo **d** Lo bueno . . . lo mezquina . . . **e** . . . lo picante . . . lo dulce.

4 **a** No te imaginas lo guapa que es. **b** No quiero contarte lo mala que era la película. **c** Lo mejor es esperar. **d** Viene lo interesante. **e** Lo difícil no era tan difícil.

5 **a** 0; un **b** 0; 0 **c** una; 0 **d** 0 **e** una **f** una **g** 0 **h** un; un; 0 **i** 0; 0; 0 **j** 0; un **k** 0; uno **l** 0.

6 **a** Paco era un ingeniero muy bueno. **b** Cierto joven preguntaba por ti. **c** No quiero repetir tal experiencia. **d** ¡Qué ruido! Salimos después de media hora. **e** Jules es francés, es médico y no tiene novia. **f** Y otra cosa – siempre lleva anillo.

7 el; unos; la; una; el; el; el; un; 0; 0; 0; 0; una; el; 0; el; lo; el; el; una.

● Key 19: Nouns

1 *f = feminine; m = masculine*
   a f; **b** f; **c** m; **d** m; **e** f; **f** m; **g** m; **h** m; **i** f; **j** m.

2 norma; víctima; trama; cima.

3 bronce; peine; fraude; aire; cine; parque; este.

4
catedral (f)	pan (m)	noche (f)	nariz (f)	planeta (m)
luz (f)	dólar (m)	día (m)	agua (f)	estrés (m)
garaje (m)	ciudad (f)	régimen (m)	lesión (f)	césped (m)
deber (m)	labor (f)	sur (m)	flor (f)	porvenir (m)
valor (m)	énfasis (m)	sol (m)	mes (m)	tarde (f)
virtud (f)	imagen (f)	mapa (m)	cárcel (f)	sed (f)

5 bares; lápices; crisis; hoteles; paraguas; deberes; exámenes; orígenes; franceses; naciones; altavoces; órdenes; meses; pies; países; cuartos de baño.

6 región; avión; quehacer; inglés; col; joven; luz; sofá; convoy; carácter; record; rubí; virgen; ilusión; violín; imagen.

7 **a** madre **b** mujer **c** alcaldesa **d** princesa **e** hembra **f** vaca **g** actriz **h** emperatriz **i** poetisa **j** reina **k** traductora **l** escritora.

8 **a** harbour; door **b** book; pound (money/weight) **c** point/spot; tip/end **d** duck; leg **e** payment; wages **f** injured person; wound.

9 **a** capital – money; capital – city **b** guide – person; guide – book **c** future; morning **d** order – arrangement; order – command/religious, military order **e** priest; cure **f** policeman; police force.

● Key 20: Adjectives

1 *1st paragraph:* incaic**os**; andin**os**; avanzad**a**; montañ* os*a; inhóspit**a**; anterior**es**; incaic**a**; ric**as**;interesant**es**.
2nd paragraph: imposibl**es**; incaic**os**; principal**es**; buen**as**; extrem**o**; sureñ**as**.
3rd paragraph: cubiert**os**; larg**o**; peligros**o**; español**es**; cansad**os**, hambrient**os**; temeros**os**; suntuos**os**; pasmad**os**.

2 **a** Cordobesas; **b** pescadora; protegida **c** izquierda **d** tremenda **e** pequeña **f** encantadora.

3 **a** trabajadora **b** dormilonas **c** juveniles **d** parlanchina **e** holgazán **f** felices **g** burlón **h** mayores
i azules **j** alemana **k** rosa **l** españoles.

4 *The correct elements are:*
a restaurante italiano **b** tercer **c** buen **d** algún **e** casa grande; playa privada **f** primero **g** mala
h tercera **i** algún **j** gran **k** palacio real **l** primer.

5 **a** revolucionario **b** español **c** viejos **d** machistas **e** nuevo **f** algunos **g** buena **h** libre **i** nuevo **j** guapo
k solos **l** muchas **m** jóvenes **n** mayor.

● Key 21: Adverbs

1 **a** perfectamente **b** inmediatamente **c** automáticamente **d** ligeramente **e** preferentemente
f cortésmente; correctamente.

2 **a** por supuesto **b** con tristeza **c** por último **d** por cierto **e** con dificultad **f** sin duda **g** de costumbre
h en efecto **i** en secreto **j** por lo general.

3 **a** arriba; abajo **b** encima **c** delante; detrás **d** lejos; cerca/aquí **e** fuera **f** dentro **g** aquí; ahí **h** aquí;
atrás **i** lejos; lejos; aquí **j** allí.

4 Antes; ahora; nunca; siempre; aún/todavía; hoy; ayer; mañana.

5 **a** bastante mal/muy mal; mucho; más **b** tanto **c** mucho; más; demasiado **d** tanto; mucho; demasiado
e mucho; bien; tan.

● Key 22: Comparison

1 **a** ... es más sabrosa que ... **b** ... es mejor/peor que ... **c** ... son más racistas que ... **d** ... piensan
menos en el dinero que ... **e** ... comen menos pescado que ... **f** ... es peor que ...

2 **a** de **b** de **c** que **d** del que **e** del que **f** de **g** que **h** de lo que **i** de lo que **j** del que **k** que **l** de la que
m que **n** de la que **o** de

3 **a** tan caro como **b** tan buena como **c** tanto café como **d** tanta verdura/tantas verduras como **e** tantas
oportunidades como **f** tanta experiencia como **g** tanto como **h** tan ambiciosos como **i** tan bien como
j tan a menudo como.

4 **a** Son dulcísimas. **b** Es riquísima. **c** Es carísimo. **d** Es larguísimo. **e** Son antiquísimas.

5 **a** la mejor **b** la mayor cantidad **c** los más obesos/gordos **d** la comida más importante **e** la mujer más vieja.

● Key 23: Demonstratives

1 **a** esta **b** estos **c** este; esta **d** esta **e** este **f** estas **g** estos **h** este.

2 **a** ése **b** ésos **c** ésas **d** ése **e** ésas **f** ésa **g** esos **h** ésa.

3 **a** aquellos **b** aquél **c** aquellas **d** aquella **e** aquella **f** aquel **g** aquellos **h** aquéllas

4 **a** éste **b** ése **c** aquellos **d** esa **e** esta **f** esos **g** estos **h** aquella.

5 **a** Esto no es difícil. **b** He leído este libro antes. **c** ¿Puedo/podría probarme estos zapatos? **d** En ese preciso momento no había nadie en casa. **e** Esto no me gusta nada. **f** Esos/aquellos bolígrafos escriben mejor que éstos. **g** Me acuerdo perfectamente de aquellos tiempos. Aquéllos eran tiempos felices. **h** ¿Por qué has dejado aquí todo esto?

● Key 24: Possessives

1 **a** Mi escritorio es muy viejo. **b** Su hermana es médica. **c** Tus amigos son muy simpáticos.
d Su habitación está reservada. **e** Nuestra casa es muy moderna. **f** Sus billetes están en la mesa.
g Vuestro coche es muy cómodo. **h** Sus ideas son muy buenas. **i** Nuestros libros son muy interesantes.
j Su opinión de Gonzalo es muy mala.

2 **a** tuyos **b** suyo **c** nuestras **d** míos **e** suya **f** nuestros **g** vuestras **h** mío.

3 **a** el suyo **b** el mío **c** la nuestra **d** el suyo **e** la mía **f** los suyos **g** los vuestros **h** las mías **i** las nuestras
j el vuestro.

4 **a** Se quitó el abrigo y se puso la chaqueta. **b** ¿Dónde he puesto el pasaporte? **c** ¿Me da su número de teléfono? **d** Sacó el dinero del bolsillo. **e** Me duele el estómago. **f** Me gustó su piso. **g** Hablamos de los hijos/nuestros hijos. **h** ¿Te has cortado el dedo?

5 **a** mi; el suyo; su; su; su; mi; mis; nuestros.
b tus; la; mis; los míos; la; suyos; los suyos; tuyos
c nuestra; las; nuestros; nuestra; su; suyos; nuestra; su.

● Key 25: Personal pronouns

1 a Tú; yo; ella **b** vosotros **c** nosotros **d** usted **e** ellos/ustedes; nosotros **f** ustedes.

2 **a** La escribió el viernes. **b** Los vi el lunes pasado. **c** Las compro en el mercado. **d** No, no lo conozco.
e Sí, las vendieron. **f** Ayer la llamé. **g** Lo he puesto en el estante. **h** No, todavía no la hemos probado.

3 **a** Montse le regaló un collar. **b** La señora no me dio ninguna respuesta. **c** Te he preparado un café.
d Nuestro padre os mandó una carta. **e** El jefe les ha explicado el problema. **f** Ellos no querían vendernos/no nos querían vender las tierras. **g** Yo siempre le digo la verdad. **h** Tenemos que darles los libros/Les tenemos que dar los libros.

4 **a** No me la dio. **b** Marta nos las mostró. **c** Roberto no os la ha hecho ¿verdad? **d** No te los puedo contar. **e** Me lo entregaron. **f** Pepe no quiere dármelas/no me las quiere dar. **g** ¿Por qué no os las quiso comprar/no quiso comprároslas? **h** Federico va a leérnoslos/nos los va a leer.

5 **a** El guía se la explicó. **b** La señora no quería vendérselas/no se las quería vender. **c** Se lo recomendé.
d Carlos se las va a pedir/va a pedírselas. **e** No pensaba devolvérselo. **f** ¿Se los pasaste?

6 *1st paragraph:* lo; pensarlo; lo; mí; comprarlo; regalármelo; él; le/lo.
2nd paragraph: le; haberlo; mí; yo; me; meterme; él; lo.
3rd paragraph: les; os; cálmate; me; nos; siéntate; escúchala; te; tú.

7 **a** ¿Quién te dio este reloj? Nadie me lo dio; lo encontré.
b No puedo darle/no le puedo dar el dinero hoy; se lo daré mañana.
c ¿Los/las has visitado antes? Entre tú y yo, no son muy amables.
d Todos te han dado/todo el mundo te ha dado algo menos ella.
e Niños, os daré los guantes; ponéoslos para salir.
f Señor, señora, ¿en qué puedo ayudarles?
g Su esposo la escuchaba mientras ella le servía la cena.
h "Os invitaré a un café" es lo que nos dijo Ricardo.

● Key 26: Relative pronouns

1 a El castillo que está en el puerto data del siglo XVI.
 b Encontramos una pensión que nos hizo recordar Santo Domingo.
 c La camarera que nos sirvió era muy antipática.
 d El hombre que contestó al teléfono me dijo que estabas fuera.
 e Devuélveme la grabadora que te dejé prestada.
 f El restaurante al que te llevé en octubre está cerrado ahora.
 g Aquéllos son los vecinos de los que me quejo.
 h Me escribió una carta en (la) que me explicó todo.

2 a quien **b** que **c** quien **d** que **e** que **f** que **g** quien **h** que.

3 a enfrente de la cual **b** del que **c** debajo de los cuales **d** por los que **e** en (la) que **f** encima del cual **g** para la que **h** entre los que.

4 a lo que **b** lo que **c** que **d** lo que; lo que **e** que; que **f** lo que **g** que **h** lo que.

5 a cuyos **b** cuya **c** cuyo **d** cuyas **e** cuya **f** cuyos **g** cuyos **h** cuyo.

6 a La excavación por paleontólogos y arqueólogos de Atapuerca, que está en la sierra de Burgos, empezó en los años 70 del siglo XX.
 b En Atapuerca se han descubierto fósiles humanos que pertenecen a seis individuos diferentes.
 c Los seis individuos, cuyos restos tienen unos 800.000 años de antigüedad, podrían haber sido los europeos más antiguos.
 d No se parecen a otros fósiles humanos encontrados en Europa, lo que revoluciona las teorías convencionales sobre la evolución de *Homo sapiens*.
 e El equipo investigador le puso a esta nueva especie el nombre de *Homo antecessor* cuyo significado en latín es pionero.
 f Han usado técnicas geofísicas avanzadas que han permitido una datación precisa del yacimiento de los fósiles.
 g En los huesos de *Homo antecessor* hay marcas por las que sabemos que era caníbal.
 h Los jóvenes arqueólogos que han hecho las tesis y cuya labor es de sumo interés general, necesitan ayuda económica para poder seguir trabajando.

● Key 27: Negation

1 a No hay nadie. **b** No tengo nada que hacer. **c** No hemos ido nunca/nunca hemos ido. **d** Tampoco voy/No voy tampoco. **e** No he visto a ninguno de tus compañeros. **f** No voy a enseñarte ninguno de mis cuadros. **g** No quiero ni té ni café. **h** Todavía/aún no tenemos los resultados.

2 a Nunca tenía dinero. **b** Nadie acompañaba al concejal. **c** En esa tienda ni vendían bolígrafos. **d** Tampoco me ayudaron. **e** Nunca viene nadie. **f** Federica nunca entiende nada. **g** Yo tampoco entiendo nunca nada. **h** Ningún científico te lo podría explicar.

3 a nadie **b** nada **c** no; ninguna **d** no; nada **e** no; ninguna **f** no; sino **g** no; nada **h** no; ni; ni **i** no; sino **j** no; nada.

4 a Nadie dejó nada en el monte.
 b No nos desviamos nunca del sendero.
 c En el grupo había fumadores y no fumadores.
 d No tiramos ni colillas ni cerillas sin apagar.
 e No encendimos hogueras tampoco.
 f No hicimos ningún tipo de fuego fuera del área indicada.
 g Nadie en el grupo sabía utilizar el fogón.
 h Pasamos el día sin ver a nadie.

5 **a** Pasé todo el día en casa sin hacer nada.
b Pablito nunca entiende nada.
c No me ha dado ningún tipo de ayuda.
d Lo que has escrito no está nada claro.
e No/ni leen los periódicos ni escuchan las noticias en la radio.
f Todavía/aún no tengo los resultados ni Jorge tampoco.
g Se marchó sin decir nada a nadie.
h Lo hizo sin dificultad/sin dificultad alguna.

● Key 28: Prepositions

1 **a** Hoy no he visto **a** Juan. **c A** mi madre no le gusta que visite **a** la tía. **e** No oí **al** profesor. **f A** mis tíos les gusta ver **a** sus hijos progresar. **g** Pablo quiere mucho **a** Isabel.

2 **a** de; a; de; a; hasta **b** desde/a; hasta/en **c** desde; hasta; de **d** de; a; de; de **e** de; de; de; hasta **f** desde; hasta; a; a.

3 **a** con; **b** según; contra **c** con; sin **d** contra; hacia; con **e** según; hacia **f** sin; sin; sin.

4 **a** sobre; **b** en; sobre **c** entre; en **d** en; sobre **e** sobre **f** en/sobre; entre.

5 **a** por **b** por **c** por **d** para; por **e** por; para **f** por; para **g** por **h** por; por; para **i** por **j** para; para **k** por **l** por.

6 **1** **a** de **b** desde **c** en **d** para **e** en **f** con **g** a **h** de **i** a **j** en **k** por **l** por **m** con **n** de **o** contra **p** según **q** en.
2 **a** según **b** por **c** para **d** según **e** de **f** para **g** con **h** a **i** de **j** de **k** por **l** a **m** de **n** con **o** con **p** en **q** sobre **r** en **s** sin **t** por.

● Key 29: Conjunctions

1 **a** Jorge **y** Javier . . . **b** ¿ . . . el negro **o** el azul? **c** . . . Fernando **e** Isabel. **d** . . . Cecilia **e** Ignacio **pero** no pudieron. **e** . . . **ni** a Paco **ni** a Alejandro. **f** . . . siete **u** ocho veces **pero** . . . **g** . . . Alemania **e** Italia. **h** . . . **sino** sudamericanos también.

2 **a** 8 **b** 10 **c** 9 **d** 5 **e** 7 **f** 3 **g** 1 **h** 2 **i** 6 **j** 4.

3 **a** Leía el periódico mientras desayunaba.
b Cuando estamos de vacaciones, nos gusta hacer algo cultural.
c Tenemos que tener esto terminado antes de que vuelva el jefe.
d No volveremos al trabajo hasta que el dinero se nos acabe.
e Nos iremos al teatro después de que/cuando lleguen los abuelos.
f No adelgazarás mientras sigas tan golosa.
g Hay que pintar la casa antes de que venga el mal tiempo.
h No me muevo de aquí hasta que salga Rodrigo Montalbán.
i Nos acostamos después de cenar.
j Hay que sacar las entradas antes de que las hayan vendido todas.

4 **a** a pesar del **b** aunque **c** aunque **d** a pesar de **e** aunque **f** a pesar de.

5 **a** en caso de que venga **b** de modo que los vendió todos. **c** Siempre que/con tal de que todo esté en orden **d** en el caso de que te haga falta/lo necesite **e** a menos que/a no ser que me envíen una invitación **f** para que conociera a Josefa **g** con tal de que progresara **h** de tal manera que lo entendimos todo. **i** a no ser que/a menos que llueva **j** para que veáis el "Guernica" de Picasso.

● Key 30: Word order

1 **a** Vinieron los tíos, los primos y alguna otra persona más.
b Te ha llamado Susana.

   c A unos dos kilómetros del pueblo se encuentra el castillo de Medina del Campo.
   d Lo que más les gusta hacer es tomar el sol.
   e Aquí la fruta que más se cultiva es la fresa/Aquí la fresa es . . .
   f Al salir el sol nos pusimos en camino.
   g Dando la vuelta al mundo tuve experiencias únicas.
   h Lo mismo dice hoy que dirá mañana.

2 a La respuesta la sabes muy bien.
   b La verdad la dirás tú.
   c Estos libros los compré en el Rastro.
   d El dinero os lo darán el lunes.
   e A Conchita le dieron el primer premio.
   f A los que lo necesitaban les dio ayuda.
   g El paquete se lo entregué al policía.
   h A nadie se lo hemos dado.

3 a También va María al concierto/María también va al concierto.
   b Siempre han venido aquí.
   c De vez en cuando hay que/tenemos que pensar en el futuro.
   d Termina pronto el trabajo.
   e Una cosa así no se hace todos los días.
   f Aquí decir la verdad sería difícil/Decir la verdad aquí sería difícil.

4 Hace millones de años se produjo la extinción en masa de la mayoría de los dinosaurios que poblaban nuestro planeta. El fenómeno siempre ha fascinado a los científicos y existen varias hipótesis sobre su extinción de las que tres tienen una base en la realidad. La hipótesis de la caída de un meteorito es la más popular. De hecho hace unos 65 millones de años un meteorito, a una velocidad de hasta 250.000 kilómetros por hora, cayó y chocó contra la costa del golfo de México. Ocasionó terremotos y maremotos de gran magnitud, lanzando a la atmósfera una nube inmensa de polvo y fragmentos de roca. Al volver a la tierra la materia sólida incandescente provocó graves incendios y el polvo impidió la penetración de rayos solares durante meses. Las consecuencias para las plantas y los animales fueron graves. Sin embargo algunas especies como las aves y los reptiles sobrevivieron.

Consolidation exercises key

Analysis 1

1 *por más túneles que se hagan* (l. 2–3): subordinate clause of concession with *por . . . que* requires the subjunctive.
se efectúen (l. 5), *vivan; entren* (l. 6); *haya* (l. 7): subjunctive in the subordinate clause as the main clause verb expresses impossibility or necessity.
permita (l. 8), *saque* (l. 11): subjunctive used in a relative clause when the relative pronoun refers back to something indefinite.
lleve (l. 13), *prueben* (l. 15), *usen* (l. 16), *hagan* (l. 17): the verb in the subordinate clause must be subjunctive as the different subject of the main clause verb expresses a wish.

2 Add the endings of the present subjunctive to the stem of the first person singular of the indicative; for **-ar** verbs, add **-e, -es, -e**, etc., and for **-er** and **-ir** verbs, add **-a, -as, -a** etc.
The irregular present tense subjunctive is *haya* from the verb *haber*.

3 *razonables* is qualifying three nouns so must be in the plural.

4 *Lo malo: lo* is used with an adjective to form an abstract noun.
lo: direct object pronoun referring to *el automóvil*.

5 **que alguien lo saque a la luz** (l. 11): **lo** refers to the car owner/potential public transport user.
lo han comprado, que prueben a usarlo (l. 14–15): **lo** refers to **el abono**.

6 **se** is used to express the passive.

Analysis 2

1 **Hay que**. **Hay que seguir trabajando** (l. 7), **hay que seleccionar** . . . **hacer presión** (l. 22), **hay que tener conciencia** (l. 23), **habrá que conservar** (l. 31).

2 *Hay que seguir trabajando*: we must continue working (l. 7).
la capa de ozono se está convirtiendo: the ozone layer is becoming (l. 7–8).
los países en vías de desarrollo continúan produciendo: developing countries are still producing (l. 15–16).
El tema del ozono . . . se va resolviendo: the ozone problem is slowly resolving itself (l. 27).

3 Present subjunctive after *para que*.
. . . para que el gobierno se dé cuenta . . . y tome medidas (l. 23–5).

4 The subjunctive is required here after a conjunction expressing time (*cuando*) in the future.

5 **a** The subjunctive is used here after the main clause verb expressing an emotion (concern).
b A passive construction *ser* + *past participle*: the past participle must agree with the noun it refers to, here *la capa de ozono*.

6 *se está convirtiendo* (l. 7–8), *el gobierno se dé cuenta* (l. 23–4), *se va resolviendo* (l. 27): *se* is a reflexive pronoun.
se usan (l. 12), *se pueden sustituir* (l. 13), *se han llevado a cabo* (l. 14): *se* expresses the passive.
se compra (l. 22): *se* is the impersonal pronoun.

7 *lo* is a neuter object pronoun referring to the previous clause: *continúan produciendo estas sustancias*.

8 *para dar cuenta* (l. 9), *para evitar* (l. 21): infinitive after a preposition.
Eliminar (l. 12), *la manera de vivir* (l. 31); infinitive functioning as a noun.

9 *sistema; periodista; problema; tema; planeta.*

Analysis 3

1 First three paragraphs, narrative context with time unspecified: imperfect tense.
Paragraphs 4 and 5, actions completed within a time context: preterite tense.

2 *había doblado su frente* (l. 3), *el sol se había dejado* (l. 11).

3 *estar* to state position.

4 Preposition + verb in infinitive. Examples in the text: *sin gemir* (l. 1), *para caer* (l. 3), *para mirarla . . . tornaba a bajarlos* (l. 5), *comenzaban a envolver* (l. 8), *se acabó de borrar* (l. 10), *al morir* (l. 11), *comenzó a dibujarse* (l. 11–12).

5 *se* is functioning as a reflexive pronoun.

6 *como si hablase* (l. 15): imperfect subjunctive after *como si*.

7 Where the verb is in the infinitive form or a gerund, the object pronoun is written on to it.

8 Within a clause, the verb usually goes before the subject, also where the subject is longer than the verb, and for stylistic effect.

9 After a preposition the form of the relative pronoun is *el que, el cual* etc., the article being in agreement with the antecedent. Where the preposition is of three syllables or more, *el cual* etc. is the preferred relative pronoun.

Analysis 4

1 The direct object of the verb is a person.

2 *no me digas eso* (l. 4), *no me lo niegues* (l. 11): subjunctive is used for negative commands and the object pronouns precede the verb in the order indirect object, direct object.

3 *las mujeres* (l. 7): collective noun; *la cabeza* (l. 8): English would use a possessive; *la vida* (l. 8): abstract noun; *el Delfín* (l. 6): article used before a nickname.

4 Main clause verb expresses a wish with a different subject in the subordinate clause.

5 Preterite of the verb *morir*; *o* becomes *u* in third person singular and plural. *Dormir: durmió; durmieron.*

6 "You have been deceived, you have been well and truly conned." This kind of English passive expression is best expressed in Spanish with the third person plural.

7 He is referring to his child.

8 *lo más común* (l. 9).

9 *Si desde el principio hubieras hablado conmigo* (l. 6): the pluperfect subjunctive is used to express an unfulfilled condition in the past – if you had spoken to me (but you did not).
la misma edad que tendría el mío si viviese (l. 15): conditional followed by the imperfect subjunctive in the "if" clause. The unfulfilled condition relates to present time – the same age as mine would be if he were alive (but he is not).

Irregular and spelling-changing verbs

⌕ Irregular verbs

The following list includes only the most common irregular verbs. Only irregular forms are given. Verbs marked with an asterisk are also stem-changing.

---

abrir *to open*

past participle: abierto

---

andar *to walk*

preterite: anduve, anduviste, anduvo, anduvimos, anduvisteis, anduvieron

imperfect subjunctive: anduviera, anduvieras, anduviera, anduviéramos, anduvierais, anduvieran

---

caber *to fit, to be contained*

present indicative: (yo) quepo

preterite: cupe, cupiste, cupo, cupimos, cupisteis, cupieron

future: cabré, cabrás, cabrá, cabremos, cabréis, cabrán

conditional: cabría, cabrías, cabría, cabríamos, cabríais, cabrían

present subjunctive: quepa, quepas, quepa, quepamos, quepáis, quepan

imperfect subjunctive: cupiera, cupieras, cupiera, cupiéramos, cupierais, cupieran

---

conducir *to drive*

present indicative: (yo) conduzco

preterite: conduje, condujiste, condujo, condujimos, condujisteis, condujeron

present subjunctive: conduzca, conduzcas, conduzca, conduzcamos, conduzcáis, conduzcan

imperfect subjunctive: condujera, condujeras, condujera, condujéramos, condujerais, condujeran

imperative: (Vd.) conduzca

---

dar *to give*

present indicative: (yo) doy

preterite: di, diste, dio, dimos, disteis, dieron

present subjunctive: dé, des, dé, demos, deis, den

imperfect subjunctive: diera, dieras, diera, diéramos, dierais, dieran

---

decir* *to say*

present indicative: (yo) digo

preterite: dije, dijiste, dijo, dijimos, dijisteis, dijeron

future: diré, dirás, dirá, diremos, diréis, dirán

escribir *to write*
past participle: escrito

estar *to be*
present indicative: estoy, estás, está, estamos, estáis, están
preterite: estuve, estuviste, estuvo, estuvimos, estuvisteis, estuvieron
present subjunctive: esté, estés, esté, estemos, estéis, estén
imperfect subjunctive: estuviera, estuvieras, estuviera, estuviéramos, estuvierais, estuvieran
imperative: (Vd.) esté

haber *to have (auxiliary)*
present indicative: he, has, ha, hemos, habéis, han
preterite: hube, hubiste, hubo, hubimos, hubisteis, hubieron
future: habré, habrás, habrá, habremos, habréis, habrán
conditional: habría, habrías, habría, habríamos, habríais, habrían
present subjunctive: haya, hayas, haya, hayamos, hayáis, hayan
imperfect subjunctive: hubiera, hubieras, hubiera, hubiéramos, hubierais, hubieran

hacer *to do, make*
present indicative: (yo) hago
preterite: hice, hiciste, hizo, hicimos, hicisteis, hicieron
future: haré, harás, hará, haremos, haréis, harán
conditional: haría, harías, haría, haríamos, haríais, harían
present subjunctive: haga, hagas, haga, hagamos, hagáis, hagan
imperfect subjunctive: hiciera, hicieras, hiciera, hiciéramos, hicierais, hicieran
imperative: (Vd.) haga, (tú) haz

ir *to do*
present indicative: voy, vas, va, vamos, vais, van
preterite: fui, fuiste, fue, fuimos, fuisteis, fueron
imperfect indicative: iba, ibas, iba, íbamos, ibais, iban
present subjunctive: vaya, vayas, vaya, vayamos, vayáis, vayan
imperfect subjunctive: fuera, fueras, fuera, fuéramos, fuerais, fueran

oír *to hear*
present indicative: oigo, oyes, oye, oímos, oís, oyen
preterite: (él, ella, Vd.) oyó, (ellos, ellas, Vds.) oyeron
imperfect subjunctive: oyera, oyeras, oyera, oyéramos, oyerais, oyeran
imperative: (Vd.) oiga, (tú) oye
gerund: oyendo

poder* *to be able to, can*
preterite: pude, pudiste, pudo, pudimos, pudisteis, pudieron
future: podré, podrás, podrá, podremos, podréis, podrán
conditional: podría, podrías, podría, podríamos, podríais, podrían
imperfect subjunctive: pudiera, pudieras, pudiera, pudiéramos, pudierais, pudieran

poner *to put*

present indicative: (yo) pongo

preterite: puse, pusiste, puso, pusimos, pusisteis, pusieron

future: pondré, pondrás, pondrá, pondremos, pondréis, pondrán

conditional: pondría, pondrías, pondría, pondríamos, pondríais, pondrían

present subjunctive: ponga, pongas, ponga, pongamos, pongáis, pongan

imperfect subjunctive: pusiera, pusieras, pusiera, pusiéramos, pusierais, pusieran

imperative: (Vd.) ponga, (tú) pon

past participle: puesto

querer* *to want, love*

preterite: quise, quisiste, quiso, quisimos, quisisteis, quisieron

future: querré, querrás, querrá, querremos, querréis, querrán

conditional: querría, querrías, querría, querríamos, querríais, querrían

imperfect subjunctive: quisiera, quisieras, quisiera, quisiéramos, quisierais, quisieran

saber *to know*

present indicative: (yo) sé

preterite: supe, supiste, supo, supimos, supisteis, supieron

future: sabré, sabrás, sabrá, sabremos, sabréis, sabrán

conditional: sabría, sabrías, sabría, sabríamos, sabríais, sabrían

present subjunctive: sepa, sepas, sepa, sepamos, sepáis, sepan

imperfect subjunctive: supiera, supieras, supiera, supiéramos, supierais, supieran

imperative: (Vd.) sepa

salir *to go out*

present indicative: (yo) salgo

future: saldré, saldrás, saldrá, saldremos, saldréis, saldrán

conditional: saldría, saldrías, saldría, saldríamos, saldríais, saldrían

present subjunctive: salga, salgas, salga, salgamos, salgáis, salgan

imperative: (Vd.) salga, (tú) sal

ser *to be*

present indicative: soy, eres, es, somos, sois, son

preterite: fui, fuiste, fue, fuimos, fuisteis, fueron

imperfect indicative: era, eras, era, éramos, erais, eran

present subjunctive: sea, seas, sea, seamos, seáis, sean

imperfect subjunctive: fuera, fueras, fuera, fuéramos, fuerais, fueran

imperative: (Vd.) sea, (tú) sé

tener* *to have*

present indicative: (yo) tengo

preterite: tuve, tuviste, tuvo, tuvimos, tuvisteis, tuvieron

future: tendré, tendrás, tendrá, tendremos, tendréis, tendrán

conditional: tendría, tendrías, tendría, tendríamos, tendríais, tendrían

present subjunctive: tenga, tengas, tenga, tengamos, tengáis, tengan *imperfect subjunctive*: tuviera, tuvieras, tuviera, tuviéramos, tuvierais, tuvieran

imperative: (Vd.) tenga, (tú) ten

traer *to bring*

present indicative: (yo) traigo

preterite: traje, trajiste, trajo, trajimos, trajisteis, trajeron

present subjunctive: traiga, traigas, traiga, traigamos, traigáis, traigan

imperfect subjunctive: trajera, trajeras, trajera, trajéramos, trajerais, trajeran

imperative: (Vd.) traiga

gerund: trayendo

venir* *to come*

present indicative: (yo) vengo

preterite: vine, viniste, vino, vinimos, vinisteis, vinieron

future: vendré, vendrás, vendrá, vendremos, vendréis, vendrán

conditional: vendría, vendrías, vendría, vendríamos, vendríais, vendrían

present subjunctive: venga, vengas, venga, vengamos, vengáis, vengan

imperfect subjunctive: viniera, vinieras, viniera, viniéramos, vinierais, vinieran

imperative: (Vd.) venga, (tú) ven

gerund: viniendo

ver *to see*

present indicative: (yo) veo

imperfect indicative: veía, veías, veía, veíamos, veíais, veían

present subjunctive: vea, veas, vea, veamos, veáis, vean

imperative: (Vd.) vea

past participle: visto

volver* *to come back*

past participle: vuelto

Spelling-changing verbs

Verbs derived from the ones below and most verbs with similar spelling undergo the same spelling changes. Imperative forms corresponding to the present subjunctive follow the same pattern.

a) **c** changes to **qu** before **e**, e.g. **buscar** *to look for*

Preterite:	**busqué**
Present subjunctive:	**busque, busques, busque, busquemos, busquéis, busquen**

b) **g** changes to **gu** before **e**, e.g. **llegar** *to arrive*

Preterite:	**llegué**
Present subjunctive:	**llegue, llegues, llegue, lleguemos, lleguéis, lleguen**

c) **-cer**, **-cir** preceded by a consonant change **c** to **z** before **o** and **a**, e.g. **vencer** *to conquer*

Present indicative:	**venzo**
Present subjunctive:	**venza, venzas, venza, venzamos, venzáis, venzan**

d) **g** changes to **j** before **o** and **a**, e.g. **coger** *to catch*

Present indicative: **cojo**

Present subjunctive: **coja, cojas, coja, cojamos, cojáis, cojan**

e) Drop **u** before **o** and **a**, e.g. **seguir** *to follow, continue*

Present indicative: **sigo**

Present subjunctive: **siga, sigas, siga, sigamos, sigáis, sigan**

f) **qu** changes to **c** before **o** and **a**, e.g. **delinquir** *to commit an offence*

Present indicative: **delinco**

Present subjunctive: **delinca, delincas, delinca, delincamos, delincáis, delincan**

g) Verbs ending in **guar** change **u** to **ü** before **e**, e.g. **averiguar** *to find out*

Preterite: **averigüé**

Present subjunctive: **averigüe, averigües, averigüe, averigüemos, averigüéis, averigüen**

Bibliography

Cited works and main works consulted in the preparation of the text are as follows:

Batchelor, R. E. and Pountain, C. J.: *Using Spanish, A guide to contemporary usage.* Cambridge University Press, 1992.

Butt, J. and Benjamin, C. 3rd edition: *A New Reference Grammar of Modern Spanish.* Edward Arnold, London, 2000.

Butt, J.: *Spanish Grammar.* Oxford University Press, 1996.

González Hermoso, A., *et al.* 3rd edition: *Gramática de español lengua extranjera.* Edelsa, Madrid, 1995.

Kattán-Ibarra, J. and Pountain, C. J.: *Modern Spanish Grammar, A practical guide.* Routledge, London, 1997.

Matte Bon, F.: *Gramática comunicativa del español, Tomo I, de la lengua a la idea.* Difusión, Madrid, 1992.

Muñoz, P. and Thacker, M.: *A Spanish Learning Grammar.* Arnold, London, 2001.

Sánchez, A., *et al.*: *Gramática práctica de español para extranjeros.* Sociedad General Española de Librería, S.A., Madrid, 1978.

Index